Dear Reader:

The book you are about to read is the latest bestseller from the St. Martin's True Crime Library, the imprint *The New York Times* calls "the leader in true crime!" Each month, we offer you a fascinating account of the latest, most sensational crime that has captured the national attention. St. Martin's is the publisher of Tina Dirmann's VANISHED AT SEA, the story of a former child actor who posed as a yacht buyer in order to lure an older couple out to sea, then robbed them and threw them overboard to their deaths. John Glatt's riveting and horrifying SECRETS IN THE CELLAR shines a light on the man who shocked the world when it was revealed that he had kept his daughter locked in his hidden basement for 24 years. In the Edgar-nominated WRITTEN IN BLOOD, Diane Fanning looks at Michael Petersen, a Marine-turned-novelist found guilty of beating his wife to death and pushing her down the stairs of their home— only to reveal another similar death from his past. In the book you now hold, A NEED TO KILL, Michael W. Cuneo examines a shocking and baffling crime—and the teenager who was responsible.

St. Martin's True Crime Library gives you the stories behind the headlines. Our authors take you right to the scene of the crime and into the minds of the most notorious murderers to show you what really makes them tick. St. Martin's True Crime Library paperbacks are better than the most terrifying thriller, because it's all true! The next time you want a crackling good read, make sure it's got the St. Martin's True Crime Library logo on the spine—you'll be up all night!

Charles E. Spicer, Jr.
Executive Editor, St. Martin's True Crime Library

Praise for Michael W. Cuneo's true crime classic . . .

ALMOST MIDNIGHT
An American Story of Murder and Redemption

"Vivid. Gripping. Undeniably potent. *Almost Midnight* barrels along like a hot rod on a twisty Ozarks road . . . a fast, furious read that leaves one plagued by disturbing thoughts every time one manages to pause before turning another page."　　　　　　　　　　　　　*—Kansas City Star*

"Crisp, informative and evocative . . . Compelling, vibrant, rich with winning details about a scuffling life."
　　　　　　　　　　　　　　　　　—The Washington Post

"Engrossing . . . disturbing noirish undertones and undeniable spiritual flair."　　　　　　　*—Kirkus Reviews*

"Cuneo handles these saints and sinners with equal aplomb."
　　　　　　　　　　　　　　　　　　　　—Playboy

"A richly detailed exploration . . . Cuneo's writing does not flinch."　　　　　　　　　　*—St. Louis Post-Dispatch*

"Cuneo's detailed descriptions of the virtues (loyalty, self-reliance, faith, family) and negatives (violence, chemical dependency, lawlessness) of the Ozarks' culture not only fleshes out Mease's personality but also vividly portrays this overlooked area of Americana. Cuneo's skillful writing allows him to convey the romantic notions of Mease's outlaw ways and travels on America's back roads, while never romanticizing the violence or the hand-to-mouth living . . . One cannot help but appreciate Cuneo's in-depth, interwoven stories of Mease and the Ozarks." *—Publishers Weekly*

Also by
Michael W. Cuneo

One Last Kiss
Almost Midnight

**from the True Crime Library
of St. Martin's Paperbacks**

A NEED TO KILL

CONFESSIONS OF A TEEN KILLER

Michael W. Cuneo

St. Martin's Paperbacks

A NEED TO KILL

Copyright © 2011 by Michael W. Cuneo.

Cover photo of Alec Kreider courtesy *Intelligencer Journal*, Lancaster, PA. Photo of house by Dan Burn-Forti / Getty Images.

For information address St. Martin's Press, 175 Fifth Avenue, New York, NY 10010.

EAN: 978-0-312-38154-7

Printed in the United States of America

St. Martin's Paperbacks edition / March 2011

St. Martin's Paperbacks are published by St. Martin's Press, 175 Fifth Avenue, New York, NY 10010.

10 9 8 7 6 5 4 3 2

To
Rebecca Cuneo Keenan

This is a true story.

Names and identifying characteristics of some
people have been altered in order to protect
their privacy.

The mall scene in Chapter Twenty-One and
several passages stemming from it have
also been created for this purpose.

PART ONE

THE KILLINGS

1

It was shaping up to be a perfect Friday evening for the Haines family. A soft breeze was blowing through their Blossom Hill neighborhood. The air was filled with the sweet fragrance of early spring. Best of all, the entire family was on hand. Twenty-year-old Maggie had just gotten back from college the day before, and both she and her younger brother, Kevin, were planning on spending the evening at home. Parents Tom and Lisa couldn't have been more pleased. They'd always treasured times such as this, when they were all together with nothing more to do than bask in the pleasure of one another's company.

They cooked spaghetti and meatballs for dinner and afterward lingered at the dining room table. Maggie talked about her sophomore year at Bucknell, the courses she'd liked and several others she'd been less than crazy about. Sixteen-year-old Kevin talked about a school-sponsored trip to Germany that he was planning on making in mid-July. Lisa gushed about the terrific bunch of kids she'd taught over the past year at a church-affiliated preschool in town.

After taking care of the dirty dishes, Lisa and Maggie sat down at the family computer and tried solving a crossword puzzle. They then hopped into Lisa's Jeep Cherokee and swung by their local video outlet. They picked up the mildly naughty romantic comedy *Because I Said So*, starring Diane

Keaton and Mandy Moore, and also a Will Ferrell feature called *Stranger Than Fiction*.

Everyone gathered in the family room at eight o'clock to watch the romantic comedy, which was Lisa and Maggie's first choice. Kevin, for his part, probably would have preferred watching just about anything else. He wandered off intermittently throughout the course of the movie, eventually abandoning it altogether and going upstairs to bed. Lisa lasted until the closing credits before likewise calling it a night. Tom and Maggie stayed up a while longer and caught the end of the Philadelphia Phillies game on TV. The Phillies won in a breeze, defeating the Cubs seven to two, and when the final out was recorded Tom also went to bed.

Maggie followed suit shortly afterward, hopeful about getting an early start the next morning. Still not tired enough to sleep, however, she curled up in bed with her laptop and watched the pilot of a new TV show called *The Traveler* and also an old episode of *Brothers and Sisters*. At midnight or thereabouts she went to the bathroom down the hall and then returned to bed and chatted online with a couple of friends from college. Finally she shut down her laptop, set it aside, and fell asleep.

Roughly an hour later, shortly past two, Maggie was awakened by the sound of yelling. She got out of bed, put on her glasses, and stepped into the hallway. The yelling, which had a menacing ring to it, seemed to be coming from Kevin's room. It was accompanied by loud thumping noises, suggesting some sort of physical struggle. Was there an intruder in the house, possibly beating up her brother?

Concerned for her own safety, Maggie retreated into her bedroom. Her door didn't close properly because the frame was warped, so she braced herself against it and tried formulating a plan of action. She'd left her cell phone on the kitchen counter, which meant that she couldn't call for help. But neither could she safely remain where she was, not if there really was an intruder on the premises. She doubted that she was strong enough to hold firm against somebody intent on breaking into her room.

Steeling her nerve, Maggie opened the door again. There was a stench of blood in the air that she hadn't noticed before. She ran the full length of the hallway and went into her parents' room. Maggie's mom, Lisa, was sitting on the edge of the bed, with Tom lying motionless beside her. Lisa seemed distressed, practically in hysterics.

"Get out of here," she said, her voice scarcely a whisper. "Get out and go get help."

Maggie charged down the stairs and exited the house through the side door. She raced to the end of the driveway and paused for the briefest of moments by the curb, not entirely certain where she should go for help. Despite having lived in the area virtually her entire life, she wasn't especially close to any of the neighbors.

She ran through the darkness to the house across the street and rang the bell. She rang and rang and pounded on the door. Just when she was on the verge of giving up and trying elsewhere, a woman turned on the porch light and let her inside.

2

Officer Steve Newman was on patrol nearby when the call came over the radio. For reasons not yet entirely clear, somebody required assistance on Peach Lane, a winding, leafy street in the Blossom Hill neighborhood of Manheim Township. For Newman, a straitlaced kid fresh out of the academy, it had already proven a difficult shift. Besides the usual Friday night complaints about rowdy teenagers, he'd had to contend with a street fight on the New Holland Pike that almost erupted into a full-blown riot. Hopefully this latest call was simply a matter of some poor soul having locked himself out of his house.

Maggie was standing watch at the neighbor's kitchen window. She saw Newman pull over at the curb and went outside to meet him. She still had on the outfit that she'd worn to bed, orange terrycloth shorts and a light blue T-shirt decorated with a picture of the comic strip character Opus. She gave Newman her name and said that she lived directly across the street. She said that she was terribly concerned about her family.

Given her moist eyes and quavering voice, Newman didn't doubt that this was so. He asked her what she thought the problem was.

Maggie told him about the yelling she'd heard and also about her mother pleading with her to go for help. She said that she'd initially assumed an intruder was in the house but now she wasn't sure. Her dad had recently undergone surgery for prostate cancer and might have suffered some sort of setback after going to bed. Perhaps this was why her mother had seemed so distressed.

A second patrol officer, Chris Keenan—a tall gregarious guy in his mid-thirties—arrived on the scene and conferred with Newman. Then both patrolmen crossed the street and rang the front doorbell to Maggie's house. They returned after a minute or two and told her that no one had answered. She seemed surprised by this, saying that her mother had excellent hearing and would normally respond to even the faintest of sounds on the property. She wondered aloud if perhaps there really were an intruder in the house and her family had taken refuge in a locked room.

The patrolmen went back to Maggie's house, this time taking her with them, and tried ringing again. Keenan asked her if she'd actually seen an intruder. Maggie said that she might have but in her panicked state she wasn't precisely certain what she saw. She said that perhaps it was all just a bad dream.

The patrolmen instructed her to go back across the street and wait for them. They then opened the front door, which was unlocked, and went inside. They switched on the light in the hallway and several times called out "Manheim Township PD." Hearing no response, they proceeded down the hallway and made a preliminary check of the rooms on the main floor. A sliding glass door leading from the kitchen into the backyard was slightly ajar, but otherwise they noticed nothing untoward.

They ascended the L-shaped staircase by the front door and saw a spot of blood on the lower landing, then two larger spots farther up. At the top of the stairs they saw bloody footprints in the carpeted hallway and, to their immediate right, a teenage boy lying facedown in a pool of blood. He was wearing briefs and a green T-shirt labeled TROOP 99—LANCASTER, PA. There was a gaping slash to the right side of his throat and a deep gash across his right cheek, as well as five obvious stab wounds to the left side of his back and numerous cuts on his forearms. The wall in front of him was spattered with blood. Judging from the position of his body, it seemed likely that he'd collapsed to the floor while trying to exit his bedroom.

Both officers drew their weapons, and Keenan called for emergency assistance on his portable radio.

The officers walked to the far end of the hallway and entered the room above the garage, which was illuminated by a lamp on a night table. A middle-aged man, his eyes wide open and lifeless, was lying supine across a queen-sized bed. He was wearing boxer shorts and a T-shirt, and there was a catheter by his side. A crimson stain was spreading across his T-shirt from a wound in his chest. His hands were raised, palms outward, in a futile gesture of self-defense.

A woman with no immediately visible wounds was curled up in a fetal position at the foot of the bed. She had on a pajama top and bloodstained briefs. She was still warm to the touch but she wasn't breathing and had no pulse. Keenan lifted some strands of hair from her forehead and shined his flashlight into her eyes, which showed not the least sign of life.

The two patrolmen retreated into the hallway and searched the rest of the second floor. They then went down the stairs, weapons still drawn, and searched the basement and the backyard. By the time they got around to inspecting the interiors of the vehicles that were parked in the driveway, more than a dozen additional cops, and nearly as many emergency medical workers, had arrived on the scene. Keenan and Newman briefed the officer in charge for that night's shift, Dave Bair, about their conversation with Maggie and also about their grim discoveries inside the house.

One of the newly arrived cops was Ray Bradley, a seventeen-year veteran of the force with a deft touch at dealing with people in crisis. At the instruction of Dave Bair, he went across the street to the neighbor's house to check on Maggie.

Maggie saw him approaching. She'd been standing at the

kitchen window with the neighbor and her teenage daughter, wondering why the process was taking so long. She met him at the door and told him who she was.

Bradley recognized her almost at once. He'd been her DARE instructor in the fifth and seventh grades at Neff Elementary School, and her appearance hadn't changed much in the intervening years. His heart went out to her now, this young barefooted woman with tousled hair and a tear-streaked face, desperately hoping for some good news concerning her family. Bradley knew, from what Dave Bair had told him, that the news was as bad as it could possibly be.

Maggie once again ran through the sequence of events that had resulted in her fleeing the house, telling Bradley how she'd been awakened by a strange voice and had eventually sprinted down the hallway into her parents' room only to find her father lying motionless in bed and her mother in a state of hysterics. She asked if he knew how her family was doing.

Bradley excused himself for a moment and went back across the street to confer with Dave Bair, who suggested that he tell her the truth about her family without going into graphic detail.

He then returned to the neighbor's house and told Maggie that both of her parents and also her younger brother were dead. He said nothing about them having been murdered but it didn't really matter. Maggie apparently drew the inference herself. The menacing voice she'd heard, the stench of blood in the hallway, the condition in which she'd found her parents—all of this could only mean one thing. If they were indeed dead, it wasn't merely by accident.

She went into momentary shock, alternately crying and insisting that Bradley must be mistaken. "They can't be dead," she sobbed. "I just saw them. I just saw my mother."

She calmed down after several minutes and slumped into an armchair. Bradley asked her if there was a friend she'd like him to contact, somebody who could help see her through the rest of the night. She said that all of her friends were at Bucknell now, and with school out for the year they were scattered across the country. He pressed her on the matter, suggesting that there must be somebody with whom he could get in touch. She said that her contact numbers were in her cell phone, which she'd left on the kitchen counter. She asked if she could go across the street and retrieve it. Bradley said that this wasn't a feasible option at the moment.

She became reflective, saying that she'd been planning on running in a race with her dad during the summer. She said that they were running partners and best buddies, and that she'd missed him a lot when she was away at college. She also said that she'd been looking forward to teaching her younger brother, Kevin, who was in the habit of wearing calf-high white socks with shorts, how to dress more fashionably. She said that she and Kevin had purchased Mother's Day cards the previous afternoon, which would now go to waste.

She then asked Bradley if he'd mind phoning her Aunt Tammy and Uncle James, who lived only two or three miles away. He rang their number and, without getting into specifics, requested that they come to Peach Lane as soon as possible.

They arrived within fifteen minutes, only to find the street blocked off by police barricades. Dave Bair directed them to the neighbor's house, and as soon as she saw them, Maggie blurted out: "My life will never be the same."

The uncle, who was one of Tom's two brothers, asked Bradley what was going on. Bradley told him that Tom and Lisa and Kevin had all been killed. Not quite believing his ears, the uncle pulled Bradley aside for a moment and asked if this were really true. The patrolman nodded in confirmation.

Bradley gave the three of them some time together, and then told Maggie that he was under orders to transport her to the police station for questioning. She asked if he could wait a little longer, saying she'd just thought of somebody else whom she wanted to try contacting.

She sat down at a computer and searched for the phone number of a young guy, Luke, who ran a campus ministry at

Bucknell. She'd started attending the ministry the previous semester upon learning that her dad had been diagnosed with cancer. She'd found Tim's spiritual counsel helpful then and hoped that he could also lend her support in this latest hour of need. She eventually succeeded in finding his number but wasn't able to get hold of him. Finally, sensing that Bradley was growing impatient, she borrowed a sweat-shirt and a pair of flip-flops from the neighbor's daughter and announced that she was ready to leave.

Maggie sat in the backseat of the cruiser during the short drive to the station. At one point, while they were stopped for a red light, she told Bradley that she recognized him as her DARE instructor from elementary school, adding that she wished that she were still eleven years old. Bradley tried lightening the mood by asking her about college and the courses she was taking. Maggie said that she was a science major, specializing in animal behavior. A bit farther along, she exhaled deeply and said: "What am I going to do? I could be in grief counseling for years."

Bradley found the remark oddly detached. Her parents and brother had just been murdered, and this was what she was thinking about? But then again, she *was* a fledgling scientist. Perhaps the remark simply reflected her analytical cast of mind.

They reached the station at half past three. The night was dark and starless, with a slight chill in the air. Bradley es-corted Maggie to a large conference room and chatted with her some more about college and the like. The aunt and uncle soon joined them, along with a minister from their church whom they'd contacted en route.

It was difficult for Bradley, sitting directly across from her, to tell exactly how Maggie was coping. Seemingly calm one moment, she'd break into a crying fit the next. She'd ask him various questions about the crime scene, none of which he was in a position to answer.

And time and again, she'd look up at him and say: "My mother was alive when I saw her. How could she be dead when the police arrived?"

3

Detective Bob Beck was awakened at three-fifteen by the ringing of the telephone. While certainly not expecting good news at so early an hour, he was hardly prepared for what Dave Bair had in store for him. A teenage boy and his parents, Bair said, had just been slain in their house on Peach Lane. The boy's throat was slashed and the father stabbed in the chest, with the precise nature of the mother's wounds yet to be determined. The only survivor was a twenty-year-old daughter, who'd fled to a neighbor's residence and was now being transported to the police station.

Beck arrived at the station shortly before four, as did Detectives Brent Shultz and John Wettlaufer, both of whom had also been called to duty. They made some coffee and contacted Patrolman Chris Keenan, who briefed them on what Maggie had told him and Steve Newman. As case officer for the detective squad, Beck was responsible for allocating assignments. He sent Wettlaufer to Peach Lane for crime scene processing and assigned Shultz the job of interviewing Maggie.

At four-twenty, Beck and Shultz retrieved Maggie from the conference room where she'd been waiting with Ray Bradley. They brought her into the squad room, introduced themselves, and offered her some coffee. She'd calmed down considerably since first being brought to the station, so much so that Beck and Shultz were at first rather taken aback. Was this really the same young woman whose entire family had just been murdered?

Shultz grabbed a pen and notebook and took Maggie into a small room furnished with a desk and two chairs. He eased into the interview by asking her how long she'd been home from college. She said that she'd just gotten home the day before but wished that she'd never left campus.

He then asked her to recount, as precisely as possible, what she'd seen and heard prior to fleeing the house earlier that morning.

Maggie told him much the same as she'd already told the patrol cops, though in more elaborate detail. She described the TV shows that she'd watched on her laptop upon retiring to her room for the evening, and also the instant messaging service that she'd used in chatting online with her friends from college. She said that after finally shutting down the laptop, she'd placed it on her spare bed. Then she'd turned off the lights and, since the evening was mild, thrown her comforter onto the floor. She said that she'd planned on rising early and going for a long run.

She described the angry yelling that she then heard and the scene that awaited her once she ran the length of the hallway and entered her parents' room. She said that she raced down the stairs at her mother's urging and left the house by the side door, which was the only door generally used by the family. "In retrospect," she added, "I should have dragged my mom with me."

She said that the lights were on upstairs at the time, though they most definitely weren't when she'd gone down the hallway to use the bathroom at midnight. She said that the door to her parents' room was open and that she vividly remembered seeing her dad's catheter lying next to him on the bed. He'd had it installed just a week or so earlier during a surgical procedure for the removal of scar tissue in connection with his prostate cancer.

At Shultz's request she drew two diagrams, one depicting the second-floor layout of the house and the other the precise positioning of her parents when she'd gone into their bed-room. She said that there was a phone in her parents' room, next to their bed, and a second phone in the guest room across from the staircase.

She then talked about her family, saying that her dad was a branch manager for Motion Industries and her mom a teacher at the Lancaster Brethren Preschool. She said that they'd been looking forward to her coming home for the summer and had driven to Bucknell the previous Sunday to pick up some of her belongings. She described Kevin as an introvert, very much into his studies, and a stalwart on the Quiz Bowl team at school. She said that he'd recently gotten his driver's license and had also landed a summer job at Dutch Wonderland on the outskirts of town.

Shultz asked Maggie if she had a boyfriend at college or if there were somebody she'd been dating closer to home. Maggie answered no on both counts. She ran a hand through her hair and talked some more about the loud voice that had awakened her earlier that morning. She described it as strange and terrifying, and said that when she'd stepped into the hall-way she could tell that it was coming from Kevin's room. She said that his door might have been slightly open but that she wasn't sure and didn't remain very long outside his room any-way. "That was a place I didn't want to go into," she said.

Shultz circled back to the subject of her family, asking if there were any problems on the home front. Maggie answered that she certainly didn't think so. She said that her family was much like the Cleavers of the classic sitcom *Leave It to Bea-ver*. Her mom and dad had enjoyed a strong marriage and had done everything possible to make a nice life for their kids. She said that she hadn't spoken much with Kevin of late but was quite confident that he'd been faring as well as could be expected of a sixteen-year-old boy.

Shultz asked her if there were weapons in the house, knives or guns or anything else. Maggie said that there defi-nitely weren't any guns because her dad was opposed to them. "Anyway," she said, giving him a puzzled look. "I didn't hear any gunshots."

He asked her about the sweatshirt that she had on, which was printed with the logo of a college different from her own. Maggie explained that she'd fled the house in bare feet and wearing only her shorts and a T-shirt, and so she'd borrowed the sweatshirt from the neighbor's daughter. She said that most of her clothing was still packed away in bags from college and waiting to be washed. She wished that she were still at college, she added.

"My life has crashed," she said, matter-of-factly.

Half an hour had passed now since they'd sat down together in the interview room, and Shultz was frankly perplexed by this slender young woman with brown eyes and lustrous brown hair. Her parents and younger brother had just been murdered and yet she seemed strangely unperturbed. Shultz understood from his brief conversation with Chris Keenan that she'd appeared upset at the crime scene, but how in the world had she made so rapid a recovery?

Shultz wasn't alone in finding Maggie's demeanor troubling. While the interview was still in progress, two more detectives arrived at the police station and sought out Bob Beck for a status report on the case. From their vantage point in Beck's office, directly across from the interview room, the newly arrived detectives had a good view of Maggie and could also hear what she was saying. She seemed to them the very caricature of a self-absorbed teenager, blithely unaffected by the horrible events of the morning.

They couldn't help but shake their heads in wonderment. Twenty-year-old Maggie, just recently returned home from college, escapes the house unscathed while her entire family is slaughtered? Imagine the odds of that.

4

If John Wettlaufer hadn't already known precisely where he was going, the glow of the flashing emergency lights in the early morning sky could have served as his guide. He wound his way to the top of the hill overlooking the town and turned onto Peach Lane.

Wettlaufer had been with the Manheim Township Police Department eighteen years, the past two as a criminal investigator, and he couldn't recall there ever being any serious trouble on Peach Lane. It was the kind of street that seemed impervious to trouble, that knew trouble only vicariously through the six o'clock news.

He parked across from the Haines house, got out of his car, and took a gulp of fresh air. He then spoke with Dave Bair and several other officers, who advised him that the folks from the coroner's office were on their way. He crossed the road while waiting for them so that he could take a closer look at the house.

It was an attractive two-story affair, with a stone façade, gray-shingled roof, and attached two-car garage. There was living space above the garage, which seemed of fairly recent construction. Thick shrubs covered most of the front yard, giving the entire place a secluded, almost cloistered feel. On the face of it, Wettlaufer thought, the house was one that most people in the area would have been proud to call their own.

Two deputy coroners arrived, looking grim in the pale moonlight. They went inside, with Wettlaufer and Chris Keenan leading the way, and examined first Kevin's body and then Tom's and Lisa's. It didn't take them long to determine that the victims had died of puncture and slashing wounds. Kevin had fared the worst, suffering multiple wounds to his back and arms and the gaping wound to his throat. Tom had suffered stab wounds to the chest, and Lisa a stab wound to the abdomen and gashes to the neck. The coroners officially pronounced the manner of death in all three cases as homicide.

Once they'd left, Wettlaufer took out his notebook and camera and got down to work. He started in the kitchen, where the sliding glass door leading into the backyard was slightly ajar. He noticed that there were transfer bloodstains on the handle and the doorframe, indicating that this was probably where the killer had exited the house.

Wettlaufer also noticed contact bloodstains on the hardwood floor at the foot of the staircase and additional stains all the way up to the second-floor hallway. He took special note of the bloody shoeprints, which were heaviest and most pronounced near Kevin's body and dissipated as they proceeded along the carpeted hallway and down the stairs.

Wettlaufer went into Kevin's bedroom, where it was immediately obvious that a horrific struggle had taken place. Blood was spattered on all four walls and also on the floor, the windows, and practically every piece of furniture. The dresser drawers were open and bloodstains were clearly visible on the clothing inside.

Wettlaufer surmised that the assailant had entered the room while Kevin was asleep and then stabbed him repeatedly. This would explain not only the five stab wounds to Kevin's back but also the cast-off blood that was on the underside of the bed. At some point in the ensuing struggle, the assailant must then have backed Kevin into a corner by the window, since the blood loss here was especially severe. Then he must have hacked and flailed away with the knife while Kevin tried crawling out into the hallway. This would explain the thick path of blood that led from the window to the bedroom door. Finally he must have finished the job with a final vicious slash, which tore a sizable chunk out of Kevin's throat.

Wettlaufer wasn't a squeamish guy. As an experienced investigator and a Gulf War veteran, he'd witnessed more than his share of human carnage. But the stench of death in that room, clinging to every imaginable surface, was almost more than he could bear. He hated to imagine the terror that Kevin must have felt while desperately attempting to fend off his attacker.

He next inspected the master bedroom, where there were three bloody footprints on the carpeted floor leading from the hallway. The assailant had almost certainly struck here first, stabbing Tom in the chest and Lisa in the abdomen, and then made his way into Kevin's room. This meant that he was in the process of attacking Kevin when Maggie awoke, got out of bed, and eventually ran down the hallway. In turn, this meant that he finally succeeded in killing Kevin outside the door to his room, after Maggie had fled the house.

The assailant must then have noticed that Lisa was still alive and gone back into the master bedroom to finish her off, tracking bloody footprints on the carpet. This would explain the gashes on her neck.

Wettlaufer went into the common bathroom on the second floor, which was located just beyond the staircase. There were bloodstains on the linoleum floor and also in the sink. Wettlaufer found it hard to believe. After disposing of his victims, the assailant had apparently been in no particular hurry to leave the house. Rather, he'd actually taken the time to go into the bathroom and rinse off his hands.

5

Allen Leed jumped out of bed and answered the phone on the second ring. It was the police dispatcher, informing him that he was urgently needed at the station.

"We've got a triple homicide, Al," he said.

"No kidding?" Leed said. "Where?"

"Peach Lane," the dispatcher said. "In the Blossom Hill neighborhood."

Leed's first thought was that the dispatcher had misspoken. Blossom Hill was just about the least likely neighborhood in the township for a triple homicide. It was probably a domestic incident instead, where some guy went berserk and threatened a couple of family members before finally killing himself. He asked the dispatcher if this was indeed the case.

"No, Al," the dispatcher said. "That's not what happened. You'd better get in here."

Leed took a quick shower and then threw on some clothes. He'd scarcely slept prior to receiving the call, having been kept up late investigating a shooting at a local tavern, but it didn't really matter. He'd long ago learned that there was nothing quite like homicide for setting the mind on edge.

Once he got to the police station, he sat down with Bob Beck and Assistant DA Craig Stedman, who'd arrived himself just moments before. The three men went over the essentials of the case while waiting for Brent Shultz to wrap up his initial interview with Maggie. As the lone survivor in what was already shaping up to be the worst crime in the history of Manheim Township, they were understandably anxious to find out what she had to say.

At five o'clock, Shultz left Maggie alone in the interview room so that he could confer with Beck, Stedman, and Leed. He briefed them on what she'd told him and also admitted to a certain uneasiness. While normally able to get a good read on people in face-to-face interviews, he found himself in this instance almost entirely at a loss. Clearly not everyone reacted to trauma in the same way, but Maggie was something else altogether. She seemed so chatty—so utterly nonchalant—that it was difficult to tell if she was feeling any trauma at all.

They talked it over and decided that Shultz should have Maggie type out a formal statement. It was imperative, after all, that they find out as precisely as possible her version of events so they could know how best to proceed with the investigation.

Shultz set Maggie up with a laptop and asked her to type out a detailed account of everything that had happened prior to her fleeing the house. She got right down to it, though not without first changing the font on the laptop.

The detectives and the assistant DA had little difficulty staying occupied while Maggie prepared her statement. They contacted John Wettlaufer by cell phone for an update on his investigation inside the Haines home. They spoke with Dave Bair again to make sure that the crime scene was totally secure. They reviewed photographs of the three bodies that the folks from the coroner's office had sent them. They made another pot of coffee and did some preliminary brainstorming based on the scant facts thus far at their disposal.

And all the while, Maggie's behavior continued to elicit concern. She'd pause occasionally from her typing to fling her head back and stroke her hair. She'd glance out into the squad room and smile. She seemed no more troubled than if she were knocking off an assignment for a favorite course at college.

Yet another detective, Cleon Berntheizel, a big soft-spoken guy in his mid-forties whom everyone simply called Bernie, came into the squad room while Maggie was working on her statement. She seemed so carefree that he wondered if she actually knew the full story about her family.

"Does she know that they've all been murdered?" he asked a couple of his fellow detectives.

"Oh, yeah," they said. "She knows."

Allen Leed hadn't yet had a chance to speak with Maggie but he could certainly appreciate the concerns of his colleagues. It did indeed seem curious that the killings had occurred just her second night back from college. And no less curious that she'd succeeded in fleeing the house without catching so much as a glimpse of the assailant. Leed knew that in cases of this sort the guilty party was quite often a family member or at least somebody—a scorned lover, a possessive boyfriend—with strategic connections to the family. Certainly nobody at this point was accusing Maggie of anything, but the detectives would be seriously remiss not to give her a closer look.

For the moment, however, Leed wasn't overly concerned. Maggie's demeanor was so odd—so contrary to expectation—that it seemed to him almost to vouch for her truthfulness. If she were somehow involved with the murders, wouldn't she want to cover her tracks by making as public a display of grief as possible? Why risk drawing suspicion to herself by behaving as if the murders scarcely mattered? Leed suspected that perhaps the only thing that she was really guilty of was having a quirky personality.

At fifty-seven, Leed was the self-described old dog of the detective squad. He'd gone into law enforcement in 1973 after having served an extended stint in Vietnam, and over the years he'd developed a style all his own. He was the kind of cop who tried treating everyone the same way that he'd want to be treated. This might mean dropping by the county jail so that he could pick up some guy he'd busted the night before and take him out to breakfast, or visiting the home of a crime victim to inquire if there was anything that he could do to help ease the pain.

With his glasses and bald pate, he looked about as prepossessing as a high school math teacher, and yet there was no mistaking when Leed showed up for work. He had the sort of unforced presence that people were quite naturally drawn to, and also a gift of gab that helped relieve the daily tensions of the squad room. Fellow detectives would gravitate to his cubicle to discuss the cases that they were working on and old buddies from patrol would invariably stop by just to say hello. The squad room somehow seemed less than fully complete on those occasions when Allen Leed wasn't on the job.

Even suspects enjoyed talking with Leed, which was a big factor in his success as an investigator. He could be sharp and aggressive if necessary but generally favored a more avuncular approach, taking the time to find common ground and build a sense of rapport. As often as not, suspects would find themselves so disarmed by his offhand style, and so eager to please, that they'd end up divulging far more than they'd initially bargained on.

There was the time, for example, when he went to the home of a high school student who was suspected of vandalizing the football coach's car. The kid denied having had anything to do with it and his parents insisted that he was telling the truth. Leed sat down with the kid and chatted with him about football and weight training and several other interests that they had in common. Finally he looked up at him and smiled.

"Listen," he said. "I'm pretty sure it was you who trashed the coach's car. All I want to know is why you did it."

"Because the guy's a jerk," the kid said. "That's why."

Leed told the kid that he didn't necessarily disagree with his harsh assessment but that now they needed to find a way to make things right.

Leed's work cubicle was stuffed with papers and documents, a couple of which held extra special significance for him. The first of these was a letter that the Texas Rangers sent his son Adam upon drafting him out of college. Adam went on to hit a three-run homer in his first at-bat in single-A ball, and though his career was eventually cut short by injury, the simple fact of his having been drafted was more than enough to make his father proud.

The second was the obituary for an old friend from high school who'd been a promising athlete before falling into a life of drug addiction and petty crime. He finally died of AIDS in 1986, having wasted away to a mere ninety pounds. Leed had kept in touch with him over the years and was profoundly shaken by his death. Every so often he'd take out the obituary and read through it while thinking: "My friend was a good man. What happened to him might very well, under different circumstances, have also happened to me."

Maggie poked her head out of the interview room and informed the detectives that she'd finished her statement.

"Okay, I'm done," she said. "You need anything else?"

The detectives printed it out and looked it over in Bob Beck's office. If a comprehensive account was what they'd wanted, Maggie had certainly delivered the goods.

She began with her arriving home from Bucknell at seven o'clock on Thursday evening. Her dad and younger brother, she wrote, were just then heading out to the local high school for a meeting concerning Kevin's upcoming trip to Germany and so she ate dinner with her mom and loafed around the house until they'd returned. Then the entire family gathered in the living room and talked about how their respective days had gone.

She watched a rerun of *Scrubs* with Kevin at eight-thirty and then part of an episode of *Grey's Anatomy* with her parents, though neither her mom nor her dad seemed quite in tune with the show's basic premise. She tried explaining it to them but they eventually lost interest altogether and drifted off to bed. She went upstairs herself at ten o'clock only to discover that she wasn't yet tired, probably because her system was still stuck on college time. She chatted online with a couple of friends and read for a while before finally falling asleep.

She got up at nine-thirty on Friday, May 11th, and spent the morning watching television and unpacking some of her stuff from college. Tom popped by at noon for a quick bite of lunch and then went back to work. Lisa came home an hour later, loaded down with presents that the kids in her preschool class had given her in appreciation of her efforts throughout the year. She helped Maggie with her unpacking for a while before sitting down to write thank-you notes to the preschool kids. Maggie, in the meantime, went online and took a couple of tests for the temp agency where she was planning on working during the summer.

By no means, she was careful to point out in her statement, was the agency her first choice for summer employment. "I'd meant to find something more 'sciency,'" she wrote. "But a job is a job and I need to make money so I can spend it at college."

When Kevin finished school for the day, he and Maggie drove to a nearby shopping center, Chelsea Square, where they picked up Mother's Day cards and a jar of spaghetti sauce. Finally, Tom came home from work and at five-thirty exactly, as was their habit, the entire family said grace and sat down to dinner.

After helping Tom wash the dishes, Lisa and Maggie spent half an hour working on a *Washington Post* crossword puzzle at the family computer. "Mom and I like to do it together," Maggie wrote. "We did it almost daily when I was home for the summer after graduating high school."

They then popped down to their local Blockbuster store and rented the romantic comedy *Because I Said So* and the Will Ferrell feature *Stranger Than Fiction*. "The romantic comedy looked good to mom and me," Maggie wrote. "We thought dad and Kevin might like the other one better."

Kevin almost certainly would have liked the other one better. He wandered in and out of the family room while *Because I Said So* was playing and finally went upstairs to bed. "I swear he's the only kid that goes to bed that early," Maggie wrote, "but he always has and probably always will."

Lisa went upstairs when the movie was over, and Tom

joined her after watching the end of the Phillies game with Maggie. "I guarantee you," Maggie wrote, "that after ten minutes up there, my parents are probably sleeping."

From this point on, her statement closely corresponded to what she'd told Brent Shultz half an hour earlier. She described going upstairs to bed herself and eventually falling asleep only to be awakened by a loud voice.

"I heard a male screaming. Not words, just screams. It sounded like it was coming from Kevin's room."

She described her tentative efforts to investigate the commotion and also the fear she felt for her own safety: "I open my door to the hallway. I step out of my doorway and turn so that I'm right at Kevin's door. I think his door was partially open. Lights are on upstairs. I don't know where they're from. I don't know if Kevin's lights were on. I sensed that there was an intruder in the house, in Kevin's room. I heard impacts like somebody was getting beat up. I thought that somebody was beating up the intruder. I don't know why I thought that. I went back into my room. I shut the door and blocked it with my body. I realized it was a possibility they could still push the door open, because I'm not terribly strong. I realized that staying in my room was not a safe option."

And then her running down the hallway and going into her mom and dad's bedroom: "Their door was open. It's usually open. Lights were on in their room. I go to the edge of their bed. My dad is lying on his back on top of the fitted sheet. There are no other sheets or blankets on the bed. He's lying still. I notice his catheter. My mom is sitting on the edge of the bed, facing the wall. She's in hysterics. She's crying, telling me to go get help or call for help."

And finally her frantic rush outside and across the street to the neighbor's house in the pitch-black darkness.

"My neighbor opens the door and lets me in. I tell her what happened and start to freak out. I desperately hope that it's a dream and that I'll wake up because I have no idea what's going on. She calls the police and I give her the details they ask for. I stay in her house until the police come. They arrive and come directly to talk to us and then go to my house. I tell them what happened and they go to the house. They tell me that they rang the doorbell and no one answered, which is weird. But maybe my family was hiding or something. They have me go over there and I tell them where my parents' bedroom is and they send me back across the street to my neighbor's. The next thing I know, Officer Bradley is at their door and asks me for information and I repeat what happened. Time passes, and police are still at my house. I start to freak out because I have no idea what's going on. Then Officer Bradley comes back and you know the rest."

The detectives read through the statement and then did so again. Some of the details they found heartbreakingly poignant. Tom taking the trouble to come home from work for lunch, no doubt for the sake of keeping his daughter company . . . Lisa helping Maggie unpack and then sitting down to write thank-you notes to the preschoolers . . . Maggie driving her younger brother to a local shopping center to pick out Mother's Day cards . . . Both kids staying home on a Friday night to watch a movie with their parents. The family seemed so innocent, so utterly sweet.

And also somewhat on the dull side. They'd apparently sit down to dinner every evening at five-thirty on the dot. And get ready for bed, even on weekends, at no later than ten or eleven. Perhaps, as Maggie had suggested to Brent Shultz, they really were like the Cleaver family of television sitcom fame.

There were other aspects of the statement that the detectives found no less striking. As often as not, they noticed, Maggie would refer to family members in the present tense, as if the murders hadn't actually occurred. "Mom and I like to do [the crossword] together," she remarked at one point. And again, this time in reference to Kevin: "I swear he's the only kid that goes to bed that early but he always has and probably always will." Was this nothing more than grammatical imprecision on Maggie's part? Or rather a matter of her still being in shock and incapable of accepting that her parents and younger brother were no longer alive?

They also noticed that she now claimed to have been awakened by the sound of screaming whereas previously she'd described it as a loud yelling. "I heard a male screaming," she wrote. "Not words, just screams." So what was going on here? Was this shift in description a cause for concern, or was Maggie simply deploying the two terms interchangeably?

There was something else. The detectives had taken special training in statement analysis. They knew that statements loaded with extraneous detail were often less than fully truthful, especially when ending on too abrupt and impersonal a note. Maggie's statement was certainly loaded with detail, some of which may very well have qualified as extraneous. She'd thrown in personal asides on everything from *Grey's Anatomy* to her preferences for summer employment. She'd talked about the bedtime routines of her family and also their tastes in film. She'd provided not so much a statement as a full-blown chronicle.

But the thing that really raised a red flag for the detectives was the manner in which she'd ended her statement.

"Then Officer Bradley comes back," she'd written, "and you know the rest."

And you know the rest. It seemed so detached, so startlingly matter-of-fact. Her entire family had just been slaughtered, and this was her concluding remark? Not even Allen Leed knew quite what to make of it.

6

It was a delicate balancing act for the detectives. They certainly couldn't assume that Maggie was telling them the full truth. To do so would have been a dereliction of duty. Their responsibility was to solve the murders, which at this point in the investigation meant taking absolutely nothing for granted.

But neither could they treat her as a suspect. Here was a young woman, after all, who'd just lost her brother and both of her parents under the cruelest of circumstances. If she were indeed telling the truth, she deserved all of the compassion that they could possibly muster.

The detectives were mindful of something else besides. There was a good chance that Maggie herself was in danger. Perhaps the assailant had planned on killing her, too, and would now be trying to track her down to finish the job. For all they knew, she may even have been the primary target.

Allen Leed suspected that there was still more they could learn from Maggie, quite apart from what she'd already told them, and so he sat down with her at a small table toward the rear of the squad room.

He began the interview by asking her about her family. Why in the world would anybody want to murder her parents and younger brother? Did the family have enemies that she was aware of? Did they owe somebody money, or have connections with drug dealers or other criminal elements? Had her mom or dad ever spoken of personal conflicts at their respective places of employment? Or dropped hints about having been involved in a sexual affair? Was there anything she could think of that might help explain why this terrible thing had happened?

Maggie said that nothing whatsoever came to mind. The family was a paragon of middle-class respectability. Her parents paid their bills on time. They went to church every Sunday. They loved spending evenings at home. The very idea of their consorting with drug dealers or cheating on one another was simply preposterous. As for Kevin, it would be hard to find a more inoffensive, straitlaced kid. His social life revolved around the Boy Scouts and the Quiz Bowl team, for heaven's sake. He hadn't gotten into anything approaching serious trouble in his entire life.

Leed asked if the murderer might be someone she herself knew. An old flame from high school perhaps, or somebody whom she'd befriended at college?

Maggie said that she highly doubted it. She didn't have a boyfriend in high school and hadn't dated much thus far at college. She got along well with her professors and classmates and the students in her dorm. She couldn't begin to imagine any of her friends or acquaintances committing so awful a crime.

Leed kept probing, asking Maggie still more questions about her family, their social networks, their likes and dislikes. No one, he reasoned, knew more about the family than she did. No one was better positioned to understand why the murders had taken place. Perhaps there was something she'd not yet thought of, some small but telling detail that would help identify the perpetrator.

The longer they spoke, the better Leed felt about Maggie. He found her smart and candid, with a core of toughness beneath the callow surface. He believed that she was every bit as committed to resolving the crime as he and his colleagues were, which partly explained why she'd thus far exhibited so little emotional distress. The demands of the moment called for dispassion, clearheadedness. She'd permit herself the luxury of grieving only after having helped the detectives as much as she possibly could. All things considered, Leed thought, she seemed a most remarkable young woman.

Everyone in the squad room anxiously awaited the outcome of the interview, no one more so than Assistant DA Craig Stedman. In his early forties, handsome, and quietly intense, Stedman was head of the county's major crime unit, a job that he'd held for nearly eight years. He wasn't quite ready to pronounce this the worst murder case of his experience, though for sheer horror it almost certainly ranked in the same league as the notorious Jesse Wise and Landon May cases.

Jesse Wise was an unemployed grocery clerk from the town of Leola who'd gone on a killing spree the previous year, bludgeoning six of his family members to death and stacking their bodies in his basement. The victims spanned three generations, the oldest Wise's sixty-four-year-old grandmother, the youngest his five-year-old cousin. Their bodies were caked in soot and grime upon being discovered by investigators.

Landon May was yet another small-town loser bent on mayhem. In 2001 he and a friend tortured and murdered a middle-aged couple, Terry and Lucy Smith, at a house in rural Lancaster County. Their treatment of Lucy Smith was especially appalling. They shot her and sexually molested her. They beat her with a claw hammer and stabbed her repeatedly and finally suffocated her. They did all of this, presumably, for the purpose of forcing the couple to relinquish the PIN numbers to their bankcards.

Stedman rarely betrayed emotion on the job, though cases of this sort privately took a toll on him. He identified closely with crime victims and was sometimes haunted by their suffering. The Landon May case was especially taxing in this respect. At one point, after having been beaten and stabbed and sexually assaulted by May and his crony, Lucy Smith managed to break free and stagger into a bathroom. Stedman couldn't help but imagine the horror that she must have felt upon seeing her reflection in the mirror. She'd have fully realized by then that her tormentors were intent on killing her and that there was little chance of escape. The image of her cringing before that mirror gave Stedman nightmares long after the trial was over.

It was this quality of empathy, and also a scrupulous attention to detail, that made Stedman a formidable presence in the prosecutor's office. He vowed that he'd never lose a case for lack of caring or lack of effort, and thus far in his tenure as head of the major crime unit he'd been as good as his word. He routinely worked through lunch and long into the evening, and he was generally one of the first officials on the scene whenever significant trouble arose. He was a favorite of criminal investigators throughout the county, all of whom admired his legal savvy and sheer relentlessness in bringing even the most stubborn of cases to closure. The role of prosecuting attorney wasn't so much a job to him as a sacred calling.

It was a calling, moreover, for which he'd seemed destined from an early age. Raised as the second of three children in nearby Bucks County, he had a strong penchant for law and order even as a schoolboy. When other neighborhood kids were tossing eggs and generally creating mischief the night following Halloween, Stedman would stand outside his family home with a hose so that he could clean up after them. Any sort of social misconduct was strictly anathema to him. After graduating high school, he attended the University of Delaware on an ROTC scholarship and then went on to Dickinson Law School. By this point he'd already made up his mind that he wanted to be a prosecutor. There was nothing else that he could readily imagine himself doing.

Stedman anxiously awaited the outcome of Leed's interview with Maggie. In the meantime, however, he had his hands full preparing an affidavit for a search warrant. It was imperative that the police gain unimpeded access to the house on Peach Lane as soon as possible so that they could scour every inch of it. Perhaps the clue that would break open the case was lurking in a dresser drawer or tucked away in a family photo album. Perhaps it was something as seemingly innocuous as a note on the refrigerator door. There was only one thing that Stedman knew for sure: If there was indeed a clue to be found, they'd spare absolutely no effort looking for it.

It was well past dawn now, and Maggie's Aunt Tammy and Uncle James were still waiting in the conference room at the police station. Several more relatives had arrived by this point, including Tom Haines's second brother, Robert.

At seven-thirty, James and Robert left the station and made the short drive to their parents' house. They broke the news to their dad out on the front porch before going inside and telling their mother. They offered whatever consolation they could, though there were, of course, no magical words for a situation so bleak.

Upon returning to the police station, they found Maggie sitting in the conference room and eating a bagel. Though the detectives hadn't yet finished interviewing her, they'd given her a much-deserved break for a bite of breakfast.

James and Robert Haines were good and decent men. They loved their niece and were prepared to lend her their fullest support. But at that precise moment they were taken aback by how unruffled she seemed. It wasn't so much that they suspected her of anything. Rather they were simply confused. How in the world was she able to pull it off? How was she able to muster such composure in the wake of so horrible a tragedy? It seemed to them utterly remarkable.

It would take some time before anyone involved with the case appreciated just how remarkable Maggie truly was.

7

Craig Stedman obtained his search warrant for the house on Peach Lane at eight-thirty that Saturday morning, which meant that investigators now had carte blanche to go through the premises with a fine-toothed comb.

At Stedman's request, the judge who issued the warrant ordered that the supporting affidavit be sealed for sixty days. There were compelling grounds for doing so. The affidavit contained sensitive information about the crime scene that Stedman wanted kept confidential lest the entire investigation be jeopardized. The perpetrator might not have realized, for example, that he'd left bloody footprints at the scene. If he were to find out about this through the news media, there was a good chance that he'd dispose of his shoes and other potentially incriminating evidence.

Half an hour later, at nine in the morning, the Lancaster County Forensic Unit entered the house and got down to work. They took photographs, video footage, and precise measurements of the various rooms. They took blood swabs from the contact stains on the sliding door in the kitchen and also on the banister on the lower landing of the staircase. They took cutouts of bloody shoeprint impressions from the carpeted hallway on the second floor and an additional cutout from the linoleum floor in the bathroom. They took swatches of fabric from a bloodstained recliner in Kevin's bedroom.

They searched under the beds, through the closets, and behind every stick of furniture. They found a bloody tissue in the upstairs bathroom and bloodstained pajama bottoms on the floor in Kevin's room. They found Maggie's laptop computer on the spare bed in her room and two desktop computers elsewhere in the house. They found a lockbox that was stuffed with family memorabilia in the master bedroom. They found two cell phones on the kitchen counter and a third in Kevin's backpack, which was propped up in a corner of the living room.

They searched through the wastebasket in the kitchen and found the receipt for the jar of spaghetti sauce that Maggie and Kevin had purchased at the mall the previous evening. They found the half-empty jar in the fridge, alongside a container of meatballs. And on top of Kevin's dresser, they found an envelope containing two Mother's Day cards. The cards were blank inside. Kevin and Maggie hadn't had an opportunity to fill them out.

Back at the police station, Bob Beck was still busy allocating assignments. Beck knew that the very early stages of a homicide investigation were of critical importance and he wanted to make sure that nothing was left to chance. He assigned a couple of detectives the task of conducting interviews with neighbors of the Haines family. He also helped arrange a police search of the surrounding area for any possible physical evidence. And he gave Detective Cleon Berntheizel the job of interviewing Maggie's two uncles, James and Robert Haines. Perhaps they'd know something of value to the case beyond what Maggie apparently did.

Bernie was a good choice for the job. He'd worked in construction for ten years before joining the department and retained a regular guy's knack for putting people at ease. He spoke with the two uncles separately at his desk in the squad room, while Allen Leed was wrapping up his interview with Maggie across the way.

The uncles had much the same to say. Their brother Tom was a gentle, mild-mannered man and a devoted husband and father. He catered to his kids and seemed as much in

love with Lisa as when they'd first gotten married. He was a
branch manager for an industrial supplies company and
gave every indication of liking his job. He never got angry
or visibly annoyed, preferring simply to smile through any
trouble that might come his way. He appeared even to have
taken his recent battle with prostate cancer entirely in stride.
Lisa, they said, was every bit as nice as Tom, though rather
less outgoing. She'd worked at the Lancaster Church of the
Brethren Preschool for the past seven or eight years, a job
that was ideally suited to her sweet disposition. She'd geared
her life around Maggie and Kevin, both of whom she was
immensely proud of. There was nothing, the uncles said, that
she wouldn't do for them.

Kevin took after his mom, they said. He was quiet and shy
and very much a homebody. He enjoyed scouting and had
been excited of late at the prospect of earning his Eagle Scout
award. He was also as smart as a whip, a member of the Quiz
Bowl team at school, and a German history buff. Maggie was
vivacious, conscientious, and a top-flight student. Everybody
liked her, and for good reason: She seemed not to have a
mean or malicious bone in her entire body. She loved competitive running and was on the track team at Bucknell. She
was especially close to her dad, who was a competitive runner
in his own right.

Maggie's uncles said that they'd spoken with Tom several
days earlier and he'd seemed perfectly fine. He and Lisa had
just returned from Bucknell, where they'd picked up some of
Maggie's belongings for the summer.

They insisted that they had no idea why this terrible thing
had happened. Tom and his family were just about the last
people in the world that anybody would want to hurt.

Bernie thanked them and, after conferring with Bob Beck,
drove to the Lancaster Church of the Brethren Preschool, on
the off chance that somebody would be there on a Saturday
morning. Bernie was familiar with the place, a low-slung, red-
brick complex with nicely manicured grounds located just off
the Oregon Pike. His children had attended the school and
genuinely enjoyed it. It was only after he'd parked his car and

tried the front entrance, however, that the grim reality hit home.

"Oh, my God," he thought to himself. "Lisa Haines is the very same woman who taught all three of my kids."

The entrance was locked up tight and so Bernie contacted his dispatcher and obtained the address of the woman who was currently running the school. He drove over to her house and told her that he had some questions concerning Lisa Haines.

"Why?" the woman asked. "Is there something the matter with Lisa?"

Bernie was in a tough spot here. The triple homicide hadn't been released to the news media yet and Bob Beck had instructed him to avoid getting into specifics.

"An incident was reported to the police," Bernie said, trying to be as vague as possible. "About something that happened at her home. We're just interested in getting information on Lisa and her family."

"What sort of incident?" the woman asked.

Bernie said that he wasn't precisely sure, though he thought that it might have been trespassing or harassment.

This seemed to put her somewhat more at ease. She said that Lisa worked with the four-year-olds at the preschool, and that she seemed pleasant enough but was a quiet person and mostly kept to herself. She said that she really didn't know much about Lisa's family situation. She suggested that Bernie speak with Karen Hope, who also worked with the four-year-olds and might be of greater help.

Bernie drove straight to Karen's and, still playing it coy, said that he needed some background information on Lisa due to a recent incident at her home.

Karen said that she'd worked closely with Lisa over the past two years, though they could hardly be described as confidantes. Lisa would sometimes talk about her two kids, as often as not referring to her daughter as "Princess Maggie." She was excited about Maggie returning home for the summer, especially since she'd spent the previous summer at college working on a biology project.

Bernie asked her if Lisa had ever indicated that she might be experiencing stress or trouble at home.

Karen said that she didn't think so. Just the previous afternoon, in fact, Lisa had seemed really quite cheerful. It was the last day of school and they'd had a picnic outside; she'd played games with the children in her class.

Bernie next went to Tom's place of work, which was also closed for the day. He checked the perimeter of the property and rummaged through a Dumpster but found no evidence related to the triple homicide. He was about to leave when a middle-aged guy pulled onto the lot and introduced himself as a business associate of Tom's. The guy said that he already knew what had happened. One of Tom's relatives had phoned him with the awful news.

They went inside and sat in a small office on the main floor of the building. The guy said that he'd spoken with several other coworkers about the killings and that they were all in a state of disbelief. Tom, he said, was one of the nicest men that he and his colleagues had ever met. Though manager of the local branch, he treated everyone as his equal. He was civil and generous and always prepared to accord his staff the benefit of the doubt. Whenever a problem arose on the job, he'd always try resolving it discreetly and hence save unnecessary embarrassment. He was the kind of boss who made coming into work a real pleasure.

Bernie was a tad skeptical about so saintly a portrait. Was there no one, he asked, whom Tom might have rubbed the wrong way?

The guy thought about this for a long moment, as if unsure about disclosing in-house secrets. Finally he said that there was indeed someone. He'd heard through the grapevine that Tom had recently taken a new salesman to task for a substandard job performance. The two men had apparently engaged in a shouting match in Tom's office. He said that the assistant manager of the local branch would know more about this than he himself did.

The assistant manager was waiting at the front door when Bernie arrived at his house. He'd already heard about the triple homicide and was obviously shaken. He, too, described Tom in glowing terms, saying that he'd never before met anyone so easygoing or respectful. He said that the killings came as a complete shock. Just three or four weeks earlier, he'd accompanied Tom to a regional corporate meeting in Delaware and Tom had seemed perfectly fine.

Bernie asked him if it were true that Tom had recently had a run-in at work with an underperforming salesman.

The assistant manager said that indeed this was so. Tom and the salesman, a guy named Bruce Smyth, had had a closed-door meeting, and things had apparently gotten rather heated. Tom had advised Smyth that his future with the company was in jeopardy unless he dramatically increased his productivity and became more of a team player.

Bernie asked if Smyth had appeared angry or upset following the closed-door meeting. The assistant manager said that he didn't believe so but maybe the guy was accomplished at disguising his true feelings. He was, after all, a salesman.

Bernie wondered if there might be something to this. Could a disgruntled employee under Tom's supervision have been responsible for the triple homicide? The motivation seemed rather thin but perhaps there was more involved than immediately met the eye. Perhaps the guy had other grievances beyond having his competency called into question. Perhaps he'd been harboring ill will toward Tom for quite some time.

It seemed rather a stretch but the possibility certainly couldn't be discounted. So far, at any rate, the police had nothing better to go on.

Upon returning to the station, Bernie learned that the search of the Peach Lane neighborhood had thus far turned up only one item of potential consequence. Two patrol officers had found a Washington Nationals baseball cap nestled in some foliage on a steep embankment in a wooded area behind the Haines home. The team logo on the front of the cap was covered with duct tape.

It was a bit of a mystery, the duct tape covering the logo. None of the detectives knew quite what to make of it.

8

Angela Kreider delivered newspapers for a living. The job required that she leave home most mornings at one o'clock or shortly thereafter. She'd normally get back at somewhere between five and six, which gave her time to relax before making breakfast for her two boys and seeing them off to school.

It was only on alternate weeks, actually, that she had to worry about seeing them off to school. Ever since she and her ex-husband Tim had split up, they'd shared joint custody of the boys, one week with her, the next with Tim. They also had a nineteen-year-old daughter who stayed full-time with Angela.

On Saturday, May 12th, she finished her morning delivery at roughly five o'clock. Fifteen minutes later she pulled into the driveway of her handsome red-brick townhouse, which was located in the Cobblestone Court neighborhood of Manheim Township, barely a ten-minute walk from Peach Lane.

A light was on in the living room, which rather surprised her. When she'd left for work several hours earlier, the house had been quiet and dark. She'd reasonably assumed that the kids were sound asleep for the night.

She went inside and found her older son, sixteen-year-old Alec, sitting alone on the couch. He was bare-chested, wearing nothing but pajama bottoms. He told her that he was feeling sick to his stomach.

Angela didn't doubt that he wasn't feeling well. He looked a bit green around the gills, and why else after all would he be up so early on a Saturday morning? She wondered if it was something that he'd eaten, or if he was perhaps coming down with the flu.

"Would you like me to give you some tummy medicine?" she asked him.

Alec declined the offer of medicine, saying that he'd try lying down again and see if the discomfort in his stomach simply passed.

Then he went upstairs to bed.

Angela also delivered the afternoon edition of the local newspaper, which most days came out shortly before noon. When she picked up her papers at noon later that same Saturday, she could scarcely believe her eyes. The front page featured a story on the slaying of Kevin Haines and his parents.

Angela knew the Haines family. Kevin was her son Alec's best friend. The two boys had hung out together since the fourth grade. They'd slept over at one another's houses more often than she could remember. They'd taken most of the same classes at school and participated in many of the same extracurricular activities. They were scheduled to be roommates on the upcoming school trip to Germany.

Angela wished that she weren't at work, that she weren't under pressure to deliver the papers on time. She wished that she were home with Alec. She hated to think of him hearing this terrible news without a parent on hand to help cushion the blow. She worried about the emotional impact that it might have on him.

She called home and got Alec on the line. She asked him if he'd heard what had happened to the Haines family.

Alec said that another of his good friends, Warren Tobin, had phoned just fifteen minutes earlier and told him that Kevin and his parents had been murdered. He'd assumed, he said, that Warren was joking.

Angela said that it was no joke, that they had indeed been

murdered. The story was on the front page of the afternoon paper.

Alec had nothing to say to this. He went quiet over the phone and then started gasping and sputtering. It was as if the breath had been knocked out of him. Then he started sighing loudly.

Angela could tell that he was in rough shape. She tried consoling him. She told him that she loved him and that the pain he was now feeling would eventually fade. She promised that she'd get home as soon as possible.

"Then I'll give you the big hug you need," she said.

About half an hour later, Angela's ex-husband Tim dropped by the house on Cobblestone Court. Their daughter had turned nineteen several days before, and Tim had arranged to pick her up and take her out for a belated birthday dinner.

At this point Tim still hadn't heard that Tom, Lisa, and Kevin had been murdered. He found out from his daughter, however, who was visibly upset upon answering the door.

Tim was stunned. Prior to the breakup of his marriage with Angela, he'd seen quite a lot of Kevin Haines. Kevin and his own sixteen-year-old son, Alec, were such good buddies that they'd sometimes seemed joined at the hip. Tim also knew Tom and Lisa, if only on a casual basis. He'd chat with them whenever they dropped Kevin off at the house, and he'd occasionally see Tom out running in the neighborhood and give him a wave of acknowledgment.

Once his initial shock wore off, Tim's thoughts turned to Alec and his state of mind. He knew that Alec was an emotionally intense kid even at the best of times and that the end of the school year, with assignments due and final examinations looming, was especially pressure-packed for him. How then would he cope with the shocking news that his best friend had just been murdered?

Tim went upstairs and found Alec alone in his room. He was lying in bed, wearing shorts and a T-shirt. Tim sat beside him and held him close. Alec broke down in tears. He seemed so distraught that he could barely speak.

Tim decided that he'd take Alec home with him for a

short while until Angela got back from work. He couldn't stand the thought of his teenage son suffering through this ordeal without the presence of a parent. The birthday dinner for his daughter would have to wait until another day.

Tim lived in a neighborhood of large single-family homes with expansive lawns and nicely manicured gardens. The neighborhood was situated on the edge of lush farmland, no more than a five-minute drive from the Manheim Township police station. His own home was an attractive split-level affair, with beige siding, green trim, and dormer windows. He'd installed a basketball hoop in the driveway not long after purchasing the place so that his two boys could get some exercise during the weeks that they spent with him.

He brought Alec inside and they sat together on the couch in the living room. Alec was still obviously upset but also very quiet. He seemed not to want to talk about the murders. After a while he stretched out on the couch and fell asleep with his head on Tim's lap.

Tim took Alec back to Angela's house at around two in the afternoon. He told him that he'd see him again the next day and suggested hopefully that the worst of the crisis might have passed by then.

Angela got home from work shortly afterward and gave Alec the hug that she'd promised him over the phone. She tried talking with him but without much success. Alec remained tight-lipped, apparently locked away from the world. Angela knew that he tended to be guarded with his feelings, but she wished that she could break through to him. She wished that she could somehow brighten his mood.

She could tell that the murders were weighing heavily on him.

She wondered if he were reminiscing about some of the good times that he'd spent with his best friend, Kevin.

9

By late Saturday afternoon, May 12th, the local community was in a state of rising panic. The murders had made not only the regional but also the national media. People feared that a lunatic was on the loose and that he might very well strike again.

It was all the police could manage simply to keep track of the tips that poured into the station. Almost everyone, or so it seemed, had seen or heard something of relevance to the investigation. Most of the tips were well intentioned. Few, if any, were actually helpful.

A woman who lived near the crime scene reported hearing odd scraping and grunting noises outside her home in the early morning. Another woman reported hearing footsteps and the sound of coughing. Yet another said that she heard screaming but had assumed at the time that it was merely a television playing too loudly. An elderly man claimed that somebody jiggled his front doorknob and then peeked through his living-room window.

There were numerous reports of suspicious characters lurking about the neighborhood on the eve of the murders. A man who lived several doors from the scene said that he saw three young Hispanic guys circling the block in a low-slung black Chevy. It seemed obvious to him now, he said, that they were casing the Haines home, most likely with the intention of breaking in later on. Another man said that two teenagers done up in full Goth garb spat and cursed at him while passing by on the sidewalk. Somebody else reported seeing several scruffy, heavily tattooed guys panhandling outside a store on the nearby Lititz Pike.

Quite a few people informed the police that they'd received threatening phone calls of late. A woman who lived around the corner from the Haines home said that just the previous day an anonymous caller told her that he planned on shooting her at the local Home Depot. "I'll blow your brains out," he reportedly said. A teenage girl said that she received a call from a raspy-voiced guy vowing that he'd track each and every one of her movements until he finally succeeded in cornering her alone.

A teacher from the local high school contacted the police with the name of a grade-ten student whom she suspected of bullying Kevin. Parents phoned with the names of kids whom they thought were involved with Satanism or drugs or other kinds of deviant activity. An anonymous caller reported an incident that had ostensibly taken place on the school bus several months before, involving a student threatening two younger students with a knife.

People called the station with rumors and innuendo, with tales that sometimes seemed spun out of thin air. One guy said that he'd heard through the grapevine that several undesirable characters had recently visited Tom at his place of work. Another said that he'd heard from a former neighbor of the Haines family that Maggie had a boyfriend whom Tom emphatically disliked. Still another claimed that Tom was a notorious slumlord and suggested that one of his aggrieved tenants had probably committed the murders.

Several callers seemed convinced that there was some sort of sexual intrigue behind the triple homicide. One woman said that she'd heard from reliable sources that Kevin had recently been seen in the company of a suspected pedophile. A clerk at a local video shop said that she was quite certain that a student from Bucknell had been stalking Maggie. A guy from a nearby town said that he'd once seen a man closely resembling Tom hanging out with some tough-looking customers at a raunchy gay bar.

People sometimes seemed only too eager to point an accusing finger at someone whom they themselves personally knew. They called the station suggesting that an old flame or ex-spouse was responsible for the murders, or a neighbor with whom they'd had a serious falling out. One middle-aged guy seemed convinced that his younger sister was the culprit. He said that she'd always had a nasty temper and was fully capable of killing with a knife. She'd thrown objects at him from her playpen when she was a toddler, he said, generally favoring metal objects with sharp points. She'd apparently taken particular delight one afternoon in striking him in the eye with a ballpoint pen.

And then there were the self-described mystics and astrologists and psychics, more than a dozen of whom contacted the station volunteering their assistance. Several of them went to the trouble of visiting the general vicinity of the crime scene, whereupon they claimed to receive visions of the killer. If nothing else, these so-called visions were impressive for their exquisiteness of detail. A female psychic from New Jersey, for example, described the killer as a lanky male in his late teens with a protruding Adam's apple and streaks of blond in his otherwise dark brown hair. At the time of the murders, she said, he was wearing a slate-gray T-shirt and blue jeans with crimson patches on the seat. She said that she couldn't precisely make out his face but was quite sure that his name was Troy.

There seemed no end to the phone calls coming into the station. People called because they genuinely wanted to help out with the investigation. They also called because they were shocked and dismayed. Crimes of this sort weren't supposed to take place in Manheim Township. Elsewhere they might, but certainly not here.

Certainly not, indeed. Manheim Township is quiet and peaceful and proudly conservative. As the most prosperous of the northern suburbs bordering the small Pennsylvania city of Lancaster, it's a community made up mostly of spacious single-family homes nestled on gracious, tree-lined streets. It's a community where people go to bed early and attend church on Sunday and generally lead their lives without fuss or fanfare. There are no strip clubs or porn shops in the township, no all-night hangouts, and only one or two bars that can be described as even moderately rowdy. It's a place where anyone up and about past midnight is practically guaranteed to stick out like a sore thumb.

The city of Lancaster is quiet and peaceful in its own right, if somewhat more frayed around the edges than its suburban neighbor to the immediate north. It's also one of the most historic cities, not only in Pennsylvania but quite possibly the entire country. Its downtown core is crowded with stately old buildings, some of them dating from the mid-nineteenth century, almost all of them remarkably well preserved. The city has a decidedly quaint feel to it that seems genuine rather than merely cultivated or contrived. Simply walking its streets or visiting the Central Market or taking in a performance at the Fulton Opera House is very much like being transported to another era.

This particular area of Pennsylvania is also a popular tourist destination. It isn't so much the architectural charms of Lancaster or the civilized graces of its suburban communities that attracts visitors, however, as the large Amish population residing on the surrounding farmland. The Amish are endlessly fascinating to tourists, for their simplicity and austerity, for their stubborn resistance to change, and for a faith that was forged generations ago in the crucible of religious persecution. Their world might seem grim and forbidding but it's also strangely alluring. Tourists sometimes can't help but entertain fantasies of dropping everything and becoming Amish themselves.

The very heart of Amish country is a scant ten-minute drive from Manheim Township. Tourists can cruise along the Old Philadelphia Pike and purchase quilts from Amish craft shops or bottled lemonade from barefoot Amish boys wearing green shirts and black pants with suspenders. They can veer north on Route 772 for a closer look at traditional

Amish farms, where horse-drawn plows work the fields and clotheslines sag with the weight of fresh laundry. Or they can marvel at the steady traffic of horses and buggies on the narrow roads winding through the lush countryside.

Not even the Amish of Lancaster County are immune to the terrors of the modern world, however. Just eight months prior to the Haines killings, the entire nation was shocked when a local dairy truck driver and father of three, Charles C. Roberts IV, murdered five Amish girls at a one-room schoolhouse in Bart Township.

On the morning of October 2, 2006, Roberts entered the schoolhouse with two loaded guns and separated the boys from the girls. He then ordered the boys outside, barricaded the doors, and lined the girls up against the blackboard. He bound them together and lashed their feet with wire and flexties. By this point several state troopers had arrived at the scene, having received a call for help from a nearby home. Roberts dialed 911 on his cell phone and advised the dispatcher that he'd kill the girls unless the troopers were sent away at once. Moments later he began executing them with shots to the back of the head, and when the troopers stormed the schoolhouse he held a revolver to his forehead and pulled the trigger. He shot ten girls all told. Two died at the scene and three more died shortly afterward at area hospitals.

The motivation behind the massacre was not immediately obvious. Roberts left a suicide note for his wife claiming that he was still distraught over the death of an infant daughter nine years earlier. He also claimed that he'd once sexually molested two younger relatives and had recently been haunted by fantasies of doing so again. When questioned by the police, however, the two relatives in question said that they had no memory whatsoever of his ever having molested them.

As if the tragedy itself weren't horrible enough, the reclusive Amish had to contend for weeks afterward with the glare of national media attention. Droves of reporters descended upon their community, disrupting not only their process of grieving but also their daily pattern of life.

Throughout all of this, however, the Amish comported

themselves with remarkable grace. They expressed not the least hint of rancor toward Roberts, preferring instead to extend him full public forgiveness. Several of them visited his wife and parents to lend sympathy and support, and a large contingent went to the trouble of attending his funeral. They also set up a charitable fund for his three children.

The schoolhouse tragedy affected just about everybody in Lancaster County, Amish and non-Amish alike, which made the Haines murders just eight months later all the more traumatic. First one inexplicable tragedy and then another: There was a limit to how much grief a small community could take.

The Amish extended forgiveness to Charles C. Roberts IV for his horrific crimes. It seemed rather doubtful that their non-Amish neighbors in Manheim Township would be in so magnanimous a mood once the Haines killer was apprehended.

10

The detectives assembled in the squad room at shortly past seven on Saturday evening. They had some important business to attend to, not least of all deciding who should assume the role of lead or primary investigator for the case. Allen Leed seemed the obvious choice, partly because of his rich experience and also because of the rapport that he'd succeeded in building with Maggie. It was hardly surprising that no one voiced objections when he volunteered for the job.

Once this was taken care of, Bob Beck handed out assignments that promised to keep the detectives busy for days to come. Despite going strong since early morning, they still had plenty of ground left to cover. They needed to contact more friends and relatives of the Haines family for basic fact-finding interviews. They needed to sort out the bogus from the legitimate leads that were pouring into the station and then follow up on the latter. They needed to find out everything possible about similar crimes that may have been committed elsewhere around the country during the recent past.

This was the biggest case with which any of the detectives had thus far been involved, and they realized that trying to solve it would take a considerable toll. Vacations would have to be deferred, family time curtailed, and less critical cases put on hold. Bob Beck, for example, had planned on taking his wife to Philadelphia for a ball game the following evening in celebration of their twenty-ninth wedding anniversary. Their kids had arranged for the occasion to be commemorated on the big electronic scoreboard in the outfield. But now the trip would have to be canceled. The Haines case had assumed pride of place on Beck's and everyone else's schedule. It was a matter of digging in for as long as it took and hopefully catching a break or two somewhere along the line.

The detectives had a couple of things going for them, including an esprit de corps that would have been the envy of most any other squad room. They could be sharply competitive at times but rarely to the point of causing hurt feelings or bruised egos. Mostly they enjoyed one another's company and they also worked well together as a team. Allen Leed was fond of saying that each detective had some particular talent that contributed to the overall effort, much like the various ingredients that go into the making of a stew. He was counting on these combined talents fully coming into play in the days ahead.

They also had a chief of police, Neil Harkins, who was savvy enough to let the men under him do the job that they were paid to do. Harkins had just recently taken over as chief of the Manheim Township force and hadn't yet had much of a chance to get to know Leed or Beck or any of the others. Since he was the person most likely to be targeted for public criticism if the investigation stalled, he might very well have been tempted to take control of it himself. Right from the start, however, he signaled his confidence in the detectives and assured them that his only concern was supporting them as best he could.

The detectives grabbed a bite from the McDonald's across the street and then got back to work. Most of them went out to chase down leads and scour the Blossom Hill neighborhood for evidence. Bernie, for his part, stayed behind to work the phones. In the interest of turning over every possible stone, Bob Beck had asked him to try contacting friends and relatives of the Haines family who lived beyond the immediate area.

The first person he got through to was an old college buddy of Tom's who was now living in Florida. The guy told Bernie that he and Tom had become the best of pals while cross-country teammates at Slippery Rock University and had stayed in touch with one another ever since. He described Tom as gentle and thoughtful, a loyal friend and a wonderful husband and father. He said that he was in shock over the murders and couldn't begin to fathom the motivation behind them.

Bernie next reached a guy who said that he'd known Tom since their days together at Manheim Township High School. He said that they'd kept in contact over the years and had last spoken by phone in late April. He said that Tom had seemed his usual upbeat self at the time, despite his recent battles with prostate cancer. He described Lisa as rather more reserved than her husband, and also more regimented in domestic affairs. He said that both of them were kind and gracious but not especially outgoing and that they very rarely entertained in their home.

He also said that he was fond of Maggie and had exchanged several e-mails with her since she started at Bucknell. He described Kevin as quiet, polite, studious, and considerably less outgoing than his older sister. He said that he'd heard rumors, the source of which momentarily eluded him, that some kids had harassed Kevin of late on the school bus. He said that he'd never discussed personal finances with Tom but was quite confident, given Maggie's enrollment in an expensive college, that money wasn't an issue with the family.

Bernie next succeeded in contacting Maggie's college roommate, who was home in California for the summer. She said that she'd heard the news about the murders and was sickened by it, knowing as she did how close Maggie was to her family.

Bernie asked her to elaborate on this.

The roommate said that during evenings in their dormitory Maggie would often talk about her family. She'd brag about her younger brother, telling everyone about his terrific grades and how proud she was of him for getting his driver's license. She'd talk about how much she loved going running with her dad and what a comfort it was as a kid knowing that her mom would be home waiting for her every day after school.

The roommate said that Maggie's parents would routinely send her packages of goodies and that Maggie in turn would phone them several times a week. She said that Maggie was so excited at the prospect of going home for the summer that she packed her car two days early so that she could get away without delay after her final examinations.

She went on to say that Maggie spent the bulk of her time at college studying and practicing with the track team. She'd occasionally hang out with friends in the common room on their dorm floor but would very rarely attend parties or go drinking at off-campus bars. She'd talk about boys with the other girls in the dorm, but hadn't really dated much or developed anything resembling a serious romantic relationship.

Bernie couldn't vouch for its truthfulness, but he thought this just about the sweetest portrait of a young woman that he'd yet come across. Imagine a twenty-year-old college student so devoted to her family that she'd talk openly about them with her dorm mates and eagerly anticipate returning home for the summer. It seemed a portrait in black and white; a relic from a simpler, more innocent era.

Bernie wasn't able to dwell on it for very long, however, as another flurry of calls from concerned and frightened citizens came into the station. A waitress at a nearby restaurant reported that half an hour earlier she'd served a guy who spoke about the killings in a gloating tone of voice, as if taking perverse credit for them. A neighbor of the Haines family reported that she'd just discovered that the tires on her car had been slashed. She worried that this was retaliation for her having spoken to the police about the killings several hours before.

A guidance counselor from the local high school called

suggesting that the police investigate a former classmate of Maggie's who was nicknamed Skunk. She said that he had predilections toward violence and seemed fully capable of committing a crime such as this. Several other people called with likeminded concerns, one of them claiming that Skunk had recently stalked her best friend's niece. Yet another claimed that Skunk had shown up on his daughter's doorstep threatening to kill her new boyfriend.

Somebody dropped off an envelope at the station, which found its way to Bernie's desk. He opened it and extracted a letter that was handwritten in green ink. "You do not know who I am but that is not important," it began.

> *I am an individual who has spiritual ability. You may know this by another name. Psychic. This gift, given by God, is to be used for the good of mankind. You may wonder why it is that I am writing unto you. When I say my prayers, I am sent forth a positive energy from my spirit. Then information is delegated unto the angels, then passed onto my guardian angel, then unto my spirit guides.*
>
> *My spirit guides did object to me seeking information about this matter. Their reason is, the graphic nature of the images of the murder victims would affect me in ways that I cannot understand at this time. However, I feel compelled to help. I respect the concern that my guides have for me and I shall proceed carefully. I trust that you will understand my position.*
>
> *I ask that you see the movie* Next. *Then you will understand how information comes to me. The movie can explain far better than I can the nature of my special gift.*

The letter went on to describe not only the killings but also four individuals who were presumably responsible for them. The first had a prosthetic leg and the second was a heroin addict. The third had a speech impediment that was caused by nerve damage suffered in the war in Afghanistan. The fourth was the leader of the group, a raw-boned youth whom the others called Andy.

Bernie folded the letter and returned it to the envelope. He certainly didn't place much stock in mumbo-jumbo of this sort but neither could he simply disregard it. What if the so-called psychic had somehow been involved with the killings, and the letter was his roundabout way of confessing? Stranger things, after all, had been known to take place in the annals of criminal investigation.

11

The detectives dubbed it the Maggie detail.

It was quite possible that the assailant had entered the house on Peach Lane intending to kill Maggie also, or perhaps Maggie primarily, and that she'd fled before he'd had a chance to do so. If this were the case, she was potentially at grave risk. The assailant might very well be awaiting an opportunity to complete the job.

The detail, then, amounted to providing round-the-clock protection. Wherever Maggie happened to be, whatever she happened to be doing, an armed police officer would be in close proximity. After the terrible events of the early morning, there was no sense taking the least chance on her safety.

For the foreseeable future, Maggie planned on staying with her Aunt Tammy and Uncle James, who lived in a beautiful two-story house with a backyard swimming pool not far from Peach Lane. She'd gone there from the station on late Saturday afternoon, May 12th, accompanied by a young patrol officer, Sarah Fitzsimmons, of the Manheim Township Police Department.

Detective Brian Freysz relieved Fitzsimmons at roughly eight-thirty in the evening. Freysz was working out of the Lancaster County Drug Task Force at the time and, with his black T-shirt, pointy red beard, and long hair tied back in a ponytail, he looked for all the world like he'd come straight from an undercover bust.

Maggie was thoroughly exhausted by the time Freysz arrived at the house, and she went to bed shortly thereafter. Her aunt stayed up for another hour or so and sat with the detective in the living room. She admitted to feeling frightened and confused. Was it really possible that the murderer might now be coming after Maggie? Did this mean that she and her family were at danger in their own home? And why was Maggie still so apparently unaffected by the tragedy? Had the deaths of her parents and younger brother not yet emotionally registered with her?

Freysz sat in the living room until almost dawn, listening carefully for any suspicious sounds. Bernie relieved him at five o'clock, having barely slept since his interviewing assignments the evening before.

Maggie came downstairs at six-thirty and sat across from Bernie in an armchair. He asked her how she was holding up and whether she'd managed to get any sleep. She said that she'd slept fitfully for about six hours, with the television and a small lamp turned on in her bedroom.

They made small talk for an hour or so, mostly about Maggie's experiences thus far at college. Maggie said that she and some of her dormmates had strikingly different outlooks, they taking easy classes and scarcely studying whereas she herself would take challenging classes and study almost constantly.

Bernie asked her if she enjoyed living in a campus dormitory.

Maggie said that indeed she did and went on to describe its physical layout. She said that she loved baking in the kitchen on her particular floor, which was located next to the common room. She added that she'd normally bake both cookies and cake, since some of her dormmates strongly preferred one to the other.

She also spoke about her parents and younger brother, their favorite pastimes and so forth, almost always referring to them in the present tense. Bernie found her really quite charming, and also uncommonly composed considering the circumstances of their conversation.

Maggie ate breakfast and puttered around the house while Bernie chatted with her aunt and uncle. At ten-thirty Bob Beck called and asked Bernie to bring Maggie to the station for yet another interview. More than a full day had passed now since the killings and Beck thought that they might be able to glean more information from her. With the benefit of some much-deserved sleep, there was a chance that she'd remember something of relevance beyond what she'd already told them.

At eleven-thirty Bernie escorted Maggie into the squad room, where she sat down at a table with Allen Leed. As was his customary style, Leed eased into the interview, consoling Maggie over her terrible loss, assuring her that he and his colleagues would stop at nothing to bring the killer to justice.

The interview covered much the same ground as the previous day's. Leed gently probed, asking Maggie if there was anything she could think of that might help shed light on the crime. Maggie professed total bafflement, saying she was no closer than before to understanding why it had happened.

Once again she went over the crucial events of two nights ago, starting with her going upstairs to bed and watching the pilot episode for a new TV show on her laptop. She mostly repeated what she'd already told the detectives, occasionally adding new details or fleshing out by now familiar ones.

She now distinctly remembered, for example, that the house was silent when she went to use the bathroom at midnight. She also remembered switching the bathroom light on and then switching it off again upon returning to her bedroom.

She clarified that she was awakened an hour and a half later by the sound of screaming, most definitely not shouting. "It was a male voice, coming from my brother's room," she said. "I just heard one voice."

And as before, she demonstrated an impressively sharp

eye for detail. She said that the door to her parents' bedroom was open when she finally fled down the hallway and that her mom was wearing blue-and-white pajamas and her dad had on boxer shorts with a light gray T-shirt.

There was one new detail that Leed found especially chilling. After running to the neighbor's house across the street, Maggie recalled, she stood watch at the kitchen window with the neighbor and her teenage daughter. They were keeping an eye out for the police but in the meantime they couldn't help but notice that the light was on in the upstairs bathroom of the Haines house. Maggie now remembered thinking that this was odd. The light had most certainly not been on when she'd fled the house. She'd made a special point, in fact, of switching it off after using the bathroom an hour and a half earlier.

Leed was intimately familiar with the crime scene. He knew that there were bloodstains in the upstairs bathroom, strongly suggesting that the killer had washed up before going downstairs and leaving the house by the sliding door in the kitchen. Did this then mean that he was actually in the bathroom washing up while Maggie was waiting for the police at the neighbor's kitchen window? And that he'd slipped away no more than a minute or two prior to the arrival of Patrolmen Keenan and Newman?

The thought of it was almost too much to bear. In all likelihood, Maggie was gazing out from the neighbor's house onto the bathroom window to her own house at precisely the moment when the murderer was inside the bathroom washing the blood of his victims from his hands and wrists.

Leed promised Maggie that he'd keep in touch and arranged for a patrol officer to escort her back to her aunt and uncle's. Then the detectives brainstormed for a while before splitting up and going out on various assignments.

They followed up on half a dozen or so new leads that had come into the station. They tracked down local troublemakers with prior arrests for violent crimes. They visited regional hospitals inquiring about anyone who might recently have sought treatment for hand or wrist injuries. They searched through trashcans and Dumpsters for physical evidence.

They were driven by a mounting sense of urgency. The investigation was still in its critical early phases but the clock was ticking. The longer it dragged on, the worse the chances of actually making an arrest.

A few times they thought that they might actually be onto something. They learned from a hospital in the western region of the county that a woman had sought treatment for lacerations on the palm of her left hand at three o'clock on Saturday morning, just an hour or so after the murders. They located the woman at a trailer park near the small city of Columbia and questioned her about the injuries. She claimed that she'd been at a drinking party on Saturday morning and had jokingly struck the bottom of her beer bottle on the top of a friend's, thinking that this would cause her friend's beer to overflow. She'd struck it too hard, however, and in the process smashed her own bottle and cut the inside of her hand. She said that her boyfriend had warned her in the past against trying this particular stunt. The detectives checked out her story and concluded that she was telling the truth.

They also followed up on a Crime Stoppers tip, which involved a conversation that a middle-aged guy claimed to have overheard the previous evening at a tavern in Ephrata. A woman at the table next to his had apparently gone on at some length about the Haines murders, telling her friends that she'd once dated the killer, an unemployed auto mechanic with an obsession for knives.

This likewise came to naught. The conversation had amounted to nothing more than drunken boasting. The woman in question actually knew very little about the murders and had never dated anybody with an obsession for knives.

While most of the detectives were conducting interviews and following up on leads, John Wettlaufer had drawn an assignment of a rather different sort. A married couple who handled tracking dogs had volunteered to assist with the investigation, and Wettlaufer met with them and their two-year-old bloodhound Nellie at the house on Peach Lane.

They let Nellie sniff some traces of blood from the upstairs bathroom and then turned her loose. Nellie zigzagged down the street and worked her way in circling motions all the way over to the Lititz Pike, where she went into a Turkey Hill convenience store and sniffed up and down the aisles before coming out again. Her handlers gave her a water break and then issued the command: "Get to work."

She went through a carwash and then crossed several busy intersections, with Patrol Sergeant Gary Sindorf stopping traffic along the way. She circled and zigzagged for another half hour, seeming at several points on the verge of picking up a strong scent trail. Finally she came to a stop, confused and exhausted, at a burger joint called the Freeze and Frizz. It was a worthwhile effort but not even Nellie seemed quite able to figure out the escape route that the killer had taken upon leaving the Haines home.

Brent Shultz returned to the station at half past six on Sunday evening and briefed Bob Beck on his investigative efforts of the past several hours. Then he helped Beck field calls from concerned citizens. People wanted to know if the police had a line on the murderer yet. They wanted to know if they were vulnerable in their own homes. And they also wanted to know what they should do with their kids. Could they safely send them to school the following morning? What if the murderer was a fellow student or even a teacher?

This was a possibility that the detectives had already considered. Indeed, they planned on visiting the high school first thing in the morning for an intensive round of interviews. In the meantime, Beck asked Shultz to try contacting some of Kevin's classmates and teachers by phone.

The first person Shultz reached was a grade-ten student who was in Kevin's mathematics class. The kid said that he also knew Kevin through the Boy Scouts but that they'd rarely hung out together otherwise. He said that Kevin was one of the smartest kids in school, which may have incited occasional jealousy among his peers. He said that he didn't really know the Haines family as a whole but had heard that they were close-knit and private.

He next reached two grade-eleven students, both of whom claimed to know Kevin primarily through their involvement with the Quiz Bowl team. They described him as serious-minded and intellectual—a "typical geek," one of them said—and obsessed with German history and culture. They said that he'd always seemed friendly enough but that he wasn't the sort of kid readily given to socializing outside of school.

Shultz sat back for a moment and thought about the Quiz Bowl, which was a game of questions and answers involving almost every imaginable area of knowledge. He hadn't participated in it during his own high school days but he was certainly familiar with the basic format. The game typically pitted a team of four or five players from some particular school against a team from another school. A moderator would ask questions and the players from each respective team would try to buzz in first with the correct answer. Shultz knew that games of this sort were intensely competitive, quite possibly to the point of arousing resentment or hostility. Was there a chance that Kevin had provoked the hostility of another player, and that this was somehow tied in with the triple homicide? The idea sounded far-fetched, but Shultz wasn't prepared at this juncture to rule out anything.

He got through to a high school teacher who'd served as academic advisor the past several semesters to the Quiz Bowl team. The teacher said that Kevin was an alternate on the team and went on to describe him as an intelligent and pleasant kid. He said that Kevin would sometimes exhibit frustration, usually when getting an answer wrong at practice. He also said that Kevin wasn't a loner or outcast and that his teammates held him in high regard, not least of all because of his helpfulness and dedication. Just recently, for example, Kevin had been trying to devise a schedule whereby team members could meet regularly for summer practice. The teacher said that he also knew Maggie, who was considerably more sports-oriented than her younger brother.

The assistant coach of the Quiz Bowl team, whom Shultz next succeeded in contacting, echoed these sentiments. He said that Kevin was bright and responsible and uniformly respected by his teammates, and that he was also a prize student in the high school's gifted program.

Shultz thought that the Quiz Bowl business might warrant revisiting but for the moment decided that he'd try getting through to a kid, Warren Tobin, whom several people had pegged as an especially close buddy of Kevin's.

Warren's mother answered the phone and said that she was rooting desperately hard for the police to solve the case. She said that Warren had been physically ill since hearing the awful news.

She then gave the phone to her son, who said that he'd known Kevin for seven or eight years and was one of his best two friends. He said that Kevin was open and honest and something of a bookworm, almost always reading or working on school assignments. He didn't date at all or socialize much with other teenagers, preferring instead to spend his leisure time at home playing strategy board games.

The kid added that Kevin got along well with everybody and, insofar as he knew, had never been targeted by bullies. He said that the entire Haines family were the sweetest and most trusting people whom he'd ever met. He said that Kevin had once told him that they very rarely locked the doors to their house unless they were away on vacation.

Shultz could tell that the kid was upset and struggling mightily to maintain his composure. He was about to ring off but then realized that he had one more question. The kid had mentioned at the outset that he was one of Kevin's best two friends. Shultz asked him who the other friend was.

The kid said that the other friend was Alec Kreider. He said that Kevin and Alec and himself were like the Three Musketeers.

12

Shultz dialed Alec Kreider's number at nine o'clock on Sunday evening and got his mother, Angela, on the line. He told her that he and the other detectives were trying to obtain as much background information as possible on the Haines family and that they'd heard through the grapevine that Alec was one of Kevin Haines's very best friends.

Angela said that this was indeed the case but that she couldn't call Alec to the phone right then since he was staying at his father's house. Shultz asked her to get in touch with Alec and have him call the station.

Alec called fifteen minutes later, catching Shultz just as he was settling back into his cubicle with a fresh cup of coffee. He told the detective that he first heard about the killings late the previous morning from his and Kevin's mutual friend, Warren Tobin. He'd assumed at the time that Warren was merely joking, but then his own mom had called with confirmation of the grim news.

He said that he and Kevin had been the best of friends for six or seven years and had often visited one another's homes. He said that they were both in the gifted program at Manheim Township High School, although this past semester they'd taken only three classes together: advanced German, algebra/trigonometry, and driver education. He said that he last spoke with Kevin at the school bus stop after Friday's classes, just ten hours or so before the killings took place.

He said that he and Kevin and Warren would have lunch together practically every weekday in the school cafeteria, quite often sharing a table with other sophomore students from the gifted program. He added that they'd talk about religion, philosophy, and politics more often than they would stereotypical teenage topics such as popular music or television.

He described Kevin as a devout Boy Scout who was extremely bright and not much interested in sports or hanging out socially. He said that both he and Kevin were fond of strategy board games such as Risk and were passionate about German history. They'd both been looking forward to the school-sponsored trip to Germany that was scheduled for July, during which they planned on being roommates.

He said that he knew Kevin's parents, if only superficially, and that they seemed very nice. They'd been excited of late about Maggie's imminent return from college, which was apparently a big event for them. He said that Kevin seemed to have a good relationship with his father, though he was very much a "Mommy's boy." His mother spoiled him with constant attention and the two of them were obviously quite attached.

Shultz asked him if there was anything he could think of that might help make sense of the triple homicide.

Alec replied that he was totally baffled by it. The Haines family had no enemies that he was aware of and seemed unobjectionable almost to a fault. He seriously doubted that they were harboring any sort of deep, dark secret.

Shultz asked him about bullies, saying the police had heard rumors of Kevin being harassed at school.

Alec suggested that the rumors were overblown. He knew of a couple of junior students in math class who'd occasionally poke fun at Kevin but that was the extent of it. The teasing had never escalated into physical violence.

Shultz thanked Alec for his help and then sat back with his coffee and reflected on these two most recent interviews. The first kid, Warren, was quite obviously distraught over the killings, to the point where simply talking about them was almost more than he could manage. Alec, in contrast, was calm and matter-of-fact, his responses measured, his tone self-assured. Of course, he may very well have been churning inside and merely putting on a brave front.

Both kids, undoubtedly, were coping with Kevin's murder as best they could and in their own distinctive ways. And both, insofar as Shultz could tell, had been cooperative and truthful in answering his questions.

13

First thing on Monday morning, May 14th, Chief Neil Harkins of the Manheim Township PD put in a call for help to the Pennsylvania State Police (PSP). Chief Harkins knew that his own detectives were working around the clock and could use a helping hand. He also knew that the PSP would be more than happy to oblige.

The PSP was one of the oldest and most prestigious state police forces in the entire country, with an absolutely top-notch criminal investigative division. Its regional headquarters in the Lancaster area, Troop J, was located just beyond the city limits on the Lincoln Highway, and the Troop J commanding officer, Captain John Laufer, answered Chief Harkins's request for help by immediately assigning seven investigators to the case.

The state guys and the Manheim Township detectives certainly didn't require formal introductions. They were familiar with one another from cooperating on other cases over the years, if none quite so vexing as this, and also from swapping war stories over the occasional beer. A few of them had friendships that went back ten or twenty years.

The initial idea was that each township detective would pair up with a PSP investigator, which was in fact the way that it mostly went. Allen Leed had something rather different in mind for himself, however. One of his best buddies in local law enforcement was a county detective named Jim Brenneman. He'd worked homicide and child abuse cases with Brenneman some years before and was convinced that their styles perfectly meshed. He thought that they should team up again now and no one saw any reason why they shouldn't.

A big yet unobtrusive man in his sixties, Jim Brenneman hadn't initially planned on a career in law enforcement. He was working as a machinist in 1968 when a cousin who was a cop with the Lancaster PD suggested that he join the force also. Brenneman did so and a scant four years later he made detective. It was at this point that he truly began to flourish. He enjoyed criminal investigation, especially on those occasions when he found himself working alongside Allen Leed.

Both men brought a nice human touch to the job. They believed that information was best obtained through gentle persuasion, with more confrontational tactics deployed only as a last resort. "It's like cooking," Leed liked to say. "You don't turn the heat up full blast right away, and you can't add too much salt." As the more loquacious of the two, Leed would generally take a more active role in interviewing while Brenneman watched and listened. Any suspect who imagined that he could put something over on them was usually in for a rude awakening. When teamed up together, the two veteran cops very rarely missed a trick.

Leed and Brenneman spent much of Monday tracking down old street contacts whom they hoped might have inside information on the crime. In the meantime, Brent Shultz and several PSP investigators visited the local high school with the intention of finding out more about Kevin.

Manheim Township High School is located just off the Lititz Pike about a mile from Peach Lane. It's a blandly functional facility, devoid for the most part of architectural ornament and surrounded by acres of student parking. What it lacks in physical charm, however, it more than makes up for in academic quality. By almost all meaningful criteria, it qualifies as one of the top two or three hundred public high schools in the entire nation.

On Monday morning all classes started with a moment of silence in honor of Kevin, and a number of students gathered around the flagpole for an impromptu prayer service. Members of the Quiz Bowl team wore their signature T-shirts as a gesture of solidarity. The school administration announced that special counselors were on hand for anyone who needed help dealing with shock or grief.

The investigators settled into a conference room by the front entrance and got down to work. They wanted to be discreet so as not to disrupt the school day any more than it was already disrupted, but they might just as well have been decked out in flashing neon signs. Everybody knew that they were there and speculation was rampant as to what they were hoping to accomplish.

They interviewed the high school principal and then quite a few of Kevin's former teachers, starting with a woman who'd had him in study hall the previous semester. She said that there were fifteen or twenty students in the class, all of whom were well-behaved, but that Kevin in particular was as quiet as a ghost. She'd heard about his murder from a neighbor that morning without even realizing at first that he'd been in her class. It wasn't until she came to school and checked her files that his name finally registered. That's how shy and unobtrusive he was, she said.

Another teacher who'd also had him in study hall said much the same thing. She told the investigators that she found out about Kevin's murder on Saturday afternoon through a Manheim Township phone chain but hadn't immediately associated him with the ultra-quiet kid who'd sat at the back of her class every Wednesday the previous semester.

Kevin had left a considerably deeper impression on his trigonometry teacher, who described him as "disciplined, respectful, and honorable" and arguably the best student whom he'd ever taught. He said that Kevin was one of several academically advanced sophomores in the trigonometry class, which was otherwise made up of grade eleven students. He said that some of the older kids might occasionally have found Kevin "a little strange" because of his intellectual precocity but that he couldn't recall any of them bullying him.

The woman who'd taught him world history the past year was also impressed. She said that Kevin sat in the back row and was mostly "quiet and reserved" but sometimes chimed in with highly insightful comments during group discussion. She said that the other kids in the class respected him not only for his intelligence but also for his humility and his willingness to help others less academically advanced than he himself was. Just recently, she added, he'd taken special effort during class breaks to help another student who'd transferred to the school and had quite obviously been struggling with the course materials.

The biology teacher likewise described Kevin as bright and respectful, and the health and physical education instructor, whom the investigators interviewed next, said that he was "very mild, meek, and polite—a by-the-book kid—who did exactly what was asked of him in class." He went on to say that quite a few students had approached him earlier that morning expressing fear about the killer still being on the loose. If such an awful thing could happen to someone as patently inoffensive as Kevin, they'd asked, did this mean that everyone was potentially at risk?

It was almost noon now, and about a mile and a half from the high school, in a small brick building tucked away in a cul-de-sac, county pathologist Wayne Ross had just finished performing autopsies on the bodies of Lisa, Tom, and Kevin. His findings mostly confirmed what John Wettlaufer and the deputy coroners had observed at the actual crime scene two days earlier.

Lisa's primary cause of death was a stab wound to the upper abdomen that penetrated and passed through the colon. She also suffered a slashing wound to the front of the neck that extended all the way to the left earlobe. Tom suffered two wounds also, both of them stab wounds to the chest, either one of which was capable of inflicting death.

It was rather more difficult to pinpoint Kevin's cause of death, since his wounds were so numerous. He suffered a stab wound to the right upper chest, which penetrated the upper lobe of the right lung; another stab wound, two inches deep, to the right lateral jaw; a gaping wound, three and a quarter inches deep, to the right side of the neck; a second gaping wound to the left side of the face and neck; a T-shaped stab wound to the left upper chest; multiple stab wounds to the upper and lower back; and fifteen cut wounds to the head, face, neck, chest, wrists, and shoulders.

At five-eleven and over a hundred and eighty pounds, Kevin was a big kid for his age, and it was obvious that he'd fought desperately hard for his life. It seemed no less obvious that his assailant, driven by some unspeakable rage, had been fully intent on completing the job that he'd started.

Back at Manheim Township High School, Brent Shultz and the PSP investigators were still hard at work. They spoke with a number of Kevin's former classmates, after first having gotten approval to do so from their parents. Several girls said that they'd always liked Kevin, not least because of his intelligence and his sweet disposition. More than a few kids described him as "nerdy" and said that he was an occasional target of schoolyard taunting. Everybody agreed that he loved German history and participating in Quiz Bowl.

The investigators reviewed several course essays that Kevin submitted shortly before the triple homicide and that were never returned to him. In one of these, a biographical reflection of sorts, he credited his mom and dad for always keeping his best interests in mind. "My parents have long recognized the importance of a good education," he wrote. "Since I was born, they have been putting money aside in a college fund for me, and they have done the same for my sister."

They also spoke with several more of his teachers, including his fifth-period English teacher, who described him as "a quiet, very well-mannered kid with superior intelligence." The teacher for the Gifted 10 class, which met once a week on Tuesdays, likewise described him as extremely bright and talented ("a top-notch student") and said that he would mostly spend his class time playing educational games such as Scrabble and Trivial Pursuit.

The family and consumer management teacher said that she didn't know Kevin very well, mostly because her course was an online affair involving minimal interaction with students. She said that it dealt with such diverse matters as career paths, personal finances, and marriage. She hadn't yet spoken about the killings in her classes, she said, but couldn't help but notice that one particular kid was wearing a bandage on his left hand. When she asked him about it, he told her that he'd cut himself with an axe. He'd always struck her as easygoing and friendly, this particular kid, but she'd thought that the bandaged hand was something the investigators should know about.

They next interviewed Kevin's German teacher from middle school, who spoke glowingly of his former student. He described him as a terrific kid, smart and respectful and blessed with impressive reserves of intellectual curiosity. He said that he'd had to work extra hard at course preparation just to keep up with him. He added that Kevin was fascinated with German history, particularly the World War II era and the exploits of Field Marshal Erwin Rommel.

The investigators asked him if he'd heard anything about bullies picking on Kevin at school.

The teacher said that he'd heard rumors to that effect over the past day or two but seriously doubted that there was much truth to them. Kevin was so endearingly modest, he said, that bullies likely wouldn't have found cause to target him for abuse. He was just about the last person in the world to flaunt his intelligence.

They asked him if there were any other rumors circulating in school about the triple homicide.

Indeed there were, he said. The most popular rumor was that the killer was someone from college who'd been stalking Maggie. The second most popular was that Maggie herself was somehow involved with the killings.

Last of all they interviewed the high school German teacher, who said that he'd taught Kevin the previous two years. He said that Kevin was passionate about German culture and history and had done quite a bit of independent reading in these areas. The students in his sophomore class were a tight-knit group, he said, having taken German together since middle school. He'd phoned their parents over the weekend to commiserate about Kevin's death and discuss the school's plans for coping with it. Of all those he had spoken with, Alec Kreider and Warren Tobin's mothers had expressed the greatest concern, which wasn't surprising considering the close friendship between the three boys. Angela Kreider said that she was especially worried about Alec because he tended to bottle up his feelings.

The investigators asked him if he could think of anyone who might have had motivation for killing Kevin.

Absolutely not, he said. Kevin was deeply involved with the Quiz Bowl and the Boy Scouts, activities hardly likely to land him in any sort of serious trouble. He'd been busy preparing for his final examinations and looking forward to the upcoming class trip to Germany. He was as inoffensive a kid as you'd ever find.

They asked him about the trip to Germany, which had come up several times already in the course of the investigation.

The teacher said that it was scheduled for July and that twenty students had planned on going, with three adults besides himself—a vice principal, a substitute teacher, and a mother—serving as chaperons. He said that there was a meeting at the school concerning the trip on Thursday evening, which Kevin had attended with his dad. The meeting dealt with a wide range of matters, from passports to packing lists to tips for the tour guide and the bus driver.

He said that students were asked to choose the person whom they'd most like to room with on the trip, which was an easy decision for Kevin.

He chose his best friend, Alec Kreider.

14

Alec Kreider's school day on Monday, May 14th, began much like any other. Dressed in khakis and a polo shirt, which was the preppy look also favored by many of his grade-ten peers, he left his father's house and walked briskly to the end of the street, where he caught the bus for the fifteen-minute ride to school. On alternate weeks he'd catch the bus from the Cobblestone neighborhood where his mother lived, but otherwise it was always the same routine: the quick shower, the hurried bite of breakfast, and then the rush to the bus stop.

By next school year, perhaps, the daily bus ride would be a thing of the past. Along with his good friend Kevin Haines, he'd taken driver education in seventh period this past semester and had just recently gotten his license. The logical progression was to pick up a car over the summer, which meant that he could then drive to school and leave it in one of the spaces allotted to students in the vast parking lot.

The day may have started with the all-too familiar routine but it was hardly, of course, just another school day. When Alec went into the classroom for first-period English, it was like entering a funeral parlor. Some of the girls toward the front were sobbing and comforting one another with hugs. Other kids stood in clusters along the side, wearing glazed looks of disbelief. They were a smart bunch, the twenty-seven students in first-period English, most of them on the Honor Roll, and they all knew Kevin Haines. Kevin was one of the star tenth graders at Manheim Township High School, perhaps the brightest star of all.

They also knew that Alec was one of Kevin's best friends and so they gravitated toward him now, girls whispering words of condolence, boys shyly shaking his hand. He accepted these gestures of concern with grim stoicism, eyes downcast, fists clenched. Some of his classmates suspected that he was fighting hard to contain his feelings. They admired him for being so brave.

The class opened with a moment of silence, as did all other classes at the high school that morning. Then the teacher gave students an opportunity to talk about the killings and also to share stories about Kevin. Only a few kids actually stood up and talked, probably because most of them were still trying to sort out their feelings. Alec sat silently at his desk in one of the middle aisles, looking glum and withdrawn.

The teacher went on to teach poetry, deciding that she'd try to make this as normal a class session as possible. Halfway through, the school principal came to the door and called Alec out into the hallway. The teacher wasn't sure at the time why the principal did this, since she was relatively new to the school and didn't know Alec personally. She only knew that he seemed a sweet and mature kid, so much so that she planned on assigning him to a group project with several girls in class. In any event, he was absent for just a few minutes before returning and settling back in at his desk.

There was a good reason, of course, why Alec was pulled into the hallway for a few minutes. A number of his teachers had already identified him as an especially close friend of Kevin's, and the principal wanted to check on his emotional well-being and assure him that the school was prepared to do everything possible to help him through this stressful time.

As the school day progressed, all of Alec's teachers addressed Kevin's death in one way or another, and they did so with impressive sensitivity. They also kept careful watch on Alec, trying to gauge his mood and ascertain how he was coping with the tragedy. Upon noticing that most of the kids in her class were quite obviously grief-stricken, for example, the biology teacher announced that anybody needing a break was welcome to take one. Alec separated himself from the rest of the class for a while and stood at the back of the room, though he didn't seem visibly upset.

During lunch period, Alec sat in the cafeteria with the same crowd as always. They were the so-called brainers, half a dozen or so kids with well-deserved reputations for being the intellectual elite among the school's tenth graders. Warren Tobin was there and so, too, were Carol Clark, Nancy Schmidt, and Joseph Browning. The only person missing was Kevin.

They sat there for the most part in abject silence, sipping juice and munching half-heartedly on homemade sandwiches. Once or twice they started to talk about Kevin but the conversation went nowhere. It was still too early, and far too painful. Somebody mentioned that criminal investigators were at the school speaking with Kevin's teachers. Somebody else mentioned that a classmate had spoken with a reporter from a national news magazine the previous evening.

The other kids in the group were particularly attentive to Alec. They knew that he went back a long way with Kevin and had always enjoyed jousting verbally with him during lunch period. They worried that the tragedy might have hit him harder than it had almost anyone else. They found it tough getting a good read on him, however. He certainly seemed sullen but this didn't necessarily mean very much. Sullenness was Alec's trademark, his special brand of tenth-grade intellectual cool. Even at the best of times, he'd dole out smiles as sparingly as if they were some precious commodity under wartime ration.

The mood in Alec's sixth-period German class was especially grim. Kevin had been enrolled in this class, too, and most of the students had studied German with him since middle school. The school psychologist was on hand and essentially took charge of the period, helping the students as a group work through their confusion and grief. She assured them that she was also available for personal counseling sessions.

The psychologist hadn't previously met Alec but knew by then that he was a good friend of Kevin's. He struck her as gloomy and depressed but not notably more so than any of the other kids in the class. His demeanor seemed altogether typical of a teenager who'd just experienced a wrenching loss.

Adding to the poignancy of the occasion, this was the day that Kevin and the group to which he was assigned were scheduled to make their class presentation. Given Kevin's track record in this regard, everyone had expected nothing less than a stellar performance. The groups to which he was assigned were almost always awarded the highest grade in the class.

Alec's group had made their presentation on Friday, with somewhat less than sterling results. Alec was forced to improvise quite a bit because one of the girls in his group hadn't shown up, but despite his best efforts the presentation faltered. The German teacher offered the group some constructive criticism and awarded them a grade of B.

This must have been a bitter pill for Alec to swallow, especially since the group that had presented the previous day, Thursday, had received not only a grade of A but also frank praise from the teacher.

It must have tasted like failure.

15

Chief Harkins was pulling out all the stops. First thing on Monday morning he'd put in a call for help to the Pennsylvania State Police. And now, just an hour or so later, he contacted Special Agent Heather Thew at the Harrisburg office of the Federal Bureau of Investigation.

In terms of reaching out to somebody for assistance, the chief could hardly have done much better than Special Agent Thew. In her mid-thirties and just recently graduated from the FBI Academy, she was smart, professional, and enormously resourceful. She also didn't believe in wasting a single moment when facing an important task.

Within minutes of hearing from Chief Harkins, she put Bob Beck and Allen Leed in touch via telephone with criminal profilers from the FBI's Behavioral Science Unit in Quantico, Virginia. Beck and Leed brought the FBI profilers up to date on the investigation and also described in considerable detail the actual crime scene.

The profilers said that this had all the earmarks of a crime of familiarity. The house wasn't ransacked and nothing appeared to be stolen, which more or less ruled out robbery as a motive. There was no sign of forced entry, which suggested that the perpetrator already knew the layout of the property. And, most telling of all, the murders were committed with a knife, which was a highly personal method of killing. The perpetrator, in sum, wasn't likely a random stranger but rather somebody who knew the Haines family and who'd entered their home specifically for the purpose of inflicting violence.

None of this was startlingly new to Bob Beck or Allen Leed. They'd been thinking along the same lines themselves. Nevertheless, it was reassuring to know that both they and the FBI were on the same page.

Special Agent Thew helped out in another important respect also. Several of the bloody shoeprints at the crime scene were very well detailed, and Chief Harkins was hopeful that the FBI Laboratory in Quantico might be able to identify the precise brand of shoe that had made them. Thew said that there was a better than decent chance that the laboratory could do so.

Sergeant William Sindorf of the Manheim Township PD emailed her digital images of the shoeprints, which she then forwarded to Michael B. Smith, an examiner with the Questioned Document Section of the FBI Laboratory who specialized in shoeprint and tire-tread evidence.

Smith negotiated a remarkably quick turnaround. Searching the FBI database, he determined that the outsole of the crime scene shoeprints closely matched the outsole of several models of shoe that were manufactured by Hush Puppies. Special Agent Thew then contacted company representatives from Hush Puppies, who advised her that most of their products with this particular outsole were "comfortable shoes of moderate styling, usually with black or brown soft leather uppers."

This was potentially a huge boost for the investigation. As the FBI was acutely aware, murderers very often held onto the shoes that they'd worn during the commission of their crimes. They'd burn their clothing and dispose of the murder weapon but as often as not they'd keep their shoes. And now Allen Leed and company knew precisely the brand of shoe that the Haines killer had worn. Of course, this was the sort of detail that needed to be kept strictly confidential. If it were ever leaked to the news media, the entire investigation might be put in jeopardy.

Monday, May 14th, had already proven a busy day. Chief Harkins had called in reinforcements from the Pennsylvania State Police and also solicited the help of the FBI. Brent Shultz and several PSP investigators had visited the local high school, where they were still conducting interviews with Kevin's teachers.

It was an eventful day in other respects as well.

In the early afternoon, Bob Beck and Bernie left the station and drove to Tom Haines's workplace. They planned on interviewing the underachieving employee with whom Tom had reportedly had a run-in shortly before the triple homicide, and several of Tom's other coworkers beyond those already interviewed by Bernie.

On the drive there, they discussed the investigation and their frustration at not yet having made an arrest. Bernie was particularly frustrated and at one point, while waiting at a stoplight, he addressed the issue with the disarming honesty for which he was known among his colleagues in the detective squad.

"Geez, Bob," he said. "There's a chance we might not be able to solve this thing."

Beck shifted uncomfortably in his seat and gave Bernie a sidelong glance.

"What do you mean?" he asked.

"We're going in so many directions at once," Bernie said. "From our meetings, our briefings, we have no clear idea on a motive. Nothing—absolutely nothing—is sticking out."

It was something that Bob Beck had already thought about. Detectives are always concerned when an investigation threatens to languish and, as case officer for the squad, he felt special responsibility for bringing this most important of investigations to as rapid a conclusion as possible.

"We stay with it," he said. "That's all we can do. Just stay with it."

Tom's coworkers, much like before, seemed almost competitive in their praise of him. One guy said that he was as fair and even-tempered a man as you'd ever hope to meet. Tom had coached Little League baseball for several years, the guy added by way of illustration, and had insisted that every kid on his team play meaningful innings, regardless of level of talent or the outcome of the game. Another co-worker went still farther, describing Tom as "the nicest person I've ever known." She said that he strongly preferred dialogue to confrontation and was always prepared to give people the benefit of the doubt. Yet a third characterized him as "the cornerstone of the business" and "consistently kind, mild-mannered, and understanding."

Bob Beck felt the same nagging doubt that Bernie had felt upon visiting Tom's place of business the morning of the murders. Why was everyone so apparently eager to nominate him to sainthood? Was there a chance, he asked the coworkers, that Tom might have been concealing some sort of secret, an extramarital affair perhaps, shady financial dealings, *anything*?

Absolutely not, they said. What you saw with Tom was precisely what you got. His life was an open book.

They next interviewed Tom's receptionist, who said that he'd often talk about his kids while at work and was quite obviously proud of them. She said that he'd mentioned several times that Maggie was planning on studying abroad in Australia next academic year. He wasn't thrilled with the idea, she said, but had apparently reconciled himself to it. She added that he very rarely went on business trips alone and always took the day off work on his wife's birthday.

They searched Tom's office and seized his Day Planner. They also found handwritten notes in his desk drawer from his meeting with the underachieving employee. There were no photos of his wife or kids in the office, which they found curious considering Tom's reputation as a family man.

Finally they met with the ostensible underachiever and asked him about the closed-door meeting with Tom. The guy characterized the meeting as cordial and insisted that neither he nor Tom had lost his temper. He conceded that he wasn't entirely happy in his present position and was considering taking another job at a business across the street.

They asked him about his whereabouts on late Friday night and early Saturday morning.

He said that he and his wife went to dinner with another couple at a restaurant in Elizabethtown, after which they hung out for a while at an arcade in a small town near Reading. They returned home at about ten in the evening and watched some television before going to bed. He said that his wife and the other couple would be more than happy to confirm his story.

Bernie and Beck talked about this last interview on their way back to the station. Bernie noted that the guy's palm was dry when they first shook hands and that he seemed perfectly calm and maintained good eye contact throughout. Beck noted that he had no visible cuts, bruises, or abrasions on his hands or wrists. They both noted that he was wearing a watch on his right wrist, which meant that he was probably left-handed. The forensics evidence strongly suggested that the assailant was right-handed.

They certainly planned on checking out his alibi but for the moment they felt confident that the guy was telling the truth.

Everybody assembled at the station house in the early evening to compare notes. Allen Leed said that he had good news and bad. The FBI Laboratory had succeeded in identifying the make of shoes that the murderer wore inside the Haines home, which was potentially very good news. On the negative side, however, he and Jim Brenneman had turned up next to nothing in their conversations with local police informants.

Brent Shultz said that the interviews at the high school had likewise yielded little of consequence. Kevin's teachers had suggested that he might not have been the most popular boy in school but that he was generally liked and respected by his peers. They hadn't been able to offer a single clue as to why he might have been murdered, beyond pointing out some kid who'd come into school that morning wearing a bandage on his left hand. Shultz added that he'd already contacted this particular kid's mother and made arrangements to interview him the following morning.

The investigators had spent the greater portion of the day looking into Kevin and Tom, trying to determine if there was anything in either of their personal histories that might help to account for the triple homicide. Now it was time, they decided, that they return their attention to Maggie and her mom.

They'd found out earlier in the day that one of Maggie's best friends from high school was a young guy who lived in the city of Lancaster. He and Maggie had mostly kept in contact through instant messaging, only rarely seeing one another in person. They'd last exchanged messages on Thursday, May 10th, shortly after Maggie's return home from college. Perhaps he'd know something of value to the investigation.

Trooper George Forsyth of the Pennsylvania State Police met with him at his residence in Lancaster later that evening. He seemed visibly shaken by the tragedy and told Trooper Forsyth that he was happy helping out in any way that he could.

He said that he'd known Maggie since the seventh grade and counted her as one of his best friends. He said that he'd met her family only once, when stopping by the house on Peach Lane a couple of years before to pick her up for a trip to the beach, but that she talked about them often and always in glowing terms. He added that she'd been especially looking forward to hanging out with them this summer since she'd spent most of the previous summer at Bucknell working on some sort of research project involving turtles.

He said that Maggie was vivacious and amazingly friendly, though she rarely dated and had never had a steady boyfriend. In one of her more recent messages, though, she'd mentioned a guy who worked in the cafeteria at Bucknell cooking stir-fry. She'd referred to him as the "stir-fry guy" and said that she'd gone out with him on a casual basis a number of times.

Trooper Forsyth asked him—"just for the record"—to

give an account of his own activities over the past several days.

He explained that he went to college in Harrisburg but came home quite often by train. He said that he had taken the train home on Thursday, got a haircut, and then spent the entire evening just loafing around the house. He spoke with Maggie via instant messaging somewhere between ten and eleven o'clock the same evening. She'd been doing a cross-word puzzle and wanted his help solving it. The next morning, Friday, May 11th, he took the train back to Harrisburg and then returned home again on Saturday.

He said that he learned about the killings from his ex-girlfriend on Saturday, after which he left several messages for Maggie on her cell phone. He said that he was still waiting to hear back from her.

Trooper Forsyth believed that the guy's story was legitimate, which of course didn't mean that he wouldn't seek corroboration of it.

Back at the station, Bernie succeeded in making phone contact with a young woman who was another old high school friend of Maggie's. She said that she last saw Maggie over the Easter break, when they'd spent an evening together at the Prince Street Café in downtown Lancaster. She said that Maggie was exceptionally outgoing but that her social circles were rather limited and she apparently saw no reason to expand them. She'd generally hang out with a select group of friends, including a couple of gay guys, whenever she was home from college.

Bernie asked the young woman how she'd characterize Maggie's relationship with her family.

Insofar as she could tell, she said, Maggie positively adored them. She loved going running with her dad and probably considered him her best friend. She might not have been quite as close with her mom but still enjoyed spending time with her. And though she worried that he was too much of a loner, she'd constantly brag about how smart her younger brother, Kevin, was.

Bernie had just gotten off the phone when Bob Beck came over and told him that they needed to pay someone a visit. A woman who lived on Peach Lane had called the station reporting that a nearby neighbor, Joyce Williams, had a son who was a heroin addict. The woman claimed that the son had moved back in with his mother several weeks earlier and that he hung out with a rough-looking crowd. She said that she'd heard quite a commotion coming from the Williams house the morning of the killings. She also said that she'd put off calling the police about this until now out of fear of possible reprisal.

Beck and Bernie drove over to the house in question and spoke with Joyce Williams. She'd lived there for almost twenty years, she said, and her adult son had moved back in with her about a month ago. She said that the son wasn't home right then but she was expecting him within the hour. She added that despite living on the same street she'd never actually met anyone from the Haines family.

The detectives decided that they'd return later on and, in the meantime, talk with some of the neighbors about the situation. They'd probably have been better off conserving their energy. Only the woman who'd called the station in the first place professed to know anything about Joyce Williams's son. Most people said that they hadn't really known the Haineses either, beyond an occasional wave of greeting on the street.

Beck and Bernie thought there something sad about this, people in such an upscale suburban community leading lives of virtual anonymity. They thought of poor Maggie racing out of her house three nights earlier and not knowing which way to turn, with one neighbor as much a stranger to her as another. It was something that you might expect of New York City but certainly not Lancaster County.

Joyce Williams's son, a lean guy in his thirties with scraggly dark hair, was waiting for them in the living room when they returned to the Williams house. He said that he'd moved in with his mom about a month ago after returning to Manheim Township from California and that he'd just recently gotten a job with a local outfit installing carpets. He said that he had spent all of Friday night at his girlfriend's place and found out about the killings the next morning when he went out for gas and cigarettes.

The detectives had a good feeling about him. He seemed confident and direct and not in the least drug-addled. He also gave them the names of several people, including his girlfriend, whom he said would be more than happy to vouch for him.

Beck and Bernie returned to the station, made a pot of coffee, and wrote up their reports. Allen Leed joined them after a while and the three men sat in the squad room and discussed the case. They still had no clear idea, three days into the investigation, why this awful thing had happened. They'd thought at the outset that they might find some explanation for it—a scorned lover, an illicit business deal—lurking somewhere in the Haines family history. So far, however, their search had come up empty. The family seemed every bit as squeaky clean as advertised.

Once midnight struck, they realized that they should probably pack it in for the evening and grab some much-needed sleep, but they couldn't bring themselves to do so. They remained in the squad room—pacing, brainstorming, drinking coffee—until the first twinkling of dawn.

16

At seven o'clock on Tuesday morning, May 15th, three scientists from the Serology Department of the Pennsylvania State Police Crime Laboratory arrived at the house on Peach Lane. John Wettlaufer escorted them inside and they got right down to work, conducting bloodstain analysis on the first and second floors of the house and the connecting stairway.

An hour and a half later, a five-man forensics team from the state police also arrived. The Lancaster County Forensic Unit had already given the house a pretty good going-over, but there was still more work to be done, especially in terms of processing for latent prints and other possible trace evidence. This was principally what the state police forensics guys were there to do.

They processed the exterior of the house using black fingerprint powder and then every imaginable surface on the first and second floors. They developed several latent prints from doorjambs and windowpanes, which they lifted with clear tape and secured to special evidence cards. They also processed the garage and the stairway leading to the basement, without developing any impressions of value.

They vacuumed the bedrooms and hallways for trace evidence and then also the upstairs bathroom, deploying separate filters for the bathroom floor, counter, toilet, and shower.

They searched the shrubbery in the front- and backyards with a metal detector and inspected under the patio stones by the rear door. They even went so far as to climb up on ladders to inspect the eaves troughs.

They did everything but turn the house upside down. If there was any evidence that they missed, it would be difficult to imagine what it might have been.

Back at the Manheim Township police station, the investigative team gathered in the conference room for the daily briefing. Allen Leed, Bob Beck, and Bernie were there, all three of them working on precious little sleep; so, too, were Brent Shultz and Brian Freysz. Most of the Pennsylvania State Police people on hand—including Sergeant Doug Burig, Corporals John Duby and Adam Kosheba, and Troopers George Forsyth, Mark Magyar, Jerry Sauers, Linda Gerow, and Shawn Swarr—had already logged long hours on the case, despite having only officially come on board the day before.

Chief Harkins and Bob Beck presided over the briefing, reviewing old evidence and proposing new avenues of attack. They realized that the investigators were anxious for a breakthrough and hopeful that this might be the day when it finally came. The chief counseled perseverance and fastidious attention to detail, both of which he knew that he could count on from this particular crew. Bob Beck handed out assignments for the day and reminded everyone to stay in touch with the command post in the event of some late-breaking development.

Brent Shultz and Trooper George Forsyth went straight from the briefing to the high school, where they'd made arrangements to interview several more of Kevin's classmates.

They started with the kid who'd come to school the previous day with a bandaged hand, and right off the top they were favorably impressed. The kid seemed shy and gentle and entirely forthright, with not the least hint of the intellectual arrogance that was in evidence among some of his peers. He said that he'd known Kevin since middle school and had generally gotten along with him, though they could hardly be described as close friends. He said that he'd always enjoyed going head-to-head with Kevin in gym class, since neither of them was especially athletic. He also said that the last time they spoke was during family and consumer management class the previous Friday. He was working on an assignment concerning pregnancy and childbearing when Kevin came over and kidded him for taking so long with it.

Shultz and Smyth asked him about his injured hand, which was still wrapped in a bandage.

The kid said that he worked every Saturday at a tourist spot outside of town that featured several antique steam engines. This past Saturday he was cutting kindling with an axe as preparation for getting one of the engines started when the axe slipped and nicked his thumb. He notified his boss of the accident, who then drove him to the hospital and gave him the rest of the shift off. He found out about the killings later that day while watching the news on television.

Shultz and Forsyth next spoke with several kids who'd allegedly picked on Kevin at various points throughout the school year. These interviews likewise yielded very little in the way of new information. The kids in question seemed uniformly distressed over the triple homicide and were able to account for their whereabouts on the night that it took place.

Finally, they met with a kid who was rumored to have visited Kevin's house on Friday after school. The kid said that he'd phoned Kevin to consult with him about a biology class project, which involved the dissection of a crayfish, but hadn't actually gone by his house. He said that they'd never really socialized outside of school and that he knew very little about Kevin's family. He'd learned about the triple homicide from the Saturday newspaper, he said.

Shultz and Forsyth had heard that this same kid was crazy about knives. They asked him if this were true, and they also asked him about a small cut that they'd noticed on the base of his left thumb.

The kid said that he did indeed like knives and had recently built up quite a collection of them but that this had nothing to do with his injured thumb. He'd cut the thumb, he said, while tearing open the plastic packaging to his new MP3 player. His mother, who was present for the interview, confirmed that this was so.

Shultz and Forsyth stopped by the principal's office to tell him that they were through for the day and then returned to the station so that they could file their reports and pick up their next assignment.

The investigators were fully alert, of course, to the possibility that the killer was somebody who lived near the Haines home and might even have known the family personally. They'd already canvassed the immediate neighborhood and now, in the interests of thoroughness, they did so again.

Troopers Linda Gerow and Mark Magyar did most of the serious legwork, going door-to-door with a three-page questionnaire that the Criminal Investigation Unit of the Pennsylvania State Police had specially prepared for the occasion. The questionnaire asked people where they worked and how long they'd lived at their current address. It asked them about their familiarity with the Haines family and their whereabouts on the night of the murders.

Most people were gracious, taking the time to fill out the questionnaire and also thanking the troopers for their efforts. Only one guy refused to cooperate. "This is bullshit," he said. "A total waste of my time. Plus none of this is any of your damned business."

After completing the exercise, Gerow and Magyar reviewed the questionnaires and found nothing in them that cried out for any sort of follow-up. They also conducted criminal history checks on everyone whose house they'd visited, which likewise yielded negative results.

It was more than three full days now since the triple homicide but tips were still coming into the station at a steady clip. A cab driver reported that on early Saturday morning, just past midnight, he'd stopped to help a woman whose car had broken down on a thoroughfare not far from Peach Lane. The woman had the look of a drug addict, the cabbie said, with scab-ridden arms and running sores on her face. She told him that her husband had been with her when the car stalled but that he'd since gone off somewhere in search of money. The cabbie apologized for not coming forward sooner, saying that he'd been out of town the past several days visiting a sick relative.

Most of the tips weren't nearly as promising as this, but the investigators could ill afford to disregard any of them. Who, after all, could tell? A tip that might at first glance seem frivolous could very well turn out to be the one that mattered most. Which meant that Allen Leed and company found themselves having to rush out the door with a renewed sense of urgency practically every time the phone rang.

And then, of course, there was also the Maggie detail, to which half a dozen detectives and patrol officers were assigned on a rotating basis. Sometimes it simply involved standing guard at Maggie's aunt and uncle's house, but occasionally it proved rather more complicated.

Patrol Officer Sarah Fitzsimmons drew the assignment on Tuesday afternoon, May 15th, having already drawn it once or twice before. At twelve-thirty or thereabouts, she accompanied Maggie and her aunt to a veterinary clinic, where they dropped off a couple of cats for grooming. Then it was off to a bookstore at a local mall, where Maggie purchased a short story collection and several fitness and running magazines. Officer Fitzsimmons made small talk with Maggie along the way and once again was struck by how calm and reserved she seemed.

Allen Leed had asked Fitzsimmons to bring Maggie by the police station in the early afternoon, and so after leaving the mall this was where they went. Leed met up with them in the conference room, carrying the lockbox that the Lancaster County Forensic Unit had found in Maggie's parents' bedroom closet. The box contained Tom and Lisa's wills and quite a few precious family keepsakes, including children's drawings and homemade birthday cards.

Maggie insisted on reading the wills right then and there,

and she did so with no apparent display of emotion. The aunt pulled Fitzsimmons aside and told her that this more or less summed up Maggie's behavior over the past several days. She said that she and her husband and other family members were concerned that Maggie hadn't yet come to terms with the triple homicide, that she'd somehow blocked the grim reality out of her mind. She said that everyone was worried that she might be headed for a terrible crash.

They carried the lockbox outside and then drove to the Charles F. Snyder Funeral Home on East King Street in downtown Lancaster. There they met with the director of the home, Chip Snyder, to discuss funeral arrangements for Tom, Lisa, and Kevin. Maggie said that she wanted Kevin buried between his mom and dad so that they could protect him. Toward the end of the meeting, just before three o'clock, somebody raised the question that had hitherto been lurking in the background. Were the bodies suitable for an open casket service?

Putting it as delicately as possible, Chip Snyder explained that Tom's and Lisa's bodies were indeed suitable but that Kevin's most definitely wasn't.

Maggie wept openly upon hearing this and struggled to regain her composure. Officer Fitzsimmons wondered if this meant that the full truth had finally sunk in, if the necessary healing process was now underway.

Fitzsimmons dropped the aunt off and then took Maggie out for a late lunch at Scooter's Restaurant & Bar in the village of Lititz. Perhaps it was the relaxed ambience of the place, coupled with the police officer's easy warmth, but Maggie's mood seemed to brighten. She ordered a salad and seafood pasta and spoke freely about her mom and dad, their pet peeves, their hobbies, their mutual affection, almost always referring to them in the present tense. She also spoke about her younger brother, though not nearly so much as she did her parents. She called him Bucko.

They stopped by the aunt and uncle's house after leaving the restaurant so that Maggie could change into her running gear. Several other relatives were also at the house and quite obviously still distressed over the triple homicide, which one of them described as "totally weird and unbelievable and senseless." While Maggie was changing, they asked Fitzsimmons if the police had any hunch whatsoever as to what might have happened.

Fitzsimmons had gotten to know these people quite well by now and she genuinely liked them. She believed them to be decent and sincere, and she appreciated all that they were doing for Maggie. She wasn't quite sure how to answer their question, however, beyond assuring them that Allen Leed and the other investigators were working around the clock in an effort to solve the case. She told them that they'd be informed right away if there was any significant progress.

The next stop on the day's itinerary was an outdoor running track at Franklin and Marshall College in Lancaster, where Maggie met up with an old girlfriend from high school. Fitzsimmons sat in the bleachers and watched as the two young women circled the track together. She could tell, by the smile on Maggie's face and the effortless grace of her movements, that coming here was a good idea. This was obviously Maggie's natural element. Gliding around the track was probably the most therapeutically beneficial thing that she could be doing right then.

Maggie ran with her friend until almost nine, after which Fitzsimmons took her to Bruster's Real Ice Cream shop in East Petersburg and treated her to a cookie dough cone. They sat at a picnic table out front and enjoyed the fresh evening breeze that was blowing in from the north. Maggie talked some more about her family, still referring to them in the present tense, as if the triple homicide hadn't taken place. She talked about some of her experiences working part-time at a Freeze & Frizz restaurant near the Lancaster airport for three years during high school. But most of all she talked about college, and especially a young professor with whom she'd worked on a project catching and studying turtles the previous summer. She described the professor as brilliant and took special pains to mention that he was just twenty-seven years old.

Officer Fitzsimmons had heard about this young professor and his research project involving turtles. The subject had arisen several times already during her chats with Maggie's relatives. The relatives had told her that Tom and Lisa had been less than thrilled with the idea of their daughter spending almost an entire summer conducting research with a professor not much older than she was, especially since there were apparently no other students involved in the project. Insofar as they knew, it was only Maggie and the professor. The relatives had said that they, too, had found this rather an unusual arrangement. Was it not possible, they'd suggested, that it might be connected in some way with the triple homicide?

Fitzsimmons made a mental note to bring this up with Bob Beck and Allen Leed. Who could tell? Perhaps it was indeed somehow connected.

17

At nine o'clock on Tuesday evening, May 15th, quite possibly the last thing on Allen Leed's mind was research involving turtles. He'd just then received a phone call that caused him to believe that the Haines case might finally have been solved.

The call was from a trooper with the North Carolina State Highway Patrol, catching Leed just as he was on the verge of leaving the station to follow up on yet another of the day's many tips. The trooper, Shawn Eller, said that he'd stopped a Jeep Cherokee with Pennsylvania plates earlier that evening for a speeding violation. The occupants of the Cherokee, two white males in their late twenties, were reluctant at first to disclose much information about themselves, providing only the sketchiest of details. Finally one of them said that they were en route to Florida and the other made some cryptic comment to the effect of their having "gotten away with murder in Pennsylvania."

The trooper said that he searched their vehicle and found some marijuana under the seat and a sheathed knife with a short blade inside the glove compartment. He noticed that the driver of the vehicle had lacerations on his right hand, which seemed still in the process of healing. When he asked him about them, the guy said that he'd hurt his hand while working at a sawmill several weeks before and had sought treatment for the injury at a hospital.

The trooper said that he took the two subjects into custody for the marijuana and that, upon further questioning, one of them remarked that they'd also recently gotten away with a home invasion in Pennsylvania. It was then, the trooper said, that he searched the National Crime Information Center's computerized database and found out about the triple homicide in Manheim Township. He thought that there was a decent chance that these two guys were involved.

Leed thought so, too. He thanked the trooper for the heads-up police work and asked him where the two guys were right now.

The trooper said that they were incarcerated at the Johnston County Jail in Smithfield, North Carolina. He gave Leed the phone number of the supervising officer at the jail, Lieutenant Rodney Watson.

Bob Beck was still at the station at this point, preparing for the next morning's daily briefing. Trooper Jerry Sauers of the Pennsylvania State Police was there, too, having just returned from interviewing an informant. They'd overheard Leed's end of the telephone conversation and could tell that this was potentially serious business.

"All right, Al," Beck said. "Don't keep us in suspense. What's the story?"

Leed was bristling with excitement. He got up from his desk and executed a nifty little pirouette on the squad room floor.

"It looks like we've got the killers," he said. "A couple of guys in a Jeep Cherokee with Pennsylvania plates. North Carolina Highway Patrol just nabbed them for speeding."

He ran the details by Beck and Sauers, who agreed that the situation seemed promising. There was the knife and the partially healed lacerations. There were the incriminating comments about having recently gotten away with *both* a home invasion *and* murder in Pennsylvania. Either one of these guys, or perhaps both of them, might very well have been involved with the triple homicide.

A sure way of finding out was to check their footwear. The FBI Laboratory had already determined that the bloody imprints at the crime scene were likely made by Hush Puppy shoes, and so Leed phoned Lieutenant Watson at the Johnston County Jail and asked him what type of shoes the two guys were wearing. Watson told him that they were both wearing sneakers.

Just to be on the safe side, Leed asked Watson if he'd mind photographing the soles of their shoes and e-mailing him the images. That way he, Leed, could compare their shoe treads with the tread of the crime scene imprints. Watson said that they didn't have the capability at the jailhouse of doing that right then but that he'd be more than happy to make a photocopy of the soles and fax it to Leed.

The fax came in fifteen minutes later, and Leed quickly determined that the shoe treads of neither subject matched the imprints that were found at the house on Peach Lane. This didn't necessarily mean, however, that these guys weren't involved with the triple homicide. They might simply have worn different shoes while committing the crime, which they'd then discarded or stashed somewhere in their vehicle.

Leed was somewhat deflated but still cautiously optimistic. He wanted to interview these subjects personally, and Jerry Sauers said that he'd be happy to come along. They went so far as to check out flight schedules before finally deciding that the more prudent course at the moment was to reach out to local law enforcement in North Carolina for additional assistance.

Toward this end, Leed contacted the North Carolina State Bureau of Investigation and spoke with Special Agent Blane Hicks. He filled Agent Hicks in on all of the relevant details and asked him if he'd question the two subjects about their whereabouts this past weekend. He also asked him if he'd obtain DNA samples from both subjects so that investigators in Pennsylvania could see if there was a positive match with DNA that had been found in trace evidence at the crime scene.

Agent Hicks said that he'd take care of it first thing in the morning and hopefully have news for Leed by early afternoon. In the meantime, he said, there was no risk of the two subjects going anywhere. Law enforcement in Johnston County would see to it that they stayed put on the marijuana charge until this matter was cleared up.

There was nothing for Leed to do now but sit back and wait. If this broke the way he hoped it would and the two subjects came up dirty, he'd be on a plane for North Carolina the next evening to take their confession.

His phone rang again, only this time it was a concerned citizen reporting that she'd seen a suspicious-looking character with a bandaged hand lurking outside a convenience store. He jotted down the information, thanked her for calling, and promised that he'd follow up on it as soon as possible. In truth, however, it wasn't easy right then working up much enthusiasm for still more tips of this sort. Not when there were two guys locked up in the county jail in Smithfield, North Carolina, who seemed a pretty good bet to have committed the crime.

It was past ten in the evening now and the squad room was uncharacteristically quiet. Leed, Beck, and Sauers gathered around a computer and did some research on Smithfield, in the event that they actually did wind up having to fly down. Located in the Coastal Plains of North Carolina thirty miles east of Raleigh, it was a sleepy little town with a population of about twelve thousand. Apart from being home to an annual Ava Gardner film festival, its chief claim to fame seemed to be an outlet shopping mall that attracted motorists from busy Interstate 95. It was a place that the detectives would not otherwise have known even existed.

"It's funny," Leed said. "Four days into this thing and now we're sitting here studying a map of North Carolina."

Beck and Sauers merely shrugged. They knew from long experience that this was how criminal investigations often went.

18

Leed and Beck drove home and tried grabbing some sleep but they might just as well have remained at the police station. At two-thirty in the morning their dispatcher called them with urgent, late-breaking news. A local guy, Frank Wright, had invaded a house in nearby Warwick Township, apparently claiming in the process that he had inside information on the Haines killings.

Beck returned to the station and contacted a detective from Warwick Township, who briefed him on the incident. Wright was a scraggly guy in his late twenties, the detective said. He'd busted into the house through the rear door and informed the terrified residents that the people responsible for the triple homicide were intent on killing him, too. Then he locked himself in an upstairs bedroom that was equipped with a telephone and called 911. He told the emergency dispatcher that he'd been shot and also made several oblique references to the Haines killings.

In the meantime, the detective said, the residents of the house locked themselves in a different room and also dialed 911. They pleaded for immediate help, saying that they were fearful for their lives.

The police arrived within minutes and removed the residents to safety. They kicked in the door to the room where Wright was holed up but he eluded their grasp by leaping from the second-floor window. He then broke into a neighboring house, so frightening the woman who lived there that she climbed out onto her roof. He was finally apprehended when he leaped from yet another window and landed in a crumpled heap on the sidewalk. The police took him to Lancaster General Hospital so that he could receive treatment for various injuries that he'd sustained during the debacle, which most certainly did not include gunshot wounds.

Beck next contacted the emergency dispatcher and arranged to listen to a tape-recording of Wright's 911 call. Wright was obviously in a state of considerable panic, which sometimes made it difficult to decipher his words, but the bulk of the call went as follows:

> WRIGHT: Help me. [Garbled] newspaper.
>
> DISPATCHER: Where are you?
>
> WRIGHT: Brooke Road. I ran down here. They already shot me.
>
> DISPATCHER: Brooke Road?
>
> WRIGHT: Yeah. Off of Loop Road. Help me.
>
> DISPATCHER: Are you inside a house?
>
> WRIGHT: Inside? Yeah. They're coming after me, these people. I got in trouble.
>
> DISPATCHER: They're coming after you?
>
> WRIGHT: They just shot me. Everywhere.
>
> DISPATCHER: Back, chest, arms?
>
> WRIGHT: In the back.
>
> DISPATCHER: Are you bleeding?
>
> WRIGHT: Yes. Help me.
>
> DISPATCHER: What's your name?
>
> WRIGHT: Frank. Frank Wright. Just come.
>
> DISPATCHER: Are you alone?
>
> WRIGHT: The people that shot me. They're going to kill me.
>
> DISPATCHER: Who are these people?
>
> WRIGHT: How do I know who you are?
>
> DISPATCHER: You called 911.
>
> WRIGHT: If I tell you, they'll kill me. They killed the mom and dad and brother.

DISPATCHER: In Manheim Township?

WRIGHT: Yes.

DISPATCHER: Why would they come after you?

WRIGHT: I was in trouble with them.

DISPATCHER: Where are you shot?

WRIGHT: In the back, the arms, and the chest.

DISPATCHER: Are you shot three times?

WRIGHT: Yeah.

DISPATCHER: Where are the people that shot you?

WRIGHT: In the house.

DISPATCHER: Where in the house?

WRIGHT: Up here. They're coming now. I was on the phone when they got me.

DISPATCHER: You were on the phone when they shot you?

WRIGHT: Yeah.

DISPATCHER: I didn't hear any gunshots. Are you locked in a room?

WRIGHT: Yeah.

DISPATCHER: What room?

WRIGHT: I'm across the street.

DISPATCHER: What's the matter?

WRIGHT: They just got me. I'm dead. Help me. Help me. Help. Help.

Beck listened to the tape several times and then played it for Chief Harkins, who'd also been summoned to the police station. Both men found the incident utterly bizarre but they weren't yet prepared to dismiss the possibility that it might indeed have some connection with the triple homicide. The homicide, after all, had thus far defied rational explanation. Perhaps it was only something as wild as this that might finally help them make sense of it.

They went outside, jumped into the chief's car, and made the drive to Lancaster General Hospital in record time. They knew that Wright had been brought in for treatment and they wanted to find out exactly what he had to say for himself.

Allen Leed was already there when they arrived, interviewing Wright in the emergency ward. He'd driven directly to the hospital after receiving the two-thirty call only to discover that he actually knew the guy. He'd gone to high school with his parents and had run into him occasionally over the years.

Wright said that he became paranoid after doing two or three lines of cocaine the previous evening, convinced that a couple of local drug dealers were intent on shooting him as retaliation for his "ratting them out" to the police. He broke into the house in Warwick Township out of panic, he said, which was also why he called 911. He said that he'd learned about the Haines killings only through reading the newspaper and wasn't entirely sure why he referred to them during his conversation with the emergency dispatcher. He certainly wasn't involved with the killings himself, he said, nor did he know anyone who was.

Leed believed that he was telling them the truth. He seriously doubted, in any event, that Wright was the sort of guy who was capable of butchering three people with a knife. Just to be on the safe side, however, he asked him if he'd object to their searching his place of residence. Wright told them to go ahead and signed a "consent to search" form to that effect. He explained that he'd actually been splitting his time between two different residences in recent months.

Leed and Beck searched both residences without finding anything of evidentiary value. They also did a timeline on Wright and determined that he was physically accounted for during the crucial hours of late Friday night and early Saturday morning. They had little option at this point but to rule him out as a suspect.

The squad room was thick with anticipation when Leed and Beck returned to the station at nine-thirty on Wednesday morning. All of the Manheim Township detectives were on hand and so, too, were the troopers from the Criminal Investigation Unit of the Pennsylvania State Police. The Wright incident had created quite a stir and everyone wanted to know if this indeed were the breakthrough that they'd been hoping for.

Leed and Beck needn't have spoken a word. One look at them and it was obvious that the news wasn't good.

"Just some knucklehead," Leed said. "The guy knows less about the Haines killings than we do."

Though understandably disappointed, the investigators realized that they had no choice but to forge onward. There was still a chance of their hitting the jackpot with the two guys who'd been busted the previous evening in North Carolina, but they knew better than to count on this. Just as likely, the murderer was somebody who was lurking in their midst at that very moment, somebody from the local community—a neighbor, a coworker, a fellow churchgoer—who'd thus far eluded even the least hint of suspicion. The challenge, of course, was in identifying who this somebody might be.

At a press conference that had been held several days earlier, on Monday afternoon, Chief Harkins had requested the help of the public in meeting this challenge. Now the Manheim Township Police Department decided to put out a news release requesting the very same thing.

"Once again," the release began, "we are appealing to the public for information relevant to the Haines family homicide."

> We are seeking a suspect who would be unaccounted for between the approximate hours of 1:00 AM and 3:00 AM (Friday night into Saturday morning), May 12th. If you know this person, you may not think they are capable of this type of crime. They may also have fabricated an alibi concerning their whereabouts during this time frame. They may not have a prior record of violence. Additionally, the suspect may have injuries to their hands, arms, or other parts of their body. If you know someone fitting this profile, please call the Manheim Township Police Department at xxx-xxx-xxxx.

"At this time," it concluded, "we have no reason to believe the incident that occurred in Warwick Township last night is connected or linked to the incident in Manheim Township."

The news release was sent out just before noon on Wednesday, May 16th, and shortly afterward Special Agent Blane Hicks called Allen Leed from North Carolina. He said that he and Trooper Chris Otto of the State Highway Patrol's Major Crimes Unit had interviewed the two subjects who were in custody at the Johnston County Jail. Both subjects had proven cooperative, he said, providing not only DNA samples but also a detailed account of their whereabouts this past weekend. What's more, he said, their stories checked out. The verdict was clear: It seemed highly unlikely that either subject was involved with the Haines killings.

Leed had sensed that this was coming but it was still tough to take. Twice now in the space of scarcely fifteen hours he'd gotten his hopes jacked sky high only to have them shot down. Twice he'd thought that they were on the verge of solving the case only to learn that they were no closer than before. He'd dealt with false alarms in the past, of course, but in a case of this magnitude they felt less like minor annoyances than they did cruel jokes.

He poured himself a cup of coffee and talked it over with Bob Beck, who seemed almost stoic in the face of the day's disappointments.

"Don't worry about it, Al," he said. "One way or another, we'll get to the bottom of this thing. Who knows? Maybe we'll even find some answers at Bucknell."

19

Bucknell was the sort of place that could induce nostalgia even among people arriving on its grounds for the first time. With its leafy pathways, green lawns, and sedate buildings, it was the perfect picture of a traditional American college. It could easily have served as the setting for any number of those life-on-campus films churned out by Hollywood during the 1940s and 50s.

By no means, moreover, was it a place of only superficial charm. It justly boasted a top-flight faculty and rigorous admission standards, making it one of Pennsylvania's most prestigious institutions of higher learning. Anyone planning on attending was well advised to bring along a complete set of sharpened pencils. There were relatively few "gift" courses at Bucknell and no athletic scholarships. The overriding emphasis was on good, old-fashioned education.

The college was located in the picturesque city of Lewisburg, about a two-hour drive from Lancaster County. Detective Brian Freysz and Pennsylvania State Police investigators Corporal Pat Quigley and Trooper Mark Magyar arrived on campus at nine-thirty on Wednesday morning, May 16th. Accompanying them was Sergeant Keith Kreider from the Patrol Division of the Manheim Township Police Department, who was an accomplished investigator in his own right.

The four men had a full day's work cut out for them. They wanted to learn as much as possible about Maggie's life at Bucknell, in the event that it was somehow tied in with the triple homicide. Was there anybody on campus who might have developed an unhealthy obsession with Maggie or her family? Somebody who might actually have harbored fantasies of violence toward them? Had Maggie been stalked or threatened in any way? And what about that research project involving turtles that had so occupied her the previous summer? What was the exact nature of her relationship with the professor who was in charge of it?

It was rather like a fishing expedition, casting about the spacious campus for clues, but the investigators had no other choice. Thus far they'd had precious little luck finding clues elsewhere.

Animal Behavior, which Maggie had declared as her major during freshman year, was housed in the Biology Department, and so this was where the investigators went first. They paired up, Detective Freysz with Corporal Quigley, Sergeant Kreider with Trooper Magyar, and spoke with quite a few professors in the department, all of whom might almost have been reading from the same script. Maggie was smart, determined, and self-disciplined, they said, the sort of student who seemed to have her priorities perfectly in order. She never missed a class or turned in a late assignment, and her performance in the biology laboratory, where she was assigned as a teaching assistant, was nothing short of exemplary.

She also had a girlish enthusiasm about her, they said, that was really quite endearing. She was sweet and whimsical, exhibiting none of the fashionable world-weariness that was only too common among her peers. She'd occasionally talk about her family during work breaks and seemed especially fond of her dad, whom she credited with instilling in her a love of cross-country running. If it weren't for her intellectual sophistication, they said, she might easily have passed for a high school student.

She seemed happy at Bucknell, they said, and had never

indicated to them that she'd experienced conflicts with a boyfriend or anybody else on campus. Indeed, they added, it was highly unlikely that Maggie had dated much since arriving at college. Romantic entanglements might have interfered with her studies, and she was far too earnest a student to risk such a possibility.

The investigators were impressed with these people, the warmth with which they spoke of Maggie, their sincere concern for her well-being. She was clearly much more to them than merely a name on a class roster. It was hardly surprising that she'd felt so very much at home in their company.

They next interviewed several professors from other departments with whom Maggie had taken elective courses over the past two years. None of these people knew her quite as well as the Biology faculty did, but they still spoke highly of her and seemed genuinely upset over the tragedy that had struck her family.

One of the people with whom they most wanted to speak, the young biology professor whose research project Maggie had participated in the previous summer, was waiting for them in his office after lunch. He was direct and cordial, saying that he'd anticipated the police wanting to talk with him ever since he first heard about the triple homicide.

He said that he initially met Maggie in the spring semester of her freshman year, when she took one of his introductory biology courses. She was the only student in the entire class, he said, to express an interest in working on his summer project, which involved studying the swimming speed of the painted turtle. She slept in a campus dorm during the two months of research, he said, and most days spent three or four hours out in the field with him and then an additional several hours in the laboratory.

The investigators asked him if he'd had much contact with Maggie since the research project of the previous summer.

He said that she once took care of the family cat while he and his wife were away for a few days but that otherwise their relationship was strictly businesslike. They'd see one another at the laboratory and biology club meetings, and occasionally she'd drop by his office for advice concerning a paper that she was planning on presenting at an animal behavior conference in St. Louis.

As for his general impressions of Maggie, he said that he found her really quite charming. She was chatty and convivial, almost preternaturally upbeat, and very obviously attached to her family. She was also passionate about physical fitness, to the point where she'd sometimes take time off for a brief run even while they were at the ponds catching turtles.

The investigators realized that they were treading on sensitive ground with their next question but there was no avoiding it. They asked if he'd ever felt a romantic or sexual attraction toward Maggie.

The professor seemed unfazed. Considering his age and how much time he'd spent alone with her, he said, it was understandable that this should arise as an issue. But there was nothing whatsoever to it, he insisted. He'd initially gotten to know Maggie as one of his students and this was precisely how he'd always seen and treated her. There'd been no ambiguity in their relationship, no murkiness, no crossing of boundaries. If anything, he said, he'd taken special pains to respect her privacy while they were conducting research together. Whomever she might have been dating, her religious beliefs, her likes and dislikes: All of this he purposely steered clear of in conversations with her.

The investigators asked him for a detailed account of his activities on late Friday night and early Saturday morning, which he willingly provided. Then they escorted him to the state police's nearby Milton Barracks, where they took his fingerprints and obtained a DNA sample via a mouth swab.

Once all of this was taken care of, the investigators conferred privately and concluded that there were no grounds for suspicion here. The professor had seemed truthful throughout the interview, not in the least defensive, and cooperative to a fault. Clearly he had nothing to hide. All things considered, they thought, Maggie was probably fortunate to have had him as an intellectual mentor.

With the semester now officially over, most of Maggie's fellow students had already dispersed for the summer. There was one more person, however, whom the investigators were especially keen on interviewing. This was the cafeteria worker—the so-called stir-fry guy—whom Maggie had apparently dated at some point during the past school year. They succeeded in tracking him down at his residence in a small town twenty miles outside of Lewisburg.

They played it coyly at first, mentioning nothing about the triple homicide, saying simply that they were interested in obtaining information on the Haines family. They asked him if he'd mind telling them what he knew about Maggie. He seemed puzzled but pronounced himself ready to help out in any way he could.

During the early stages of the fall semester, he said, he'd see Maggie almost daily in the cafeteria, where he was in charge of preparing and serving the stir-fry. He finally worked up the nerve to ask her out on a date, though technically this violated college rules governing employee conduct. Altogether they went out seven or eight times over a several-month period, generally not doing much on these occasions beyond walking around the campus or relaxing in Maggie's dorm.

It never reached the point, he said, where they became anything other than casual friends. They were both fairly conservative in their values and hence not much interested in sexual intimacy merely for its own sake, and Maggie's dedication to her studies left little time for the cultivation of a serious relationship. They stopped dating by mutual consent toward the end of the fall semester, and shortly afterward he left the cafeteria job to pursue other interests.

The last time he saw Maggie, he said, was in early April, after having been completely out of touch with her for several months. He'd driven to Lewisburg for a job interview and afterward surprised her with a visit. They hung out for a while in her dorm and exchanged phone numbers but hadn't bothered contacting one another since.

The investigators could tell from his body language and tone of voice that he truly had no idea what this was all about. Seeing little point at this juncture in keeping him in the dark, they told him about the triple homicide.

The poor guy seemed shocked. He stood up and stared out the window and wiped tears from his eyes. He pleaded with them for assurance that Maggie was safe. He asked if there was anything that he could do to help her.

The drive back to Lancaster County seemed to take forever. Dark clouds hovered in the evening sky, matching the mood of the investigators. They'd hoped that the trip to the Lewisburg area would result in some discernible progress. Instead they'd once again come up empty. The two people whom they'd most wanted to interview had proven not only sympathetic but also entirely above suspicion.

Never before had they encountered a case quite like this one. There seemed not even a ghost of a promising clue.

20

The satellite trucks were the first thing that Allen Leed noticed upon arriving at the police station on Thursday morning, May 17th. The Haines killings had made CNN and several other major news outlets the previous day, turning what was hitherto primarily a local story into a full-fledged national curiosity. As if the situation weren't difficult enough already, Leed thought, there was now the added pressure of operating under the glare of a big-time media spotlight.

He parked around back, dodged a scrum of reporters and cameramen, and ducked into the station. He checked in with Bob Beck and then went down the hallway to visit with Sergeant Tom Rudzinski, an old buddy from patrol who was serving as media liaison for the case. Rudzinski said that the news people were starting to get antsy for some tangible answer as to why the murders might have taken place. Leed said that he couldn't imagine them being half as antsy as the guys in the squad room were.

The heightened media attention certainly hadn't done much to allay fears within the local community. People were still calling the police station at a steady clip, worried that a maniac was on the loose. They were afraid to fall asleep at night, afraid to let their kids out to play. They were adding deadbolts to their doors and installing floodlights on their property. Security firms were hard-pressed simply keeping pace with the sudden demand for their services. The president of one such firm told a reporter for a national newsmagazine that sales of residential security systems in Manheim Township had risen eight hundred percent in the aftermath of the triple homicide.

The investigators were well aware of all this, though it wasn't something that they generally talked about amongst themselves. They realized that the community would breathe easier only when a suspect was arrested and put behind bars. They hardly needed reminding that it was precisely their job to bring this about.

After the morning briefing, Leed sifted through a stack of investigative reports while most of his colleagues went out on interviewing assignments. There were still people connected in some way or another to the Haines family whom they'd not yet spoken with. Perhaps one of them might have a glimmer of an idea as to why this awful thing had happened.

Bernie's first interview of the day was with the pastor of Otterbein United Methodist Church, which was located in the east end of Lancaster. The Haines family had worshipped at Otterbein for close to two decades, with Tom serving as a church trustee for a stretch during the late eighties and early nineties. A memorial service for Tom, Lisa, and Kevin was scheduled there two days hence.

The pastor ushered Bernie into his study, where they talked for a while about the theological challenge of making sense of tragedies such as this. Bernie was a devout Catholic with a reflective cast of mind. He appreciated hearing the Methodist minister's thoughts on the matter.

The pastor apologized for not knowing the Haines family as well as he might have. He said that since first arriving at the church four years ago he'd always found them rather aloof. They'd sit in the balcony during Sunday worship services and leave immediately afterward by the side door. Very rarely would they stick around to socialize or participate in after-worship fellowship activities.

He said that he knew Kevin best of all, mainly by virtue of helping him prepare for his religious confirmation several years previously. Which in itself was hardly an easy process, he added. The poor kid was so painfully shy that he dreaded the prospect of standing up in front of the entire congregation when it came time for the actual confirmation ceremony.

Insofar as he could tell, the pastor said, the Haineses were fundamentally decent and well-meaning people. He'd heard no rumors to the contrary, nothing whatsoever about their having skeletons in the closet. He certainly couldn't imagine anybody wanting to cause them harm. Was there a chance, he mused, that the killer had somehow targeted them by mistake?

This was an intriguing possibility, which the pastor was by no means alone in suggesting. Later that same day, for example, Detective Brian Freysz and Trooper Jerry Sauers interviewed a guy who was a close neighbor of the Haines family. He told them that he'd been involved in highly competitive business ventures for almost a decade now, during which time he'd accumulated more enemies than he cared to count. Just recently, he said, he'd run afoul of a rival business faction whose leadership definitely wasn't averse to playing it rough. Though he hadn't as yet received any explicit death threats, he said, it would come as no surprise if some of his enemies had reached the point of wanting to kill not only him but perhaps also his entire family.

This was the first thing, he said, that crossed his mind upon hearing of the Haines killings. He was out of town on business at the time and when his wife phoned his hotel with the news, he immediately thought to himself: "Maybe they went to the wrong house. Maybe that was supposed to be me and my family that got killed."

Might this be it, then? Was it possible that the killings were really nothing more than a case of mistaken identity? That the murderer had somehow gotten the wrong address? Confused the Haineses for some other family?

Freysz and Sauers agreed that this deserved looking into, though for the moment they had more pressing business to contend with. Several local residents had reported seeing an unkempt guy wandering about in the vicinity of the Haines home over the past day or so. They claimed that he had a wild look in his eye and scratch marks on his arms and wrists. They thought that he was probably a drug addict.

The investigators found the guy at a sandwich shop on the Fruitville Pike, sitting alone at the counter with a cup of coffee. They identified themselves and took him to the rear of the shop for greater privacy.

The guy spoke in a faltering tone, tugging nervously on a strand of greasy hair. He said that he'd been going through a rough patch of late, having gotten fired from his job and then evicted from his apartment. Given his unsettled circumstances, he said, it was little wonder that there were rumors linking him to the triple homicide. Nevertheless, he insisted, there was absolutely no truth to them. He'd spent all of Friday evening and Saturday morning hanging out with an old girlfriend at his aunt's house, where he'd been staying for the past couple of weeks. The girlfriend and aunt would be more than happy to vouch for him, he said.

Freysz and Sauers asked him about the scratches on his arms, which seemed of fairly recent vintage. He said that he'd gotten drunk a few days ago and fallen into some rose bushes in his aunt's backyard. They asked him if he'd be prepared to provide a DNA sample for comparison against DNA that was collected at the crime scene. He said that he was prepared to do anything in the interest of clearing his name. He intended to straighten out his life, he said, which would be a tough assignment with a cloud of suspicion hanging over him.

Freysz and Sauers got in touch with the guy's aunt, who confirmed his alibi and attested to his good intentions. They then returned to the station, where they'd arranged to interview several more of Maggie's acquaintances from high school.

All of them spoke highly of Maggie. She was that rare individual, they said, for whom high school seemed not the least bit troublesome. She seemed to breeze right through. She was brainy but not nerdy, opinionated but not judgmental, and self-confident without an ounce of arrogance. She got along well with almost everybody, avoiding the cliques and petty animosities that consumed so many of her peers. If there was indeed such a thing as an exemplary high school student, they said, Maggie almost certainly fit the bill.

Trooper Mark Magyar of the Pennsylvania State Police spent most of Thursday afternoon on the telephone with various Bucknell students, most of whom lived in the same campus dormitory as Maggie. They described her as smart and convivial, with a sweetly innocent temperament. She'd bake goodies for everyone on the dorm floor, they said, occasionally telephoning her mom for some special recipe.

Magyar asked them if they thought it possible that somebody on campus had become dangerously obsessed with Maggie.

They said that they had no reason to believe so. Maggie led a fairly regimented life on campus, they said. She spent most of her time attending classes, studying, and practicing with the track team. She rarely stayed out late, never all night long. She had severely limited opportunities for running into somebody who might be dangerously obsessive. Plus she'd certainly never mentioned anything of the sort.

Bernie returned to the station in the early evening with the intention of typing up his notes from the half dozen or so interviews that he'd conducted throughout the course of the day. He'd barely sat down at his desk when the phone rang. It was a man on the other end, his voice low and gravelly.

"Look into the mother," he said.

"Are you referring to Lisa Haines?" Bernie asked.

"Yes," the man said. "Look more closely into her."

And then he abruptly hung up.

21

The kung fu center was located in a strip mall just off Route 741 on the western fringes of Manheim Township. It was a nice, comfortable space, decorated in red and green with a mirror running the length of one of the side walls.

Alec Kreider bobbed and weaved in the middle of the floor, practicing his shadowboxing. *Strike . . . kick . . . block . . . strike . . . kick . . . block.* He was just now beginning to work up a good sweat, beginning to find that perfect harmony of mind and body, the promise of which had drawn him to kung fu in the first place. *Strike . . . kick . . . block . . . strike . . . kick . . . block.* It didn't matter that he wasn't alone, that there were five other kids shadowboxing alongside him on the vinyl floor. *Strike . . . kick . . . block . . . strike . . . kick . . . block.* He was getting into the zone, losing himself in the rhythm of his movements. At that precise moment, there might just as well have been no one else for miles around.

The proprietor of the center, an intelligent, soft-spoken guy in his thirties, stood off to the side and watched. He regarded Alec as one of his prize students, if not indeed his very best student ever. Rarely, he thought to himself, had he encountered a young man of such honor and integrity, a young man so thoroughly committed to the cultivation of excellence in the martial arts. He caught the eye of the woman who was Alec's personal instructor and who likewise regarded him highly. They both nodded approvingly.

Alec normally attended martial arts class on Tuesday and Thursday evenings. Sometimes he'd stop by Park City Mall on his way home, which is what he decided to do this particular Thursday evening.

The mall was a large, upscale shopping complex within easy walking distance of the kung fu center. It featured a movie-and-music store and the usual assortment of trendy clothing outlets, making it a favorite after-school hangout for teenagers.

Alec strolled along the main concourse, checking out his reflection in the store windows. He felt bored, uninspired. It was scarcely a week now since Kevin's murder, and yet already his life was settling back into its old routines. He yearned for something new.

He took the escalator to the food court on the lower level and spotted them right away. Amanda and Caroline. They were sitting with their backs to him at a table along the far wall, sharing a soda and an order of fries. He'd gotten to know the two girls during visits to the mall over the past year or so, though not as well as he might have preferred. He knew that they went to school in the city of Lancaster but otherwise their lives were mostly a mystery. They hadn't volunteered much in the way of personal information and he hadn't bothered asking.

He considered approaching them but instead lingered by the escalator. He'd wait for them to notice him and wave him over. Far better to play it cool than risk appearing overanxious.

After a while they did indeed notice him and wave him over. Still he waited several beats before responding, not wanting to join them until they'd finished their fries. The sight and sound of people chewing ranked high on his list of annoyances. Not even cute teenage girls were exempt.

He sat down at their table and went into full brooding mode, which was standard for him in social situations of this sort. The two girls, for their part, behaved much the same as they always did whenever he saw them. Amanda gushed and giggled, making a public display of her cheerfulness. It wouldn't have bothered him so much if he thought that it were merely an act but she really did seem cheerful, certainly more so than anyone had a right to be.

Caroline was more to his liking. She sat there with a sweet smile on her face, perfectly content to let Amanda do most of the talking. She had a serious side to her, which he found immensely appealing. She was the kind of girl he longed for, the kind of girl he dreamed of making his own.

Later that evening, sitting alone in his room, he felt good about how things had turned out. He'd finally worked up the nerve to ask Caroline for her phone number, which she'd seemed only too happy to provide. Perhaps there was something new in store for him after all.

22

The anonymous tipster with the gravelly voice had advised the police to look more closely into Lisa Haines. The next morning, Friday, May 18th, another guy called the station with essentially the same message.

He said that Lisa had sometimes driven to the nearby city of Elizabethtown in order to visit an old female friend from college. This particular friend lived just down the block from a middle-aged businessman, Ray Diener, who'd been shot to death outside his home scarcely a week before the Haines killings. Was there not a decent chance, the guy asked, that the two incidents were somehow related?

The Manheim Township detectives were well aware of the Diener murder, which at that point was still unsolved. They'd assumed that it was an isolated incident, with no connection to the triple homicide beyond proximity in space and time. They certainly weren't opposed, however, to re-thinking the matter.

Later that morning, Bernie and Trooper Shawn Swarr met with the friend in question at her home in Elizabethtown. She said that she and Lisa had gotten to know one another while college students thirty years before and had stayed in close contact ever since. They'd spoken as recently as the week of the murders, she said, with Lisa telling her how excited she was at the prospect of daughter Maggie coming home for the summer.

Bernie asked her if Lisa knew Ray Diener, or if she'd ever mentioned anything about experiencing marital problems.

Absolutely not on both counts, the friend said. Lisa wouldn't have known Ray Diener from Adam and her marriage was the next best thing to perfection itself. There was no infidelity, no significant tension, no diminution of affection. Lisa and Tom had been getting along just as splendidly as they ever had. Lisa most likely would have told her if this weren't the case, she added.

She provided names of several other women with whom Lisa had kept in touch since her college days. Bernie and Trooper Swarr spoke with each one of them in turn without learning anything strikingly new. Lisa was basically a homebody, they all said. Aside from making an annual pilgrimage to New York for dinner and a show, her life revolved around Tom and the kids. She seemed perfectly content, moreover, in her dual role as wife and mother. If she had any complaints or misgivings, she'd certainly kept them to herself.

One woman mentioned that she'd spoken with Maggie on May 12th, the day immediately following the triple homicide. She said that Maggie seemed to be struggling with survivor's guilt, questioning why she alone was still alive.

Bernie and Trooper Swarr compared notes afterward and found themselves in essential agreement. All of these women seemed not only truthful but also really quite delightful. It was hardly surprising that Lisa had maintained close friendships with them over the years.

In the interest of thoroughness, Bernie returned to the station and telephoned several of Lisa's relatives, all of whom he'd already spoken with a few days earlier. This time he questioned them pointedly about the state of Tom and Lisa's marriage. Had the couple seemed genuinely happy? Might either one of them have been involved in an extramarital affair?

The relatives said that Tom and Lisa were like two peas in a pod. They shared the same values, the same optimistic outlook, the same vision of the good life. They were as happy together as newlyweds. The idea of either one of them having an affair was simply preposterous.

Maggie contacted the squad room on late Friday afternoon with a list of family keepsakes that she wanted put on display at the memorial service, which was scheduled for the next day at Otterbein United Methodist Church.

Bob Beck took the list to the house on Peach Lane and went inside. He retrieved several stuffed animals and Lisa's wedding ring, which he found on top of her dresser. The last item on the list was a large map of Germany that was prominently displayed on the wall next to the window in Kevin's bedroom.

Beck realized that the map meant a great deal to Maggie, that it reminded her of her younger brother and his love for Germany. He realized that she was counting on him to remove it from the wall and deliver it to her aunt and uncle's house. He also realized that there was no way he could do so.

The map was evidence. It was spattered with blood.

23

Otterbein United Methodist Church is an imposing stone structure with stained glass windows and a bell tower. It occupies the southwest corner of East Clay and North Queen Streets in Lancaster as if by divine right: solid, austere, and unmoveable.

On Saturday morning, May 19th, Corporal Richard Townsend of the Pennsylvania State Police sat in an unmarked car on the opposite corner with a surveillance camera in hand. He had a good view of not only the front but also the side entrance to the church. Quite a few people were already making their way inside and he wanted to be certain of catching every single one of them on film.

Corporal John Duby and Trooper Brendan McAnally of the Pennsylvania State Police Criminal Investigation Unit circled the block several times before finding a parking spot for their Crown Victoria. They gave Townsend a nod of acknowledgment and then entered the church through the side door and went directly to the pastor's study, where they introduced themselves and laid out their plans. They'd stand by the front vestibule, they told the pastor, and keep an eye on the proceedings. In the event of anything untoward, they'd waste no time swinging into action.

Duby and McAnally had drawn the rather delicate assignment of helping to protect Maggie at the memorial service.

If the murderer had indeed meant to kill her also, he might see this as an ideal opportunity to finish the job. He might think that striking at a church gathering would afford a certain element of surprise. It was Duby and McAnally's responsibility to stand guard against such a possibility, and to do so as unobtrusively as possible so as not to compromise the solemnity of the occasion.

No one could reasonably claim that the two men weren't up to the challenge. The state police's Criminal Investigation Unit seemed to have a penchant for attracting a particular kind of individual, of which Duby and McAnally might very well have served as exemplars. Both were tenacious and dedicated, with an unassuming style that nicely understated their sharpness of mind. They also possessed the flexibility of talent and temperament that permitted them to adapt to the demands of the moment.

Corporal Duby was the more senior of the two and also co-supervisor of the Troop J Criminal Investigation Unit. For this particular case he was chief liaison between Troop J and the Manheim Township Police Department, which meant sitting in on daily briefings and making sure that the township guys got whatever resources they needed. Trim, dapper, and boyishly handsome, he could easily have passed as an anchorman for a local television station.

Trooper McAnally was a career cop who'd never dreamed of doing anything else. He'd joined the Haines homicide investigation during its second day and had already participated in numerous interviews. He was soft-spoken and serious, and he possessed the physical size and grace of a high school athlete, though he was rapidly approaching his fortieth birthday.

Corporal Duby and Trooper McAnally stationed themselves by the rear vestibule, weapons at the ready beneath charcoal-gray suit jackets, and watched as the sanctuary filled to standing-room-only capacity. A contingent of Boy Scouts from Kevin's troop had shown up for the occasion and so, too, had dozens of students from Manheim Township High School. The boys sat awkwardly in the wooden pews, arms crossed, eyes downcast. The girls exchanged meaningful glances and rummaged through their purses for handkerchiefs.

Just before the service was scheduled to start, Allen Leed led Maggie and several of her relatives into the sanctuary from a door off to the side. They sat in a front pew, Leed immediately next to Maggie, who was wearing an ankle-length dress and a silver necklace. Leed glanced backward to survey the congregation and made fleeting eye contact with Corporal Duby. The two men knew and respected each other, having worked together on various cases over the years. Each felt better simply knowing that the other was on the scene.

The pastor took to the pulpit and made the best of an impossible situation, discoursing on the mystery of evil and the fragility of earthly existence and the eternal hope of redemption. Every note was on key, perfectly pitched for the occasion. Then Maggie's uncle on her mother's side, who'd traveled from out of state for the service, went to the pulpit and spoke passionately about the impact of this sort of crime on family survivors and community morale.

The uncle concluded his address by imploring the perpetrator of the triple homicide "to come forward and ask forgiveness of Maggie" and her family. "I say this to you," he said, "knowing full well that the killer of our loved ones might be in the audience today."

The words sent a palpable chill through the congregation. Was it possible that this was true? That the killer was somebody who was sitting in their very midst? A wolf in sheep's clothing?

At the conclusion of the service many of the high school kids gravitated toward the back of the church, not far from where Corporal Duby and Trooper McAnally were stationed. One of the boys caught McAnally's attention. He was about sixteen, this particular kid, tall and lean with a mop of thick blond hair. He was with two other boys of roughly the same age and physical appearance but there seemed something peculiar about him. While his two friends exchanged hugs of condolence with some of the girls, he hung back on the periphery, aloof, awkward, as if not quite part of the group. Several girls eventually made a special point of going over to commiserate with him, which only accentuated the oddness of his behavior. He scarcely acknowledged them and seemed almost to freeze when they tried giving him a hug.

McAnally pointed him out to Corporal Duby, who likewise found his behavior curious. Was the kid simply socially inept, or was he being purposely standoffish?

The two state police investigators didn't realize it at the time, of course, but the kid in question was Alec Kreider. And there may very well have been a reason for the stilted behavior that they observed.

During the service Alec had sat next to his German teacher in a pew toward the front of the sanctuary, and at one point he'd gotten visibly perturbed. "Look at all these high school kids making a public display of their grief over Kevin's death," he'd thought. "What a bunch of hypocrites! How many of them actually gave a damn about Kevin when he was still alive?"

There was something else that Duby and McAnally didn't realize at the time, nor might they reasonably have been expected to. The high school had arranged for grief counseling sessions in the church basement after the service. Quite a few of the kids in attendance took advantage of this arrangement, going downstairs for thirty minutes or so of therapy.

Alec Kreider was one of those kids.

24

The investigators had heard rumors concerning Alec Kreider over the previous day or so. They'd heard that he and several other students at Manheim Township High School had palpable leanings toward Nazism. So far there was no evidence that this was true, nothing that the rumors might actually be pinned to. Still, Bob Beck decided that they were worth following up on, and so after the morning briefing on Sunday, May 20th, he gave Trooper Jerry Sauers and Corporal Adam Kosheba of the Pennsylvania State Police the job of interviewing Kreider at his mother's house.

Sauers and Kosheba were two of the most experienced and talented investigators assigned to the triple homicide. Big, good-looking men who favored old-school blue suits with white shirts, they took pride in their proven ability to cut through nonsense and see things for what they really were. Sauers was a twenty-five-year veteran of the force with a highly personable style. Kosheba was the younger of the two by ten years and, along with Corporal John Duby, co-supervisor of the Troop J Criminal Investigation Unit. Together they made a formidable team.

While en route to Alec's mother Angela's house, they reviewed what they thus far knew of Alec Kreider. They knew that he was a good friend of Kevin Haines, quite possibly his very best one. They knew that he was a star student at the local high school and passionate about German history and culture. They knew that Brent Shultz had interviewed him shortly after the killings, and that nothing whatsoever about the interview had given Brent cause for concern.

They arrived at the house on Cobblestone Lane at ten o'clock only to discover that Alec wasn't there. His older sister answered the doorbell and told them that he was at his father's house right then. He wasn't scheduled to return to Cobblestone Lane until later that afternoon, she said.

They turned their car around and made the short drive to Tim Kreider's house, talking about the rumors involving Nazism along the way. Sauers speculated that the rumors might have gotten started simply because of Alec's unabashed fascination with German history and culture. With a kid his age, he said, people were sometimes quick to imagine the worst. In any event, he went on, this was something that the local school authorities would have been certain to nip in the bud. Manheim Township had a significant Jewish population and also a long tradition of civility and tolerance. There was little chance that the authorities would have stood idly by while one of their own students propagated a hateful ideology.

Kosheba agreed that this was probably so but suggested that they keep an open mind on the subject. To this point, after all, they hadn't been able to tie the murders to sex or drugs or any of the other usual motives. Who could tell? Perhaps the motive that would finally make sense of the crime was precisely a hateful ideology such as Nazism.

They found Tim Kreider at home with his fiancée. They said that they were conducting follow-up interviews with friends of Kevin Haines and asked if they could speak with Alec.

Tim said that Alec was still sleeping. He invited the two men inside and told them to make themselves at home while he went upstairs to get him.

Sauers and Kosheba weren't surprised that Alec was still in bed. The running joke among investigators working the case was that all of these high school kids awoke precisely at the crack of noon on weekends.

Alec came downstairs with his dad after a few minutes, wearing jeans and a T-shirt. His hair was disheveled, his eyes still bleary from sleep.

They sat in the living room, Sauers and Kosheba side-by-side on a couch, Alec and his dad across from them in a couple of armchairs. The fiancée excused herself and went into the kitchen.

Sauers was struck by how similar in appearance Alec was to several other high school boys whom he'd interviewed in connection with the case. All of these kids—tall and skinny with a mop of fair hair—seemed cut from the same mold.

He told Alec that they were interested in obtaining more background information on Kevin.

Alec said that he was happy to help out in any way he could. After all, he added, he and Kevin had been the very best of friends.

He said that the last time he actually spoke with Kevin was immediately following classes on Friday, May 11th, at the school bus stop. They'd planned on hanging out together over the weekend.

Kosheba asked Alec if he'd sometimes sleep over at Kevin's house.

Almost always on Kevin's birthday he would, Alec said, and occasionally at other times also. He said that Kevin's parents enjoyed hosting sleepovers. In any event, he added, it was four or five weeks now since he'd even stepped foot inside the Haines house.

Kosheba asked him if Kevin had any enemies, or if there were students at school with whom he simply didn't get along.

Alec said that quite a few kids would poke fun at Kevin, mostly because he came across as a stereotypical nerd. He gave the investigators the names of three grade eleven students whom he described as habitual offenders in this regard.

Kosheba asked him how he'd characterize Kevin's relationship with his older sister Maggie.

Alec said that Kevin rarely spoke to him about Maggie. He'd always been under the impression, he said, that they weren't particularly close.

To this point Sauers had let his partner handle most of the questioning. Now, however, he leaned forward and made direct eye contact with Alec.

"Do you know anyone who would ever want to hurt Kevin?" he asked point-blank.

Alec paused before answering, his gaze level and sure.

"No," he said.

The investigators shifted gears, telling Alec that they'd heard rumors about him and several other Manheim Township High School students dabbling in Nazism. They asked him if the rumors were true.

Once again he took his time answering, as if the question called for some serious mental calculation.

"Absolutely not," he finally said. "Such a thing would never be tolerated at my high school."

They probed some more, asking him why he thought the rumors had picked up steam in recent days and where they might have stemmed from.

Alec's answers were clear and convincing. He said that he wasn't sure where the rumors stemmed from, though he imagined that his involvement in the German club at school had played a role. People sometimes mistakenly assumed that anyone fascinated with Germany must also have a predilection for Nazism, he said.

It was half an hour now since the interview began, and Tim Kreider's fiancée came into the living room and asked the investigators if they'd mind moving their car. It was blocking the driveway and she had to get out to run some errands. They were just about finished anyway and so Sauers and Kosheba thanked Alec for his help and promised that they'd be in touch again if anything else came up.

Tim Kreider walked them outside and wished them luck in solving the crime. Sauers noticed a Harley Davidson parked next to the garage. An avid motorcyclist some years before, he chatted with Tim about the virtues of the all-American Harley before joining his partner in their car.

They headed back toward the Manheim Township Police

Department, dissecting the interview along the way. Both men had gotten a favorable impression of Tim Kreider, who was exceedingly pleasant throughout. They realized that interviews of this sort could be especially hard on parents, and Tim was as cooperative as any parent whom they'd thus far encountered during the course of the investigation.

Alec had struck them as cooperative also, not to mention a pretty cool customer for a kid his age. Here was a sixteen-year-old who'd been rousted from bed on a Sunday morning for a grilling at the hands of two seasoned investigators. Yet he'd betrayed not the least hint of nervousness. He'd seemed relaxed, almost nonchalant, while answering their questions, not a waver of anxiety in his voice, a flicker of doubt in his eyes.

If there was anything amiss with Alec Kreider, they thought, he was doing a splendid job of disguising it.

25

FBI Agents Ray Carr and Kevin McShane didn't talk much about the case during the drive from Philadelphia on Monday morning, May 21st. There seemed little point in doing so. They already knew the essentials and once they arrived in Lancaster County, Bob Beck and Allen Leed would be more than happy to fill them in on the finer details. The important thing at this juncture was keeping an open mind and avoiding making any premature hypotheses. Keeping an open mind while assessing all available evidence was precisely what they'd been trained to do.

Both men seemed tailor-made for the job. Lean, fit, and handsome in an unfussy, square-jawed sort of way, they actually looked like FBI agents. They were also smart, funny, and street savvy, with a disarming knack for putting people at ease. Ray Carr was the older of the two by several years, and rather the more outspoken. He first joined the Bureau in 1989, worked out of the Buffalo office for a couple of years, and then moved to Philadelphia, where he became a fixture with the Violent Crime/Fugitive Task Force. In 1996 he shifted over to the Newtown Square office without skipping a beat. Kevin McShane, for his part, grew up in the suburbs of Baltimore wanting nothing more than to become an FBI agent. He was assigned to the Philadelphia office upon graduating the academy in Quantico in 1996, where he quickly distinguished himself as a top-flight investigator.

Normally the FBI will only get involved with a local investigation upon receiving a specific request for help, which was precisely what happened in this case. Manheim Township Police Chief Neil Harkins initially reached out to Special Agent Heather Thew at the Bureau's Harrisburg office for help identifying the bloody shoeprints found at the crime scene. Now the chief wanted Agents Carr and McShane actually to walk through the crime scene on the chance of their noticing something that his own detectives might have missed. In the world of criminal investigations, it was rather the equivalent of calling in the cavalry.

Carr and McShane exited the turnpike and drove south on Route 222 through lush farmland. They turned off at the Oregon Pike and wove their way to the Manheim Township police station, which was a low-slung red-brick building on manicured grounds located directly across the road from a McDonald's restaurant. Everything about this corner of Pennsylvania struck the agents as peaceful and orderly, a far cry from the rush and roar of Philadelphia.

Agent Thew was waiting for them at the front door. Since helping out with the bloody shoeprints the previous Monday, she'd kept close tabs on the investigation, driving in every morning from Harrisburg for the daily briefing. She greeted Carr and McShane, both of whom she held in high regard, and escorted them inside. They checked in with Chief Harkins and then walked down the corridor to the detective squad room.

It was potentially a touchy situation, a couple of hotshot feds coming in from Philadelphia ostensibly to save the day. Any other detectives might understandably have felt a bit resentful, not wanting to admit that they could use some help, but the Manheim Township guys rolled out the red carpet. Bob Beck and Allen Leed and the rest of the team were delighted to see the two FBI agents. They weren't in the least concerned with protecting their turf or proving themselves competent. Their only concern was in solving the case, and toward this end they were only too happy to accept any help that came their way.

It certainly didn't hurt that Agents Carr and McShane were genuinely good and decent men. They'd spoken several times over the previous week with Agent Thew about the case. They knew how vexing it was, a triple homicide with no apparent motive, and they appreciated how hard the local guys had been working trying to solve it.

Beck and Leed sat down with the agents in the squad room and brought them fully up to speed on the investigation. Then they drove over to Peach Lane together, donned protective gear, and went inside the Haines house.

They walked through the main floor first and then went upstairs, where the sheer horror of the slaughter was still very much in evidence. Even Carr and McShane, seasoned pros though they were, had never before encountered anything quite like it. The trail left behind by the bloody shoe-prints, the spatters of blood on the walls: It was almost as if the crime had taken place just moments before.

The atmosphere was so grim, so overbearing, that nobody spoke for a while. Agent McShane tried loosening things up with some gallows humor. Noticing that it was a left-footed shoe that had made most of the bloody prints on the carpet and floor, he said: "Well, at least we've pegged our suspect."

"What do you mean?" Allen Leed asked.

"It's obvious," McShane said. "The killer's a one-legged man."

The crack proved the perfect tonic. Everybody laughed and the house was suddenly less suffocating.

The FBI agents found it remarkable how easily they could track the movements of the perpetrator, his progression from room to room, simply by following the trail of blood that he'd left behind. He'd started in the parents' bedroom, quite possibly viewing Tom and Lisa as an immediate threat that needed dispelling, and then gone on to kill Kevin. He'd then returned to Tom and Lisa's room and washed up in the second-floor bathroom before going downstairs and exiting the house through the sliding glass door in the kitchen.

It was Kevin's bedroom that the agents found most telling. Whoever killed the teenager, they thought, had done so with unspeakable rage. Rage was written all over the blood-spattered walls, the bloodstained floor. It clung to every corner. This wasn't a random crime, they thought. The killer had entered the house with the specific purpose of killing Kevin and whomever else he encountered along the way, after which he'd carried out the deed with alarming ferocity.

They discussed all of this with Bob Beck and Allen Leed immediately upon leaving the house. They said that stabbing was a highly personal method of killing to begin with, and that this particular crime seemed intensely personal. The perpetrator most likely knew Kevin, who was quite obviously the principal target of the attack, and seemed to have taken particular relish in murdering him.

The folks at the FBI's Behavioral Science Unit in Quantico had already suggested as much to Beck and Leed over the telephone. Here again the two detectives were grateful for the input.

Back at the station, Beck and Leed showed the agents a copy of Maggie's statement, explaining that several of the investigators working the case had serious concerns about it. The agents suggested emailing the statement to the FBI's National Center for the Analysis of Violent Crime in Quantico. No one was better equipped than the center's expert analysts, they said, for assessing the integrity and coherency of witness statements.

The agents ate lunch with Corporal John Duby at a restaurant just down the road from the station, which proved a nice interlude in their day. They swapped theories about the triple homicide and also discussed current developments in the fields of criminology and criminal justice.

Upon returning to the station, they discovered that the analysts in Quantico had already gotten back to them with a report on Maggie's statement. They'd gone over the statement, the analysts had, without finding any evidence of glaring deception in it.

At four o'clock, all of the Manheim Township detectives assembled in the conference room for an afternoon briefing. Bob Beck spoke for a while and then gave the floor to Agents Carr and McShane.

The agents reiterated what they'd already told Beck and Leed at the crime scene, elaborating here and there as they saw fit. The crime was almost certainly not a random act of violence, they said. In all likelihood, the victims were specifically selected for a reason. The perpetrator, moreover, seemed familiar with the house, perhaps having previously spent time in it. He knew the layout of the rooms and had a plan of escape at the ready, which involved slipping out through the rear door. This wasn't alien territory to him. Rather he was operating in a kind of comfort zone.

There was a good chance, the agents said, that the perpetrator lived within relatively easy walking distance of the Haines home. That he was somebody whom neighbors might actually have seen from time to time in the course of their daily activities. They recommended that the detectives extend the perimeter of their neighborhood investigation by several blocks in the event that this was so.

They also recommended that the detectives continue to focus on the victims, and especially Kevin in this regard, who was quite clearly the primary target of the attack. What specifically had caused them to become victims? Was there something about Kevin or his parents that might shed light on the matter?

The agents realized that the detectives were frustrated at not yet having uncovered a motive for the crime. With this in mind, Ray Carr counseled patience and perseverance.

"There's always a motive," he said. "Sometimes at first it's only known to the offender. But there's always a motive."

26

Tuesday morning, May 22nd: It was a week and a half now after the triple homicide, and the investigators seemed no closer than before to making an arrest. Frustration was mounting, nerves beginning to fray. Arguments over how best to proceed with the case had started to erupt in the squad room. As often as not, these arguments concerned Maggie.

Some investigators still thought that Maggie might know more than she'd thus far told them. Perhaps there was a critical detail that she'd neglected to mention, or that she'd not quite gotten right. Perhaps there was something in the family background about which she'd not been entirely forthcoming.

These investigators realized that the FBI's expert analysts had found no evidence of deception in her statement. But this, they believed, was rather beside the point. Maggie was the only survivor of the attack, the only person who might reasonably be counted as a witness. They'd be seriously remiss not bringing her into the station for yet another interview.

Allen Leed was opposed to this, and so, too, was his partner Jim Brenneman. Both men believed that Maggie had already been stretched to the limit. She'd answered every imaginable question concerning those fateful hours of a week and a half ago, and she'd done so as candidly as possible. What more, realistically, would she be able to tell them?

Leed and Brenneman were also concerned with the signal that they might be sending Maggie in calling her in for another interview. Would she interpret this to mean that they didn't believe her story, that in their view she was somehow involved with the killings? Such an interpretation, they thought, would not be entirely unreasonable.

The two detectives found themselves outvoted, however, and so at eleven o'clock on Tuesday morning Leed called Maggie at her aunt and uncle's house and asked if she'd mind coming to the station for some more questioning. Maggie sounded less than thrilled with the idea but agreed nonetheless. Anything, she said, in the interests of furthering the investigation. She arrived an hour or so later, accompanied by her police escort du jour.

The interview took place in the main conference room. Leed and Brenneman sat across from Maggie at a narrow table, with two other investigators observing from across the room. Unlike the previous interviews of Maggie, this one was videotaped.

The investigative team as a whole had prepared a list of specific questions for Leed, who was charged with presiding over the proceedings. Some of these questions were of a rather delicate nature, calling into doubt the accuracy, if not outright veracity, of Maggie's previous statements. Leed realized that getting through them would require as much tact as he could muster.

Adopting his most solicitous tone, Leed once again asked Maggie to recount precisely what happened when she first left her room upon being awakened on the night of the murders. Maggie did so, describing the strange voice and the thumping noises that she heard in the hallway outside Kevin's bedroom.

"I also remember smelling blood," she said. "It smelled like a lot of blood."

"Were you ever previously in a position where you smelled a lot of blood?" Leed asked.

"I am a girl," Maggie answered curtly, "and I have my period."

She then described how she retreated to her bedroom for a brief spell before running down the hallway and entering her parents' room. Neither parent, she said, seemed visibly wounded at the time.

"My mom was in hysterics," she said. "She said that I needed to go for help. She looked at me when she said this. My mom was extremely upset. She ran over a cat a couple of years ago and she was upset then. This was a notch above the cat incident."

"Did you ask your mother why you should go for help?" Leed asked.

"No," Maggie said. "I just went. You wake up and you hear all the commotion and then you see your mom in hysterics and your dad not moving. I just went for help."

She described racing across the street to the neighbor's house for help and then the agonizing wait while the police searched her family home.

"Finally Officer Bradley came back over," she said, "and now we get to the absolutely worst moment of my entire life. He tells me that my parents and brother are dead. I just look at him. I may have said, 'Are you kidding me?' He repeats and confirms what happened."

"Did he tell you how it happened?" Leed asked.

"No," Maggie said.

Leed asked her about the campus ministry that she tried contacting prior to leaving the neighbor's house for the police station.

"It's a prayer group I go to at college," she said. "I wanted to talk with the guy, Luke, who leads it. I did not have his phone number. I made my neighbor's daughter take me to a computer to try and find it."

"Tell us more about the campus prayer group," Leed said.

"My dad was diagnosed with prostate cancer," she said, "and right before he was going to have surgery I was very nervous and concerned. I told a friend at college about my dad having prostate cancer. I was really upset and she talked me into going to the group. I went, once a week for about a month, and it somewhat helped to an extent. We talked about how I could apply the Bible and religion to my life. It went okay."

Her eyes filled with tears at this point and she took a few seconds to regain her composure.

"Anyway," she went on, "after Officer Bradley told me that my parents and brother were dead, I wanted to talk to Luke to find out why this has happened. Why would God have let this happen? I never did get ahold of Luke. I was being told that I needed to go to the police station. I borrowed flip-flops and a sweatshirt and went with Officer Bradley to the station."

Upon arriving on the scene the night of the killings, Patrolmen Chris Keenan and Steve Newman thought that Maggie might have mentioned actually seeing an intruder in the family home. Leed now asked her if this were true.

"I don't remember telling them that," Maggie said. "I actually did not see anyone. I just knew there was an intruder in my house. It was a gut feeling."

"Why did you not look into Kevin's room when going to your parents' room?" Leed asked.

"I just wanted to get out of the house," Maggie said. "I saw my mom and I went into her room."

"One of the initial officers on the scene," Leed said, "thought he heard you say that the noises you heard might have had something to do with your father's recent surgery."

"I was freaked out," Maggie said. "I did not know what was going on. I tried to come up with some explanation for why the events were occurring. I thought that maybe something went wrong with the whole catheter thing and I was just trying to grasp at something for a reason."

They went back and forth on this theme for a while longer until Leed abruptly shifted gears.

"Could someone have peered into your room while you were still asleep?" he asked. "Without your being aware of it?"

"Yes," Maggie said. "I am a very heavy sleeper."

Leed asked her about several of the friends with whom she was in the habit of communicating via instant messaging. Then Detective Brenneman chimed in with a question of his own.

"How do you think your parents and brother died?" he asked.

This was something, as obvious as it might seem, that the police had not explicitly covered with Maggie in previous interviews.

"I assume that they were stabbed to death," Maggie said. "I think I heard Detective Leed or someone at the station say that. At one point you guys asked me if there were any knives in the house."

"Do you have any idea why this happened to your family?" Brenneman asked.

Maggie shifted in her chair and looked directly at him.

"I have no idea," she said.

Maggie had raised eyebrows in certain quarters with her seemingly matter-of-fact approach to life over the past week. Prior to the triple homicide she'd been planning on presenting a paper at an animal behavior conference in St. Louis and then studying abroad in Australia. She was still planning on going ahead with these endeavors, despite the tragedy that had befallen her family. The investigative team had urged Leed to raise this with her.

"Tell us about your plans to go to Australia," he now asked.

"I want to study abroad in Australia," Maggie said. "I think that it would be fun. A lot of my friends at Bucknell are studying abroad this spring. I didn't want to be the only one left at Bucknell. I haven't filled out all of the paperwork yet. I've been discussing this throughout the past year. I've discussed it with my parents."

"And the St. Louis trip?" Leed asked.

"I am actually presenting at the joint meeting of the Ichthyologists and Herpetologists in St. Louis," Maggie said. "I'll fly out and stay at the Hyatt with a girl from another college who's also presenting. I'll meet my professor from

Bucknell out there. He's only twenty-seven, and he's very, very smart. He's married, kind of dorky, a really good guy. I'll fly in on July 13th and leave on July 16th. I'm presenting on the Sunday."

"How would you describe your parents' marriage?" Leed asked, once again shifting gears.

"It was wonderful," Maggie said. "They would bicker but would never full-out fight. There was no screaming."

"What kind of a relationship did you have with your mother?" Leed asked.

"It was fairly close," Maggie said. "I think that she missed me more than I missed her. I felt bad about that. I was able to go away to college."

"Would your mother have confided in you if she were having an affair?" Leed asked.

Maggie's responses to this point had mostly been crisp, her manner brusque. At this last question, however, she flared in indignation.

"I think that it's utterly ridiculous that she would have an affair," she said. "I think that I would know about it if she was. There was nothing going on with my parents and someone else."

Leed exchanged glances with Jim Brenneman. He took off his glasses and folded his hands on the table.

"What kind of a relationship did you have with Kevin?" he next asked.

"I did not have a close relationship with him," Maggie said, still sounding rather miffed. "We are four grades apart. He is my little brother. I am a big sister. I would call home and talk with my mom. I would talk with Kevin if he was there."

"Do you think that he had problems with any other kids?" Leed asked.

"No, not really," Maggie said. "He was not Mister Popular. He did his own thing. Nobody had any issues with him."

Leed asked several more questions about Kevin and then backtracked, once again raising the issue of what Maggie might or might not have seen prior to fleeing her house on the night of the murders.

"Do you feel that it's possible that you did in fact see this intruder and you're now blocking it out?" he asked.

"I think that anything is possible," Maggie said. "It is possible. There is no way for me to really know."

Leed and Brenneman wrapped things up soon thereafter and thanked Maggie for coming into the station at such short notice. Once she'd left, they conferred with the two investigators who'd been sitting in as observers.

Leed and Brenneman thought that Maggie had been truthful throughout the entire interview, if not exactly pleased at having to endure it. They believed that she was just as perplexed as they were by the killings.

Their two colleagues weren't so certain. They thought that she might still know something of vital importance to the case that, for whatever reason, she wasn't revealing.

27

Wednesday, May 23rd, was the last day of classes at Manheim Township High School before final examinations.

Alec Kreider began the day with a flourish.

Several weeks earlier, his first-period English teacher had assigned him to a group of girls for a class project. The teacher hadn't done so merely by accident. She regarded Alec as not only smart but also as just about the sweetest boy in the entire class. She had every confidence that he'd comport himself appropriately.

Alec had rewarded the teacher's trust in him, making a significant contribution to the project and behaving like a complete gentleman throughout. And now, on this the last day of the semester, he came to class with a bouquet of flowers for each of the girls in his group. The teacher was impressed, not least of all by the beauty of the bouquets. Alec had most likely gone to the trouble of purchasing them at a first-rate florist's shop. The kid really was a sweetheart.

The remainder of the school day proceeded rather less eventfully.

The tenth-grade biology teacher closed off the semester by having students fill out course evaluation forms. Alec wrote in his that he no longer enjoyed studying subjects such

Mug shot of Alec Kreider.

Photo courtesy of Manheim Township PD.

Maggie Haines. One frame taken from her videotaped testimony at Alec Kreider's sentencing hearing.

The Haines family residence.
Photo courtesy of Manheim Township PD.

Covered bridge in Lancaster County.
Photo courtesy of Brenda Michelle Cuneo.

Amish horse and buggy in Lancaster County.
Photo courtesy of Brenda Michelle Cuneo.

Piece of local color in Lancaster County.
Photo courtesy of Brenda Michelle Cuneo.

The Manheim Township PD detective squad. Left to right: Detective Robert Beck, Detective John Wettlaufer, Detective Cleon Berntheizel, Lieutenant Douglas Sing, Detective Allen Leed, Detective Brent Shultz, Detective Richard McCracken, Detective Sergeant Keith Kreider, and Detective Brian Freysz. Photo courtesy of Dan Jerchau.

Detective Allen Leed.

Photo courtesy of Brenda Michelle Cuneo.

Lancaster County District Attorney Craig Stedman.

Photo courtesy of Brenda Michelle Cuneo.

Alec Kreider shortly after his arrest, being escorted by Trooper Mark Magyar of the Pennsylvania State Police.

Photo courtesy of *Intelligencer Journal*, Lancaster, PA.

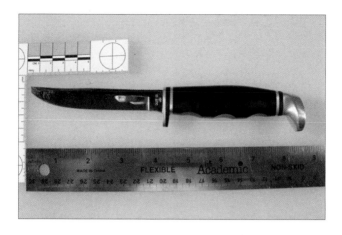

The murder weapon that was recovered from Alec Kreider's father's house.

Photo courtesy of Manheim Township PD.

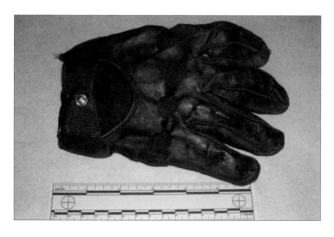

One of the gloves that Alec Kreider wore during the killings.

Photo courtesy of Manheim Township PD.

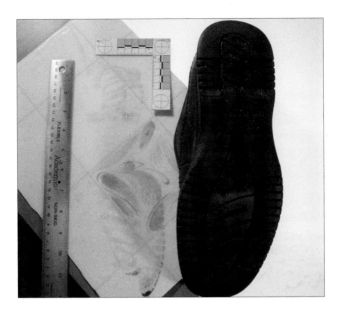

Police match the tread on Alec Kreider's shoe with a bloody shoeprint impression from the crime scene.

Photo courtesy of Manheim Township PD.

The baseball cap (with duct tape covering the logo) that police recovered in a ravine near the Haines home.

Photo courtesy of Manheim Township PD.

Lancaster County Prison.   Photo courtesy of Dan Jerchau.

Alec Kreider's cell, Lancaster County Prison.

Photo courtesy of Lancaster County Prison staff.

Communal area outside Alec Kreider's cell, Lancaster County Prison.

Photo courtesy of Lancaster County Prison staff.

as biology. He'd recently learned, he went on, that it was far more important simply to seize each and every day and live life to its fullest.

He ate lunch in the school cafeteria with the usual people, Warren and Joseph, Carol and Nancy, none of whom seemed especially cheerful. It hadn't been quite the same at lunch since Kevin's death. Kevin and Alec had always enjoyed jousting verbally over their juice and sandwiches, arguing about war and politics and religion, pushing one another to the limit. Their debates had energized the entire table. Now everyone simply sat there struggling to make small talk, like distant relatives at a funeral parlor.

This was true even of Carol and Nancy, both of whom under normal circumstances were bright and vivacious. Prior to the killings, they'd often tease Alec about his sullen demeanor, saying that he needed to lighten up and have more fun. Not entirely in jest, they'd formed what they referred to as the "Happy Club," the singular purpose of which was to induce at least one smile from Alec every school day. But this seemed an eternity ago now. In recent days smiles were in short supply from just about everybody in the tenth grade at Manheim Township High School.

Alec's thoughts were actually elsewhere during this particular lunch period. The previous evening he'd finally worked up the nerve to call Caroline, the cute girl from the mall. The conversation had gone remarkably well and he'd arranged to meet her at the food court after his kung fu class the next day. Sitting there now at the lunch table with his schoolmates, he felt a pang of longing that was unfamiliar to him. He thought that it might be love.

Later that afternoon, a student from Alec's sixth-period German class approached him in the hallway with a yearbook in hand, which he asked him to sign. Alec did so and beneath his signature he inscribed a brief message.

> *I will be going away for a long time.*
> *Have a good summer.*

The fellow student had no idea in the world what this meant, nor did he bother asking. He knew that Alec was sometimes purposely enigmatic.

28

Patrol Sergeant Jeff Jones of the Manheim Township Police Department had become a mainstay on the Maggie detail in recent days. It was a challenging assignment, involving as it did an unusual combination of roles. Performing it well meant not only serving as bodyguard but also as friend and counselor. It meant not only protecting Maggie but also consoling her and keeping her company.

A soft-spoken, charming, and intelligent man in his early forties, Sergeant Jones was ideally suited for the assignment. He liked and respected Maggie, and was prepared to take whatever steps necessary to keep her out of harm's way. He was also fond of her aunt and uncle, both of whom he thought had comported themselves with uncommon dignity in the wake of the tragedy.

For more than a week now, Jones had been a veritable shadow to Maggie. He'd accompanied her to the lawyer's office for a reading of Tom and Lisa's will, and to the undertaker's for final burial arrangements. He'd accompanied her to the shopping mall and to the supermarket and to the outdoor running track at Franklin and Marshall College. He'd accompanied her almost everywhere.

Upon arriving at the aunt and uncle's house early on Wednesday afternoon, May 23rd, Jones found Maggie in the backyard swimming pool. She seemed perfectly at ease, lounging on an inflatable raft in the deep end. The aunt came outside and invited the officer to make himself at home, saying he was virtually part of the family by now. He took off his shoes and socks and sat on the edge of the pool with his feet dangling in the water, all the while keeping a wary eye on the perimeter of the property.

Later that afternoon, as a light rain was starting to fall, Maggie told Jones that she wanted to visit a friend from high school who lived in the nearby village of Lititz. The two of them got into the police cruiser and headed north on the Lititz Pike. Maggie chatted about college along the way, her favorite courses and professors, her aspirations for junior year.

Eventually she began talking about her parents and younger brother, referring to them in the present tense. This was something to which Jones had become accustomed. She'd often talk about her family, especially her dad, always speaking of them as if they were still alive.

This time, however, there was a brittleness to her voice that Jones hadn't heard before and the voice soon petered out altogether. Jones looked over and noticed that she was crying, ever so softly. He stopped the car at the next corner and reached over and took her hand.

"It's okay, Maggie," he said. "You can let it out."

She immediately began to sob loudly, clutching the dashboard with her free hand. Jones sat quietly, watching beads of rain collect on the windshield, reluctant to interrupt this outpouring of emotion. Finally she stifled the sobs and looked over at him.

"I heard my brother dying," she said. "I'm the big sister. Big sisters are supposed to protect their little brothers. I didn't do that."

Jones realized, of course, that Maggie's carefree manner since the triple homicide had given some people cause for concern. Was she in denial, not yet prepared to accept the grim truth of the crime? Or, worse, was she herself somehow implicated in it? Jones, for his part, had resisted trying to read much of anything into Maggie's manner. For all he knew, she might simply have been putting on a casual front for the benefit of others while suffering her grief in private.

Hearing her now, however, he thought that he truly understood. Maggie was afflicted with survivor's guilt. She'd been blaming herself all this time for Kevin's death, thinking that there must have been something she could have done to prevent it. Her apparently blithe demeanor since the triple homicide was nothing more than a coping device, a way of allaying this terrible burden of self-recrimination.

Jones tried saying all the right things. He told her that by all accounts she was a wonderful daughter and big sister. He told her that Kevin would have been proud of her for the courage that she'd shown throughout the ordeal.

He told her that there was nothing—absolutely nothing— that she could have done differently that awful night.

29

Things seemed destined to get progressively worse before they started getting better.

With the month of May winding down, the investigators of the triple homicide were still completely baffled. They had no leads, no suspects, not even a whisper of a motive. As if not under pressure enough already, they now had to contend with some unanticipated complications.

The first of these came about on Thursday, May 24th, when the Lancaster County coroner, Doctor Gary Kirchner, made some inflammatory comments about the case in an interview with a television reporter.

Kirchner, who had a reputation within local law enforcement circles as something of a loose cannon, had drawn the ire of the DA's office once or twice previously with ill-advised pronouncements. This time he seemed determined to set a new standard for himself in the ill-advised department.

He first of all described the crime scene for the reporter, saying that the victims had been stabbed multiple times and that the killings were the worst that he'd ever seen.

"They're gruesome," he said. "They're awful. They're bloody. They're unbelievable."

He then went on to offer his own theory about the person responsible for the murders.

"My theory is probably that this is a psychotic killer," he said. "And that means that the whole motivation for the killing is in his head. It's not out among people."

Asked to elaborate, he said that he had every reason for believing that the perpetrator was psychotic. The police had thus far failed to uncover a rational motive for the crime, he said, and the investigation had gone absolutely nowhere. There was a good chance, he suggested, that the killings would remain unsolved.

"They're not coming up with anything," he said. "No motives. No people. I mean we're down to interviewing kids at school. They've gone to Florida to visit the daughter's college roommate."

The investigative authorities were outraged upon hearing these comments, and not merely because of the mistaken information about the police having traveled to Florida for the purpose of interviewing a college friend of Maggie's. In revealing graphic and hitherto confidential details of the crime scene, the coroner had potentially jeopardized the entire investigation. And in surmising that a psychotic killer was on the loose in the community, he'd risked inflaming the fear and panic that so many local people were already feeling.

The DA's office, in conjunction with the Pennsylvania State Police and Manheim Township Police Chief Neil Harkins, tried counteracting the damage with a withering press release:

> Doctor Kirchner has once again compromised a major criminal investigation by publicly disclosing to media outlets detailed information about victim injuries that only the killer would know, and he has done so for no legitimate reason. To compound his obstruction, the coroner has now decided to offer a profile of the killer even though specific information about the criminal investigation has been intentionally withheld from him and he has no expertise as a behavioral scientist.

"Doctor Kirchner's assumptions," the release concluded, "are irresponsible and not worthy of consideration."

Matters took another turn for the worse two days later when a guy walked into a local bar in the wee hours and opened fire with a pistol, critically injuring one patron and grazing another in the back of the head.

Rookies Sports Bar & Grill, the scene of the shooting, was located in a shambling motel complex on Keller Avenue on the southern fringes of Manheim Township. It was the last thing that the township detectives needed at this point, yet another violent crime in their jurisdiction. Bob Beck assigned Brent Shultz to the case as lead investigator, hopeful that Shultz would succeed in making quick work of it.

In the larger scheme, of course, developments of this sort amounted to little more than minor distractions. The investigators were living and breathing the triple homicide, playing every imaginable angle, leaving absolutely nothing to chance.

They'd set up an evidence table at the back of the squad room, where they spent hours at a time searching through case reports and other documents for something that they might have missed, a hidden clue perhaps, an elusive detail.

Thanks to some nifty legal maneuvering on the part of Assistant DA Craig Stedman, they had the complete financial profile of the Haines family at their disposal. The bank records seemed perfectly in order, with no suspiciously large deposits or withdrawals having been made in recent months. The family credit history was likewise unremarkable, and Tom's annual salary was more than adequate for the family's needs.

Everything they looked at suggested the same conclusion. The Haineses were a stable, close-knit, middle-class family without a single known enemy. They were modest and unpretentious, preferring simple homespun pleasures to anything else. Their only fault, if such it may be described, was a tendency toward domestic insularity, a seeming reluctance to extend themselves socially.

On balance, they seemed thoroughly innocuous.

Tips continued to come into the station, mostly far-fetched, occasionally promising. Even the more promising invariably fizzled out. Late one evening, for example, Bob Beck took a call from a man who'd recently moved from Lancaster to Indianapolis. He said that he was hanging out at a gym not far from his new home when he saw a guy whom he vaguely recognized as also being from Lancaster and with whom he subsequently engaged in conversation. The guy had a scabbed-over wound on the palm of his right hand and seemed visibly agitated, saying that he'd left the Lancaster area because of police harassment and was now working undercover on "a mission against towel-heads."

Beck contacted the Indianapolis PD, who picked the guy up for questioning and quickly determined that he'd had nothing to do with the Haines killings.

Then there was the strange letter with no return address that showed up on Bernie's desk one morning. Its author apparently suspected a nineteen-year-old kid whom he or she knew of being the killer and had enclosed a smudge of the kid's blood so that the police could test it for DNA and see if it matched the DNA found at the crime scene. "Profile of a young man" is how the letter began:

> A 19-year-old with known obsessive-compulsive disorder, untreated; few friends, in room upstairs for hours or entire weekend, never goes anywhere by himself . . . mathematically adept, fascination with knives and swords . . . forges his own intricate knives with detailed, carved, hardwood handles . . . involved in martial arts, destructive of property, very poor hygiene, shows no emotion, close-minded, never smiles, poor eye contact, no consideration for others . . . smokes and uses alcohol (although never witnessed to be intoxicated), potential drug-seeker; family history of mental illness . . . no history of self-harm or harm to others . . . He was not home during the hours of the Haines's murders . . . However, I do not know of any motive . . . It is very important that I maintain anonymity at this time.

The letter concluded with a request that the police disclose the result of the DNA test in the classified section of the local newspaper.

Bernie showed the letter to Bob Beck and Allen Leed, who agreed that it possessed an especially poignant quality. Was this a mother writing about her very own son, worried to death that he might be the killer? The detectives followed up on it, only to run into yet another dead-end. The nineteen-year-old who was the subject of the letter might indeed have been troubled but he'd almost certainly had nothing to do with the triple homicide.

The investigation was a collaborative effort in the truest sense, with dozens of people—state and local alike—working practically around the clock on it. All of these people were committed to solving the case, regardless of cost in time and energy to themselves personally. This was acutely so of the guys in the squad room, the Manheim Township detectives. This was primarily their case, after all. The crime had been committed on their turf and finding the killer was more to them than merely a job. It was the ultimate test of their worth, the toughest professional challenge that any of them were ever likely to face.

As the investigation dragged on without resolution, the detectives would sometimes lose patience with one another. They'd argue about suspects and evidence. They'd argue about basic investigative strategy. But the disagreements never once turned ugly. They never once got in the way of the job at hand. Throughout everything, the squad room remained a place of civility and mutual respect.

The detectives were an impressive group.

There was Allen Leed, of course, savvy veteran and inspirational leader of the squad. But there was also Bob Beck, an alert and articulate man with a sophisticated understanding of police work, not to mention an encyclopedic knowledge of Major League Baseball. Beck was a consummate gentleman, considerate, courteous, and tolerant. He was also the sort of cop who could take suspects by surprise, coolly reflective on the surface but tough as nails underneath.

Cleon Berntheizel, or Bernie, was quiet and earnest, whereas Brent Shultz, at forty-one the second youngest of the detectives, was brash and irreverent. With his shaved head, sharp suits, and devil-may-care manner, Shultz gave the appearance of being on loan from some big-city police department elsewhere in the country. In his own way, however, he was as indispensable as Leed and Beck were. As tensions mounted during the investigation, Shultz could generally be counted on to lighten the mood in the squad room with a burst of salty humor. He was also fearless, precisely the sort of guy you'd want as backup in a tough situation.

John Wettlaufer was classy, conscientious, and a top-flight crime scene man. Much like Shultz, moreover, he played a crucial role in bolstering morale and relieving tensions during the tough going. A part-time artist of no small talent, he'd produce amusing comic strips featuring his colleagues in various work situations, which he'd then bundle together and circulate throughout the squad room under the title of *Wett News*.

Brian Freysz was the newest detective on the squad, a recent transfer from the county's Drug Task Force. A slender man with an acerbic sense of humor, Freysz was approaching forty but could easily have passed for ten years younger. He comported himself with quiet intensity, rarely missing a thing while letting others do most of the talking. He was as smart as a whip.

There were also Detective Rich McCracken and Lieutenant Doug Sing. A big, friendly man and a Vietnam veteran with a passion for motorcycling, McCracken was the department's resident evidence specialist. And Lieutenant Sing, commander of the detective division, was a calm and gracious presence in the squad room even when the investigative waters were most turbulent.

The person ultimately responsible for keeping the ship afloat, however, was Chief Neil Harkins. The chief was still in a transitional phase at the time of the Haines killings, having just recently taken over the department after spending a lengthy stint as chief of the Falls Township PD in suburban Philadelphia. He didn't yet have a cell phone, an official vehicle, or a computer in his office. He didn't yet know most of the people in the department, and most of them didn't yet know him.

Late one evening the week of the triple homicide, patrol officer Dave Bair saw some guy he didn't recognize—a big, middle-aged guy in a suit—standing by the parking garage at the rear of the station. Bair approached the man and demanded to know what he was doing lurking about on police property. When the guy identified himself as Neil Harkins, the new chief of police, Bair was instantly apologetic, saying he certainly hadn't meant any disrespect. The chief assured Bair that he'd done nothing wrong, that vigilance of the sort he'd shown was precisely the hallmark of a good cop.

Chief Harkins treated the detectives in a similar fashion. He gave them the latitude to investigate the triple homicide as best they could, even if this meant their stepping on some toes along the way. He kept close tabs on the case, attending daily briefings and offering strategic advice, but rarely interfered with day-to-day operations. In handling relations with the media himself, moreover, he ensured that the detectives had a working environment mostly free of distractions.

Leed and the others appreciated the trust that the new chief placed in them. It made them that much more determined to solve the case. The last thing that they wanted was to disappoint the boss.

In happier days the detectives would look forward to visiting one of the many affordable restaurants in the area for lunch or dinner. Since the killings, however, they hadn't had time for simple pleasures of this sort. They were either out chasing down leads or sequestered in the squad room poring over investigative reports. Their efforts in this regard did not go unrecognized in the wider community. Restaurants would routinely send platters of food free of charge to the squad room, and ordinary citizens would sometimes deliver batches of homemade cookies.

There was a coffee shop in a nearby shopping plaza where

several of the detectives had enjoyed hanging out prior to the triple homicide. One evening a waitress from the shop came by the station with coffee and pastries for the entire squad room. Making the gesture all the sweeter, she'd written a message for them on a napkin, which all of the other waitresses had signed.

> Brent, Wet, Bernie,
> Oh, yeah, and Allen
> You guys don't have time to come to us.
> So we decided we'd come to you!
> We love you

It gave the detectives a good feeling, knowing that so many people in the local community were out there rooting for them.

30

During the last weekend in May, a caseworker at the local juvenile detention center contacted the Manheim Township PD with some intriguing information. A kid in custody at the center, a sixteen-year-old nicknamed Teeter, claimed to have personal knowledge of the Haines killings. Not only that, but the kid seemed open to the idea of talking with the police about it.

Allen Leed and Brent Shultz drove to the center and met with Teeter in a small conference room. He was small and blond, with a history of petty criminal offenses. He seemed not only open to talking with the detectives but downright eager to do so.

Here's what he told them.

Shortly past midnight on Saturday, May 12th, he received a phone call from an African-American kid, Amani, with whom he'd dealt drugs in the past. Amani said that he'd just invaded a house in Manheim Township and "taken care of the people" who lived there. Now he wanted to know where rich white people normally kept their money. Teeter asked him what he'd meant—"taken care of the people"—but Amani ignored the question and abruptly ended the conversation.

The next afternoon, Teeter went on, he met with Amani outside a pharmacy in downtown Lancaster. Amani showed him a bloodstained knife that was wrapped in a washcloth.

He said that he'd driven to Manheim Township the night before hopeful of robbing a house as part of his initiation into a street gang. He found a house that was unlocked and went upstairs and into a bedroom where a couple were sleeping. But then the couple woke up and everything went awry. He panicked and wound up stabbing both of them, killing the man instantly with a thrust to the chest. Next he went into a bedroom down the hallway where a boy was sleeping. He pulled open a dresser drawer and was rifling through it when the boy woke up. He fought with him and finally succeeded in stabbing him to death, too. He left the house shortly afterward upon getting frightened when a door slammed shut.

Teeter told the detectives that Amani had asked for his help disposing of the knife but that he'd begged off, claiming family commitments later that afternoon. He said that he'd neither seen nor heard from him since.

Leed and Shultz could scarcely believe their ears. The story seemed perfectly in accord with the actual crime scene. Tom had indeed been fatally stabbed in the chest. A dresser drawer had indeed been left open in Kevin's bedroom. These were details that the police had purposely kept from the media, that only the killer or somebody he'd confided in might reasonably be expected to know. And what about the sound of the door slamming shut, which purportedly spooked Amani into leaving the house? Might this not have been Maggie fleeing for help?

The story had an irresistible ring of truth to it. The detectives—Leed especially—could hardly contain their excitement.

They'd gotten their hopes up before, of course, only to see them deflated. There was the home invasion in Warwick Township, for example, and also the two guys pulled over for speeding in North Carolina. Both of these incidents, so promising at first, had ultimately proven illusory, the criminal investigator's equivalent of fool's gold. But perhaps this was different. Perhaps now they were actually on the verge of solving the crime.

And why not? Why shouldn't the crime have gone down

exactly as Teeter was telling them that it did? Thus far they'd gotten nowhere operating under the assumption that the killer was someone with a personal connection to the Haines family. Perhaps it really was just some punk hitting a house at random for the sake of robbing it and thereby winning a measure of street credibility.

The detectives—Leed and Shultz and the others—met with the folks at the DA's office and formulated a game plan, which they wasted no time implementing. First they received assurances from Teeter that he was fully committed to cooperating with the investigation. Then they obtained a court order that authorized his release from the detention center into the custody of his grandfather. Finally they arranged for the Drug Task Force to outfit him with a wire so that they could eavesdrop on his conversations with Amani.

It was then that the fun began.

For almost two weeks Allen Leed and a couple of operatives from the Drug Task Force played a kind of hi-tech tag, following Teeter to various locations in Lancaster where he'd scheduled meetings with Amani. They followed him to the market and to the train station. They followed him to the barbershop and to the park and to various restaurants. They followed him everywhere.

At every location Teeter tried coaxing an incriminating statement out of Amani. He asked him about the layout of the house on Peach Lane. He asked him about the mother and the father and the boy. He asked him about the murder weapon. Not once did Amani say anything even remotely incriminating, at least insofar as the Haines killings were concerned. He'd talk freely about drugs and guns and girls, but the triple homicide? It was as if he'd never heard of it.

Leed and the Drug Task Force guys were perplexed. Had Amani somehow been tipped off? Was he smarter perhaps than they'd assumed him to be? And yet they kept at it, working out of a van without air conditioning in the midst of a heat wave. Several times their electronic surveillance equipment malfunctioned. Once they got a flat tire. Never did they hear anything actually worth hearing.

It became a bone of contention in the squad room after a few days, this whole Teeter business. Some of Leed's colleagues insisted that his story had been too good to be true from the very start. That he'd fabricated it and merely gotten lucky with some of the details regarding the crime scene. That he'd probably seen it as his ticket out of juvenile detention.

Leed conceded the possibility but was opposed to pulling the plug on the operation. They'd taken it this far, he reasoned. They might as well follow it through until they knew for certain whether or not it was a dead-end.

So back into the surveillance van he went for another painstaking week, listening in on conversations that never went where they were supposed to go.

Investigators from the state police, in the meantime, were working on a rather different front. They'd heard that for quite some time now a local man—a middle-aged musician—had been on unusually friendly terms with one of Kevin's schoolmates, Warren Tobin. He'd taken Warren under his wing several years before as a sort of mentor. They'd also heard that he'd subsequently become close with Kevin, bringing him to the shooting range and the bowling alley and sometimes even out camping.

Under ordinary circumstances, this might not have aroused much concern. These, of course, were anything but ordinary circumstances.

The investigators spoke first of all with the musician in question, who struck them as cordial yet guarded. He said that he'd been involved with various outreach programs for teenagers over the years, which was how he'd initially gotten to know Warren, and that through Warren he'd also gotten to know Kevin. He said that Kevin was painfully shy when they first met and so he decided to take him on as a project.

The investigators asked him if he were in the habit of doing this sort of thing.

He said that he enjoyed helping teenage boys overcome obstacles and realize their full potential, which was precisely what he'd had in mind for Kevin. He'd take him on excursions and talk with him over the phone once or twice a week, all for the purpose of drawing him out of his shell. He said that Kevin's parents appreciated his efforts in this regard and had come to view him as a friend of the family.

He said that he was visiting his own parents in a neighboring town during the weekend of the triple homicide and found out about it through the news.

They asked him if he had any idea why the crime might have occurred.

None whatsoever, he said. The Haineses were among the sweetest people whom he'd ever met. He said that rumors circulating on the Internet—that the killings were somehow connected to Lisa having an affair, or Tom a clandestine gay lover—were totally absurd. To know Tom and Lisa was to know how devoted they were to one another.

The investigators thought there was something odd about all of this. Why should Tom and Lisa entrust their teenage son to an adult male with whom they had no prior history? Did they not realize the potential for mischief in such an arrangement? Were they really so naïve?

The investigators asked the musician if he'd submit to a polygraph and willingly provide a DNA swab and finger as well as palm prints.

He said that he would, but not without expressing dismay at being treated as a suspect. His friendship with Kevin had been thoroughly innocent, he insisted. He'd wanted nothing more than to help the teenager emerge from his cocoon and spread his wings.

The investigators next spoke with the musician's parents, who vouched for his whereabouts on the weekend of the triple homicide. Finally they spoke with Warren and several other boys in his circle with whom the guy was also on friendly terms. The boys were unanimous in their praise, describing him as smart, honest, and completely selfless. One boy said that in his entire life he'd never met a more impressive person.

The musician had gotten along well with all of Kevin and Warren's friends, another boy said.

With one possible exception.

He'd apparently not been fond of Alec Kreider.

31

The investigators decided that they should speak with Alec Kreider yet again. As Kevin's best friend, perhaps he'd thought of something critical to the case since last being interviewed. If nothing else, perhaps he'd be able to shed light on this odd business involving the middle-aged musician.

Trooper Linda Gerow of the state police drew the assignment this time, dropping by Tim Kreider's house early in the evening on Thursday, May 31st.

They sat in the living room, Trooper Gerow, Alec, and his dad. There was nothing especially dramatic about the occasion—just one more follow-up interview among dozens that the police were conducting.

Was it really true, Gerow asked Alec, that he, Kevin, and Warren Tobin had been the very best of friends?

Yes, Alec answered. Since the fifth grade, when they first met. The three of them would hang out together at one another's houses playing strategy games and pool. Sometimes they'd go bowling or simply sit on a bench at the park and talk.

Gerow eventually worked the conversation around to the subject of the middle-aged musician, asking Alec how well he knew the guy.

Only superficially, Alec said. The musician was principally Warren and Kevin's friend. He'd met him only a couple of times, and the two of them hadn't exactly hit it off. He'd received the distinct impression that the guy didn't much like him.

And why might that have been? Gerow asked.

Tough to say, Alec said, though it might have had something to do with his passion for German history and culture. The musician apparently loathed Nazism and might have suspected him, Alec, of having leanings in that direction.

Trooper Gerow saw no reason to delve more deeply into this. Gerry Sauers and Adam Kosheba had covered the topic of Nazism during their interview of Alec ten days previously.

In any event, Alec went on, Warren and Kevin would never invite him over to their respective houses if they knew that the musician was going to be there. Nor would they talk much about the guy with him.

Gerow asked if this had bothered him at all, being excluded from so many social occasions involving his two best friends.

Not in the least, Alec said, mainly because he himself didn't much care for the musician. Insofar as he was concerned, the guy had a discomfiting air of arrogance about him.

Now that the Haines killings were three weeks old, Gerow asked, did he have any theories about what might have happened?

No, he didn't, Alec said. For his own sake, he tried not even thinking about the killings.

PART TWO

THE KILLER

32

Alec Kreider had gotten a new job for the summer. It was at the McDonald's on the Lititz Pike near Millport Road, just up the street from his high school. The previous summer he'd worked at a car wash on the Manheim Pike. The Mc-Donald's was closer to home, and the hours more flexible.

On Monday, June 4th, he donned his uniform for the first time and went in for the five-to-nine evening shift. He spent a couple of hours in basic orientation, watching McDonald's employee videos and the like, and then joined a more experienced worker at the grill.

He could hardly wait for the shift to end so that he could call Caroline, the sweet girl from the mall. Their phone conversations in the late evening had become a regular occurrence of late, the one thing that he truly looked forward to. Nothing else much mattered to him nowadays. Talking with Caroline had become the governing factor in his life, his primary reason for existing.

It wasn't that he'd lost interest in other girls. He found some of the smarter and cuter ones in his grade immensely appealing, and he certainly wasn't averse to casting gestures of affection their way. He'd brought those flowers to English class on the last day of the semester, for example, and the very same day he'd given a girl in another class a silver ring with a turquoise stone.

Nor had he grown indifferent to his studies. He'd aced his final exams and was looking forward to finishing high school and going on to a top-flight college. He had a track record of academic excellence, which he had every intention of keeping intact.

There was no denying it, however. School, family, the cute girls whom he'd met in class: Everything paled in significance to his love for Caroline. He'd become obsessed with her, and his every waking moment was a torment because he wasn't yet certain how she felt toward him.

He worried that he'd pushed her too hard in recent days and shown more of himself than might have been prudent. He worried that perhaps he'd scared her off.

The phone call this past Saturday evening was the worst. Why in the world had he thought that he could win her over with a display so utterly gloomy? He'd started off by complimenting her on her ear for music but then gone on to lament his own lack of musical or artistic talent. He'd said that there was only one work of art that he could ever see himself accomplishing. This would involve his signing a blank canvas and then blowing his brains onto it with a gun. The work could be entitled *Suicide*. It would be his true masterpiece.

The conversation went downhill from there. He said that he'd contemplated suicide several times of late, with only his love for her preventing him from going through with it. He asked her if she loved him and she said yes, probably by this point because she was too terrified to say anything else. He then chastised her for seeming overly calm on her end of the phone. He was pouring his heart out to her, after all. Shouldn't she be more emotional?

She asked him if he'd discussed his state of mind with either of his parents, and he answered that discussing anything of the sort with them would be a total waste of time. Neither of them truly understood him. Neither of them realized how unhappy he was, or that he actually had two personalities. He told her that his dad in particular was clueless, clinging to the belief that everything was fine and that the divorce hadn't adversely affected his kids.

Caroline tried cheering him up, talking about the flowers that were in fresh bloom at the park and the garden that she was planning on starting in her aunt's front yard. Her efforts eventually paid off and the conversation ended on a much lighter note.

Afterward, Alec worried that he might have botched his chances with her by coming on too strong, and so first thing on Sunday morning he sent her a reassuring text message.

The birds are singing again.
I feel peaceful now.
Good luck with gardening.
I think it's going to rain.
To my dearest friend,
XOXO
Talk to you later.

He called her again on Sunday evening, and the tone of the conversation was mostly upbeat. He told her that he was scheduled to start his summer job at McDonald's the next day. He also told her that he'd not mentioned to anyone else that he'd been contemplating suicide of late. In any event, he added cryptically, he was rather an accomplished liar.

Now it was Monday evening and here he was, stuck at McDonald's and desperate to speak with her again. His shift finally ended and he wasted no time getting home to his mom's house, where he was staying for the week. He went upstairs to his room and rang her number.

They chatted amiably at first, mostly about his first day's work at McDonald's, but then he started banging his fist against the door to his room. She heard the banging and asked him what was going on.

"It's really weird," he said. "I usually do this when I'm all alone and now you can hear it over the phone."

"What is it?" she asked.

He explained what he was doing, which seemed to alarm her. She urged him to talk with his parents about whatever it was that was bothering him.

"No need to," he said. "They'll find out eventually."

Thinking this might mean that he was planning on killing himself, she asked if she could speak with his mom. He told her no, saying that he thought it a bad idea. She asked him to promise that he wouldn't hurt himself, and he said that he couldn't make any such promise.

She tried cheering him up but the conversation ended on a sour note, with Alec still dropping hints that he intended to harm himself. He sent her a text message early on Tuesday morning, saying he desperately wanted to talk with her after he got home from his job at McDonald's later that evening. Then at two in the afternoon on Tuesday, he sent her another text message.

So sorry you got caught in this.
I'll make it up to you someday.
Talk to you later.

Alec went to work at five o'clock on Tuesday, and this time the manager put him on the grill for the entire shift. He performed well, doing everything precisely as he'd been trained to do it the previous evening.

The manager was impressed. This kid learned fast. He promised to be a good pick-up for the summer.

33

Alec called Caroline at ten on Tuesday evening, not long after arriving home from his second shift at McDonald's. He told her that he found the new job immensely boring and wished that he didn't have to work at all. He also said that he had a special request of her.

She asked him what it was.

"I need you to carry my life and make my decisions," he said.

She said that she wasn't quite certain what this meant, whereupon his tone of voice immediately grew more desperate. He said that he seriously doubted that he'd make it through the week, and that he had a loaded gun in his hand right then, which a friend of his mom had lent him several weeks before.

Caroline heard her aunt come into the house. She slipped downstairs with her cell phone and whispered that she was talking with a boy whom she'd met at the mall. She said that the boy had a loaded gun and was hinting that he might kill himself. She wrote his name and address on a scrap of paper. The aunt told her to keep him on the phone, adding that in the meantime she'd drive over to his house and alert his mother to what was going on.

The aunt left at once, and Caroline turned her full attention back to Alec. She pleaded with him to put the gun away but he said that he didn't want to. She heard a loud click and asked him what it was. He said that he'd just racked the slide. What else did she think it might be? He went on to say that he respected guns far more than he did people, and that he also spent quite a bit more money on guns.

He then said that he'd just had an idea. Perhaps he'd kill three other people and then himself afterward. She knew from their previous conversations that his mother and sister and brother were in the house with him. Was he now thinking of killing them, too? She asked him if this was what he'd meant.

He ignored the question and continued playing with the gun, loading and unloading it. She wasn't sure if he was deadly serious or if this was some sort of macabre game. She warned him that she'd hang up if he didn't unload it and keep it unloaded.

"So hang up then," he said.

But she didn't, choosing instead to keep him on the phone in the hopes of calming him with small talk about summer jobs and the like. The strategy proved partly effective, as he did indeed calm down for a short while and seemed actually to make an effort at civility.

The aunt eventually returned home and communicated with Caroline through gestures and whispers. She said that she'd spoken with Angela Kreider, Alec's mom, who'd had no idea that any of this was going on under her roof. Angela had thanked her and then immediately called 911.

Caroline kept Alec on the phone, still trying to distract him with small talk. She chatted about gardening and music and movies until Alec interrupted, saying that he had a proposition for her. She'd teach him all about gardening and in return he'd teach her all about guns. She said that she wasn't much interested in guns but he rambled on about them anyway, discussing the relative merits of various models. Finally he let out a loud gasp.

"Oh, my God," he said. "I just looked down the barrel of a loaded gun."

She pleaded with him once again to unload it, which he

agreed to do. But a minute or so later, she heard the sound of a click.

"What was that?" she said, almost too afraid to ask.

He told her that he'd just put the unloaded gun to his temple and pulled the trigger. He then said that he yearned for the destruction of the entire world so that he'd no longer have to live in it. He said that he couldn't take any more pressure and knew that the end was near. He said that he'd once heard a song by Elton John, whose title he wasn't sure of, that he wanted played at his funeral.

The police had made telephone contact with the aunt by this point. They wanted to know if Caroline could somehow persuade Alec to leave his room and go downstairs. The aunt relayed the message to Caroline, who tried talking him into going down to the kitchen for a snack. He refused, saying that he didn't understand why his having a snack was so important to her. In any event, he said, he was starting to feel queasiness in his stomach.

He said that he wouldn't kill himself if she remained on the phone. Otherwise who knew what might happen. He then talked some more about his emotional state, saying that he felt neither happiness nor sadness inside but rather total emptiness.

"Here were those parents I knew who died in a horrible way, and I feel nothing," he said.

He said that he'd once confided his suicidal fantasies to a couple of kids from school, neither of whom seemed overly impressed. Then he spoke at some length about a girl from his neighborhood, Monica, whom Caroline had never heard him mention before. He called her a bitch and a whore and said that he despised her for always seeming happy.

"I almost killed Monica and her family," he said.

Then he dropped yet another bombshell, telling Caroline that just the day before he'd thought seriously about killing her also.

Caroline was flabbergasted. She clutched the cell phone to her ear, wondering how he could possibly top this.

"You know what I mean?" he asked.

"Yes," she said.

Alec said that he couldn't stand the thought of living in this world any longer because the only thing that he was truly passionate about was killing people. He said that he'd once tried strangling his younger brother and was still upset that he hadn't succeeded in doing so. He promised that one day, when the time was right, he'd tell her about some other things that he'd done.

She asked him about his mother's work, once again in hopes of lightening the mood, but this only seemed to annoy him. She wondered if the police were close to arriving at his house.

Much as he had during the phone conversation on Saturday evening, he reproached her for seeming so calm. How could she maintain her composure when he was laying bare his very soul to her?

"You seem fake to me," he said.

It was past midnight now and Alec found himself stifling yawns. He told Caroline that he'd better get ready for bed. He said that he had things to do in the morning and was afraid of sleeping in.

So what was she to make of this? One minute he's hanging over the precipice, and practically the very next planning on tucking in for the night so that he can get an early start in the morning. What about his desperate state of mind, and the torrent of confessions that he'd unleashed over the course of the evening? Was all of this merely a sham? A bizarre cry for attention?

He left his bedroom and walked down the hallway, telling Caroline along the way that he was going into the bathroom to brush his teeth. Then he told her that he'd just glanced downstairs and noticed that the front door to the house was slightly ajar. He said that he'd better go and shut it.

A few seconds later Caroline heard a man's voice, and then Alec's phone went dead. She assumed that it was the police, arriving on the scene and taking matters under control.

She was grateful that the ordeal was finally over.

34

The call came over the radio at roughly eleven-thirty on Tuesday evening. A sixteen-year-old kid in the Cobblestone Court neighborhood of Manheim Township was barricaded in his room with a loaded pistol.

Patrol Officers Jason Myers, John Barto, and Mike Naff arrived on the scene scant minutes later. Angela Kreider was standing outside her house with her nineteen-year-old daughter when they arrived. She told them that her son Alec had apparently threatened suicide while talking with a girl on his cell phone. She told them that she found out about this from the girl's aunt, and that insofar as she knew Alec was still on the phone with the girl.

The officers asked her if it was true that Alec was locked in his room with a loaded pistol. She said that this was indeed the case, and that just before leaving the house with her daughter she'd heard what sounded like Alec racking a round into the chamber. They asked her if anyone else was inside the house right then. She said that Alec's thirteen-year-old brother was asleep in an upstairs bedroom across the hallway but that otherwise the house was empty.

She said that Alec had been upset of late over the loss of his close friend Kevin Haines, who had been brutally murdered several weeks before. She'd had no idea, however, that he was in the throes of an emotional crisis. He'd seemed fine when she'd picked him up from work earlier that evening. Certainly he hadn't given any indication that he was feeling particularly depressed or considering suicide.

The officers asked her about the gun, and she said that a friend had lent it to them a couple of weeks previously, mainly because Alec had expressed interest in purchasing a similar model and wanted to get a feel for it. She added that she herself had also wanted a gun in the house for security reasons.

Dave Bair had arrived on the scene by this point, and so, too, had Lieutenant Wayne Wagner, the consummately cool-headed commander of the Manheim Township PD's patrol division. The three responding officers assured Bair and Lieutenant Wagner that this was no false alarm. There was indeed an emotionally disturbed kid with a loaded gun in the house, and his thirteen-year-old brother was asleep in the room across from him. The lieutenant said that the department's crisis negotiator had already been notified of the situation and was on his way.

The crisis negotiator was Allen Leed.

Leed arrived shortly afterward and immediately established cell phone contact with Caroline's aunt, which gave him at least some line of communication—however indirect—with Alec Kreider. He told the aunt that he wanted Caroline to try coaxing Alec downstairs, perhaps by suggesting that he get something to eat in the kitchen. This would get him off the second floor, thereby putting his younger brother out of harm's way. It would also provide a good opportunity to take him safely into custody.

Several additional officers were on the scene by then, including Steve Newman and Ray Bradley. Dave Bair told them to don tactical gear. Then he cracked open the front door to the house and told them to position themselves on either side of it. Finally, after a longer wait than they'd anticipated, Alec came down the stairs with his cell phone still clamped to his ear.

He appeared to be unarmed but the officers in staging position couldn't tell for certain that this was the case. They stormed through the front door and ordered him to freeze and raise his arms above his head. He continued down the stairs much as before and so they rushed forward and tackled him. Then they handcuffed him, helped him to his feet, and escorted him outside.

Allen Leed saw the skinny teenager in shorts and a T-shirt coming through the front door, with a patrol officer on either side. Leed knew quite a bit about the kid without ever having actually met him. He knew that he was a star student at the local high school, with a passion for German history and culture. He knew that he'd been one of Kevin Haines's very best friends. He knew that investigators had interviewed him on three separate occasions in the weeks since the triple homicide.

Leed went over, intercepted the kid, and led him to the street corner, where his mother and older sister were standing. He wrapped an arm around his waist and asked him if he was all right.

"You threw a real scare into us," he said.

Alec nodded and lowered his gaze.

"Can you tell me what's wrong?" Leed asked.

Alec shrugged.

"Because I promise I'll listen," Leed said.

Alec raised his eyes and stared across the street.

"This world's a horrible place," he said.

"I agree with that assessment," Leed said. "Most cops probably would."

"There are some terrible people in the world," Alec said.

"I agree with that, too," Leed said. "No question about it."

"It's a terrible place," Alec repeated.

He grimaced, twisted his torso, and for the briefest second broke free of Leed's grasp. Dave Bair and Ray Bradley, both of whom were stationed nearby, stepped closer just in case he were thinking of trying to flee.

"All of these negative thoughts surfaced just recently," Angela Kreider said to Leed. "After the murder of his best friend, Kevin, and Kevin's parents."

Leed had expected as much. Any sixteen-year-old might feel emotional distress in the wake of so terrible an event.

Angela stroked her son's hair and whispered something to him, whereupon Alec grew visibly agitated.

"I'm not a bad person," he said to her.

"No," Angela said. "You're not a bad person."

"You don't know what I've done," Alec said.

Angela spoke softly to him, offering a mother's words of support, which only seemed to increase his agitation.

Leed pulled him aside at this point and tried calming him down, telling him that things might look better tomorrow, that time had a way of easing pain. Then he handed him over to Officer Steve Newman, who was charged with transporting him to Lancaster General Hospital.

You don't know what I've done. Dave Bair and Ray Bradley had heard this remark and wondered what it meant. They assumed that Allen Leed had heard it also, but he hadn't. Leed was so intent on comforting the kid and getting the situation under control that the remark had passed him by.

In the meantime, Officers Myers and Naff had gone upstairs to Alec's bedroom, where they found a Beretta nine millimeter pistol sitting in a blue plastic case. They also found a clear plastic bag containing twenty-eight rounds of nine millimeter hollow-point ammunition, three pistol magazines, and a gun cleaning kit. The magazines were empty and the pistol unloaded. It was not immediately obvious that the kid had been serious about killing himself. Myers and Naff seized all of these items for the purpose of entering them into safekeeping at the police station.

The drive to the hospital was mostly uneventful. Alec sat in the back of Officer Newman's police cruiser, with Angela following in her own vehicle.

It may have been because Newman himself was so young, but Alec seemed surprisingly relaxed, and more than a little chatty.

He asked Newman if the township police were involved in very many operations of this sort.

"Not very many," Newman said. "But it does happen."

He complimented the police on the stealth with which they'd carried out the operation, saying he didn't even realize that they were outside his house.

"You guys were amazingly quiet," he said.

"That's part of the idea," Newman said.

Next he asked about basic strategic options. Might the police have gone into the house at some point? Or would they have waited indefinitely for him to come down the stairs?

Newman told him that this depended entirely on how the situation would have played out.

Alec considered this for a moment, and then asked something of more immediate concern.

"What now?" he said. "Do you know what's going to happen?"

Newman explained that he was transporting him to Lancaster General Hospital, after which the medical professionals would take charge of the situation.

They stopped for a red light, and all of a sudden Alec seemed curious about Newman.

"How long have you been a cop?" he asked.

"For just about a year," Newman said.

"Do you like your job?"

"Yes," Newman said. "It's something different every day."

"Are you from Lancaster County?"

"I've lived in the area all my life," Newman said.

"Did you go to college?"

Newman said that indeed he had and told Alec where.

As they drew closer to the hospital, Alec became more reflective. He asked about his father. Had anybody bothered to contact him? Would he be there waiting when they arrived?

"I'm not sure," Newman said. "We'll have to see."

There was something that Newman was curious about also. He'd been one of the cops in staging position outside the front door to Alec's mom's house. He'd seen Alec walk down the stairs with his cell phone in hand and had wondered who was on the other end of the line.

"When you came down the stairs?" he asked. "Who was it you were talking to on your phone?"

Alec was quick to dismiss the question.

"Don't worry about it," he said.

35

Pennsylvania law allows for the involuntary commitment of individuals who have attempted suicide or threatened to do so. Alec Kreider was committed to the psychiatric ward at Lancaster General Hospital in the wee hours of Wednesday, June 6th. His mother, Angela, filled out the necessary paperwork.

Later the same day he was moved to Philhaven, a private facility located in the bucolic village of Mount Gretna in Lebanon County, Pennsylvania. Opened in 1952 as an explicitly Christian mental health center within the Mennonite tradition, Philhaven boasted an excellent reputation locally and nationwide. Its medical staff was first-rate, and its treatment programs absolutely state of the art. Anyone compelled to spend time in a psychiatric facility could do far worse than spending it at Philhaven.

Alec Kreider hated it.

He hated the regimented living and the intensive, personalized attention that was accorded high-risk patients. He hated the doctors and the nurses and the support staff. He hated the treatment programs, all of which he deemed a complete waste of time. He especially hated group therapy, which required that he sit among people whom he regarded as clearly inferior to himself.

Alec spent much of his time trying to plot his way out.

How could he convince such and such a doctor that there was really nothing wrong with him? Or win over another who seemed somehow resistant to his charms? Or put on a convincing show during group therapy? What steps might he take to make this intolerable confinement as short as possible?

When he had time alone in his room, he mostly spent it writing. Some of this was in the form of journal or diary entries, a sort of daily chronicle of the torments he was forced to endure in this most wretched of places. But there was much else besides. He wrote letters to several of his closest friends from school. He wrote a lengthy missive to Caroline, with whom he was still deeply obsessed, and then another one to her aunt. The prose throughout was precise and polished, easily the equivalent of an advanced undergraduate's.

The actual content of most of this material, however, was something else altogether. Alternately self-pitying and preachy, it was a narcissist's delight. In one paragraph he'd lament his current plight, describing Alec the beleaguered victim, lonely, bereft, misunderstood, stuck in circumstances not of his own choosing. Then in the very next he'd dole out nuggets of wisdom as if he were a New Age guru. *Loyalty is the noblest of virtues ... Video games are the devil's playground ... God's love must never be taken for granted.*

Perhaps the most ominous piece that he produced during this period was a "Last Will and Testament." In the event of his death, he wrote, his family and also his best friends from school could take whatever of his belongings they so desired. Anything left over after this, he added, "should certainly not be auctioned off but rather given away." He also provided precise instructions for the disposition of his mortal remains. "I want my body to be cremated," he wrote, "and along with my body I want a single stem with two lily flowers, no more and no less, at the height of their growth." If he were ever to fall into a vegetative state, he concluded, he wanted his family "to pull the plug" so that he might get as fast a start as possible on his next life.

Some forty-odd miles away, the Manheim Township detectives were still chasing down leads and exploring new angles. They'd given up on the kid from the detention center, whose story they now realized was a total fabrication, but several other possibilities had arisen in the meantime.

The most promising of these involved a woman who'd contacted the police convinced that her boyfriend was the murderer. Several nights earlier, she said, he'd gotten drunk and gone on at length about the crime scene, describing in exquisite detail the positioning of the bodies and so forth. She'd wondered at first how he knew so much about it but eventually everything started to add up. She remembered reading in the newspaper shortly after the killings that a bloodhound had tracked a scent to the Freeze and Frizz on Lititz Pike. Hadn't her boyfriend lived right around the corner from the Freeze and Frizz at the time, and also been a frequent customer at the place? And hadn't he once dated a woman who lived on Peach Lane, just a stone's throw from the Haines home? And hadn't he sometimes in the past shown a propensity toward violence?

John Wettlaufer and Brent Shultz tracked the boyfriend down and read him his Miranda warnings. He vehemently denied having had anything to do with the killings and expressed astonishment that anyone should think otherwise. He said that he'd spent the night in question at his mother's house and knew no more about the crime scene than what he'd pieced together from news accounts and casual conversations with drinking buddies. He also said that he'd happily submit to a polygraph examination if it meant clearing his name.

Wettlaufer and Shultz carefully appraised the guy, his tone of voice, his body language, even the make and size of his shoes, and felt confident that he was telling them the truth. They planned on doing some follow-up investigation on the matter but for the moment it seemed nothing more than yet another in a long line of dead ends.

And then there was the Lancaster postal worker who'd taken to writing letters of condolence to Lisa's mother. The mother found the letters troubling, not least of all because she'd never once met the guy writing them. She discussed the situation with Allen Leed, who thought it worth looking into. Perpetrators of grisly crimes were sometimes known, after all, to derive perverse pleasure from contacting friends and relatives of their victims.

The guy seemed genuinely mortified when Leed showed up at his apartment and asked him about the letters. He said that he'd meant them as a gesture of sympathy and support and certainly hadn't intended to make a nuisance of himself. He said that writing letters of this sort was something of a hobby for him.

Leed believed that the guy was probably guilty of nothing other than loneliness and a certain eccentricity. He gently suggested that he consider finding some other way of filling his spare hours.

At just about the same time, as if things weren't tough enough already, the entire investigation was dealt a potentially crippling blow. Assistant DA Craig Stedman had known for several weeks that *People* magazine was preparing a story on the triple homicide, and that the magazine had enlisted the help of a local reporter in digging up information. Now, on the eve of its publication, Stedman found out that the story made explicit mention of the bloody shoeprints that were found at the crime scene.

Stedman was horrified. This was a detail that the DA's office and the police had zealously guarded from the media. There was a decent chance that the perpetrator still had the shoes that he'd worn during the commission of the crime, not realizing that he'd left behind those damning prints. He'd almost certainly dispose of them, however, if he were to find out about the prints through *People*. The very best evidence from the crime scene was on the verge of being compromised.

And how had this happened? How had *People* gotten hold of information so sensitive? Stedman thought that the local reporter assisting the magazine with the story might have had something to do with it. The guy was well known in Lancaster County for his tenacity and resourcefulness. But from whom would he have gotten the information? Was there a leak somewhere in the law enforcement pipeline? The entire business was terribly vexing.

Stedman contacted *People* and pleaded with them to kill the story, or at least edit out the telling detail concerning the bloody shoeprints. He explained that the ultimate outcome of the investigation might very well hinge on this being kept confidential. His efforts, however, came to naught. The story appeared in the June 11th, 2007, issue of the magazine, with the bloody shoeprints given prominent play.

Craig Stedman was of sturdy stock. Very rarely would he succumb to doubt or despondency. But this latest development was tough to take. He'd been thoroughly engrossed in the criminal investigation, attending daily briefings, reviewing evidence with Bob Beck and Allen Leed. He could hardly have been more committed to solving the case if the victims had been his own flesh and blood.

But, again, this was tough to take. They still didn't have a suspect almost a full month into the investigation and now their most valuable piece of evidence might very well have been rendered worthless.

So where to go from here? Craig Stedman wasn't entirely sure.

36

Alec Kreider desperately yearned for two things. The first was contact with Caroline. She hadn't written. She hadn't phoned. Was it possible that she'd forgotten about him already? Or that she simply didn't care?

The second was his freedom. It was Tuesday evening, June 12th, and he'd been at Philhaven for a full week now. The restrictions of the place were wearing him down, eating away at his spirit. And earlier that day he'd learned that he was probably stuck there for another week more.

He'd anticipated getting out on Thursday, which was the original idea. His dad had planned a cookout for family and friends in celebration of his returning home. But the folks at Philhaven had told him that very morning that he wouldn't be released until they'd had a chance to arrange appropriate outpatient therapy. Which meant another week of torment. Which meant missing out on the cookout, to which he'd planned on inviting Caroline.

His more immediate concern, however, was the session of family therapy that was on tap for that evening. His mom and dad would be there. Perhaps they'd be able to expedite his release. Perhaps they'd even have some word from Caroline. They knew how important she was to him.

An attendant escorted him along a corridor and into the room where the session was scheduled to take place.

His parents were already there, waiting with his therapist. He gave each of them a hug of greeting and then everybody sat down.

They made small talk for a couple of minutes, and then his parents mentioned that they'd spoken with Caroline's aunt. They realized that this was a delicate subject but thought that he should know the truth prior to his coming home from Philhaven.

The aunt had told them, they said, that Caroline was too young for a serious relationship and that she and Alec could be friends but nothing more than that. She'd also told them that this was what Caroline herself wanted.

Alec's demeanor changed. His eyes darted and he squirmed in his chair. He let out a strange laugh. Then he looked at his parents and told them to leave, indicating that he wanted to speak with his therapist alone.

"You'd better get out of here," he said.

Tim and Angela left the room and waited in the corridor, wondering what in the world was going on. After a few minutes the therapist opened the door and beckoned them back in.

They returned to the room and sat down again, looking first at Alec and then at the therapist, who had a stricken look on her face.

"Alec has something to tell you," she said.

"What is it, Alec?" Tim asked.

And so he told them. He told them that he'd killed Kevin and his parents. Crept into their house in the wee hours several weeks earlier and killed them in their bedrooms.

A terrible silence fell over the room. Tim and Angela could scarcely believe their ears. They wondered if he were merely making this up, perhaps as a result of his distressed emotional condition. The therapist also wondered if this was so.

"Are you imagining that you did this, Alec?" she asked. "Rather than actually having done it?"

Alec shook his head no.

Angela asked him if he was so upset over the death of his

best friend that he somehow felt compelled to take responsibility for it.

Again he shook his head no.

Then he gave precise details of the crime, just to prove that he was indeed telling the truth.

He said that he made his preparations immediately after his mom left for work. He got dressed in dark clothing, including a dark trench coat. He put on a dark baseball cap, but not without first disguising the logo by covering it with duct tape. He put on thin black driving gloves. He retrieved a flashlight from his dresser, and also an old hunting knife that his dad had given him years before. He wore the same Hush Puppy shoes that he almost always wore, and which he had with him right then in his room at Philhaven.

He said that he took a wooded area to the Haines house, which he entered through an unlocked door. He went upstairs, thinking that he'd kill Kevin by smothering him, but instead went into the parents' bedroom first and knifed them to death. Then he went into Kevin's room and killed him.

He described his state of mind while committing the murders, saying he felt rage and detachment simultaneously. He knew what he was doing, and yet it almost felt as if he were somebody else.

He said that killing Kevin was quite a struggle and that he finished him off in the hallway outside his bedroom. He also said that he didn't realize at the time that Maggie was already home from college. For some reason he hadn't expected her to return for another day or two.

He then said that he fled the house through the sliding door in the kitchen and took the same wooded area back to his mom's house. Somewhere along the way he lost his baseball cap and flashlight.

He said that he washed his clothes upon arriving home. Then he stayed awake until his mom got back from work, the rage that he'd felt during the killing spree now replaced by a fearful tension in the pit of his stomach.

Tim and Angela were too aghast to press him for additional details. Tim did, however, try asking him why. Why on earth had he wanted to kill his best friend? He tried asking but couldn't get a definitive answer in return.

Alec spoke vaguely about how Kevin had been annoying him of late. He'd chew his food too loudly in the school cafeteria, for example. He'd argue a point too strenuously during one of their political debates.

Was this it then? Was this actually why Alec Kreider had wanted to murder his best friend?

Because Kevin had been annoying him of late?

Tim and Angela drove home from Philhaven in a state of shock, still not fully believing what they'd just heard.

Later that same evening, Tim phoned Alec at the facility and asked him if it was really true. Had he really killed Kevin and his parents?

Yes, Alec answered.

He'd really done it.

37

Late afternoon on Wednesday, June 13th, James Grumbine of the Lebanon County Detective Bureau received an anonymous phone call from somebody who was affiliated in some capacity or another with Philhaven. The caller told Detective Grumbine that she'd heard some disturbing news through the facility's grapevine.

Just the previous evening, she said, a young male patient at Philhaven had apparently confessed to the Haines killings in a family therapy session. This same patient had then apparently told staff members that he'd had fantasies about killing again and had conducted research on the Internet about how to do so without getting caught.

The caller hung up on that note but then phoned Grumbine again scant minutes later. She'd just spoken with several staff members at the facility, she said, who told her that they'd noticed what looked like healing cuts on the patient's hands. One of these staff members, moreover, claimed that the patient had threatened to kill his own parents and siblings. The patient's name, the caller said, was Alec Kreider.

The name meant nothing to Grumbine but he was certainly familiar with the Haines triple homicide, which was big news everywhere in Pennsylvania. He immediately contacted the relevant authorities in Lancaster County and then drove over to the Manheim Township PD, where he met personally with Craig Stedman, Allen Leed, and several investigators from the Pennsylvania State Police.

Stedman and Leed and the others weren't entirely sure what to make of this information. They knew, of course, that Alec Kreider was one of Kevin's best friends and that he'd recently created quite a stir by threatening suicide. They knew that investigators had interviewed him on three separate occasions, without the kid showing so much as a twinge of nervousness. If he had indeed committed the murders, he certainly possessed remarkable sangfroid for a sixteen-year-old.

They also knew that the information was quite likely false in at least one respect. None of the people who'd interviewed Alec Kreider had noticed cuts on his hands or wrists, which was something that they'd have routinely looked for.

They decided that it would probably be best at this juncture if a couple of investigators went up to Philhaven to snoop around.

Brent Shultz and Corporal John Duby drew the assignment, arriving at the facility at nine o'clock in the evening. They introduced themselves to the receptionist and asked to speak with a supervisor. While waiting for him, they noticed that a sign-in sheet for visitors was sitting in plain view on a counter in the lobby. They glanced at it and saw that Alec Kreider had had three visitors earlier that day. Two of these were his parents, who'd signed in at four forty-five and then signed out at shortly past seven. It was the third visitor, however, that grabbed Shultz and Duby's attention.

Jack Kenneff.

The investigators exchanged knowing glances. Everybody in local law enforcement knew who Jack Kenneff was. At one time a top gun in the DA's office, he was now one of the most prominent criminal defense attorneys in the entire county. He'd signed in at four forty-five also and stayed until almost six-thirty. A visit of such length from Jack Kenneff was surely no mere happenstance. This was serious business.

A middle-aged man came into the lobby and introduced himself to Duby and Shultz as Philhaven's evening manager.

They showed him their badges and asked him if he knew why they were there.

"Yes," he said.

The investigators could see fear and concern in the guy's eyes. They could hear it in his voice.

He escorted them to a private room on the main floor of the facility and invited them to sit down.

"What can you tell us right now?" Duby asked him. "Without violating confidentiality or anything of the sort?"

The guy said that he was prevented by facility rules from discussing any particular patient.

"Just for purposes of clarification," Duby said. "Is the particular patient in question here Alec Kreider?"

"Yes," the guy said.

He phoned Philhaven's chief executive officer, who said that he'd be there within half an hour.

In the meantime, Shultz and Duby contacted Manheim Township PD. They spoke with Stedman and Leed and told them what they'd thus far found out. Jack Kenneff had spent close to two hours with Alec Kreider and his parents earlier that evening. Detective Grumbine's anonymous tipster had apparently been on to something.

Philhaven's CEO arrived at nine-forty and told Shultz and Duby that he wasn't at liberty to discuss the matter with them. Instead he arranged a conference call with the facility's chief legal counsel.

The legal counsel told the investigators that there wasn't much that he could tell them right then, mainly due to privacy protections enshrined in the Mental Health Procedure Act. He did say, however, that he was amenable to speaking with someone from the District Attorney's office about the matter first thing in the morning.

When Shultz and Duby returned to the police station, the place was buzzing with excitement. All of the Manheim Township detectives were on hand and so, too, were most of the state police investigators. At long last they seemed on the verge of nailing the killer.

Here's where matters stood at this juncture:

Sixteen-year-old Alec Kreider had apparently told his parents in a family therapy session the previous day that he'd killed Kevin, Tom, and Lisa.

Kreider's parents still hadn't gone to the police with this information. Perhaps they were planning on doing so eventually, but they certainly hadn't yet. Rather, they'd kept quiet about it and retained the services of a prominent local attorney.

Kreider lived with both parents, alternating weeks at their respective houses. Critical evidence related to the killings was quite possibly hidden away somewhere in these houses. The police had no reason in particular to suspect that Tim or Angela Kreider might try disposing of such evidence. Nevertheless, any parent in a similar situation might be tempted to do so.

Captain John Laufer, commanding officer of the state police's Troop J barracks, knew precisely what was needed in order to prevent anything of the sort from happening. He contacted one of his top men, Corporal John Comerford, with instructions to conduct round-the-clock surveillance on both Tim and Angela Kreider.

Comerford was ideally suited for the assignment. A smart, gregarious, and ruggedly handsome guy in his late thirties, he'd spent years in cloak-and-dagger operations, as often as not tracking the movements of hardened criminals. Compared to his usual stints in the field, this shaped up to be a walk in the park.

He got down to work immediately, setting up undercover surveillance details at both Angela's house and Tim's. At eleven o'clock that same evening, one of his men reported that Angela had come out onto her deck carrying a small white plastic bag, which she'd tried tossing into a Dumpster. She'd missed the mark, however, with the bag landing against a fence in her yard.

"Keep your eye on it," Comerford said. "For the moment that bag stays exactly where it is."

Two and a half hours later, at one-thirty on Thursday morning, Angela left the house and got into her car. With Comerford following at a discreet distance, she drove into the southeastern section of Lancaster City and parked at a loading dock. Comerford was puzzled at first but then realized that she was merely picking up her newspapers for morning delivery. He stayed on her tail for the next few hours while she made her rounds, filling up one newspaper box after another at various locations throughout the city.

She returned home at four-fifteen and brought her dog outside for a bathroom break. After the dog was finished, she retrieved the white plastic bag from her yard and threw it into the Dumpster.

"No need for a search warrant now," Comerford thought to himself. "The bag's ours."

She came outside yet again at seven-forty in the morning, nicely dressed in a skirt, blouse, and jacket. Just then, a plainclothes trooper who was stationed at Tim's house reported that Tim had also come outside, wearing a button-down shirt and blazer. He'd started his car and was sitting in it at the end of the driveway, the trooper said.

Angela got into her car and drove over to Tim's house, with Comerford once again following at a safe distance. She joined Tim in his car and they headed toward the city. They took Duke Street all the way down and circled the block by the courthouse, apparently looking for a parking spot. Comerford assumed that they had an appointment with an attorney, probably Jack Kenneff.

An hour or so later, Comerford went undercover on a trash truck and picked up the Dumpster that contained the white plastic bag. He opened the bag at an out-of-the-way location, half expecting to find something of evidentiary value to the case, perhaps even the murder weapon.

It was filled with dog poop.

38

Corporal Comerford was correct in assuming that Tim and Angela had an appointment with an attorney when they drove to the courthouse on Thursday morning, June 14th. But it wasn't with Jack Kenneff.

Kenneff had initially planned on representing not only Alec but also Tim and Angela. On second thought, however, he worried that such an arrangement might constitute a conflict of interest and so he'd put in a call for help to an old friend.

The old friend was Robert Beyer, a supremely sharp and articulate man who'd likewise worked out of the DA's office for a spell before turning his talents to criminal defense. After discussing the matter with Kenneff, Beyer agreed to meet with Tim and Angela with a view to representing them, and also to help out with Alec's defense in any way that he could.

So it was Robert Beyer that Tim and Angela went to see first thing on Thursday morning, and afterward the attorney did some expert calculating. He knew that Alec would almost certainly be tried as an adult, though he was exempt from the death penalty because of his age. The challenge was formulating a defense strategy that gave him the best chance of avoiding a lifetime behind bars.

It was quite possible, of course, that Craig Stedman

would try to convict Alec of first-degree murder, which is deliberate or premeditated killing. But Stedman might also try to convict him of second-degree or felony murder, which in Pennsylvania is any homicide that occurs during the commission of a serious felony. In the event of a guilty verdict, the mandatory sentence in either case would be life without parole.

Beyer realized that there was a strategic advantage in having Stedman pursue first-degree rather than second-degree murder charges, since this would allow the possibility of a psychiatric or diminished capacity defense. In Pennsylvania a defense of this sort cannot be offered for anything other than first-degree murder. Beyer decided that this was what he and Kenneff should shoot for. They'd negotiate with Stedman, tell him that Alec's parents would cooperate with the prosecution on the condition that he, Stedman, take second-degree or felony murder off the table and pursue first-degree murder instead. This way they could have Alec examined by defense-friendly mental health experts and then argue diminished capacity at trial, providing of course that the experts actually found something wrong with him.

If the diminished capacity defense was successful, it might result in a conviction for third-degree murder, which would most likely involve Alec being sentenced to twenty years for each of the three killings, with the sentences running consecutively rather than concurrently. He'd still be facing sixty years in prison but with the possibility at least of sometime seeing the light of day, which wouldn't be the case if he was convicted of felony murder and sentenced to life without parole. Not only that, but he stood a significantly better chance of receiving a commutation somewhere down the line for a third-degree rather than a felony murder conviction.

Bob Beyer ran all of this by Jack Kenneff, to whom it made eminently good sense, and then he ran it by Alec's parents. Now it was simply a matter of contacting Craig Stedman and opening negotiations.

Stedman had actually called Jack Kenneff late the previous evening, after Brent Shultz and Corporal Duby reported seeing the attorney's name on the sign-in sheet at Philhaven.

"Jack, we want to talk to Alec Kreider," he'd said. "And you know why."

There was a long moment of silence on Kenneff's end, after which he'd said, "I'll get back to you," and then hung up.

Now it was Thursday morning and Bob Beyer called Stedman, reaching him at his office in the county courthouse. He explained that he was representing Alec Kreider's parents but that Jack Kenneff had given him authority to speak on behalf of Alec also.

"Do you want to take a walk?" he asked.

"Sure," Stedman said. "It's a nice day."

There was a good reason why Beyer proposed going for a walk. He wanted to speak with Stedman alone, not with Stedman and one or more of his detectives, which would almost certainly have been the case if they'd arranged to meet in the courthouse.

The two men walked for an hour and a half through downtown Lancaster, all the while talking about Alec Kreider and the Haines killings. They'd pause for a bit here and there—the Central Market, Trinity Lutheran Church, Fulton Opera House—and then start walking again.

Beyer laid out his proposal. In return for the cooperation of Alec's parents, he wanted Stedman to agree to pursue first-degree rather than second-degree murder, which would open the door for a diminished capacity defense.

Stedman wasn't especially surprised that Alec's parents seemed open to the idea of cooperating. He knew that Alec was scheduled to be released from Philhaven within several days, which meant that they were facing a terrible dilemma. Did they bring their son home, where he might possibly pose a risk to the entire family? Or did they take steps instead that could very well result in his lengthy imprisonment? It seemed clear that they'd chosen the latter option.

Stedman told Beyer that he'd call a meeting with the

Haines family members to discuss the matter and get back to him within an hour or two.

The meeting took place at the Manheim Township police station. Allen Leed was on hand and so, too, was Chief Neil Harkins. It was brutally hard on everybody. Several family members knew Alec Kreider by virtue of his close friendship with Kevin. They were shocked to learn that he was the killer. Maggie seemed especially shaken. Alec had been a frequent guest in her home, somebody whom the family had liked and trusted. How could he possibly have done this?

Nevertheless, the family comported themselves with their customary class and dignity. There were no cries for vengeance, no clamoring for blood. Most of them expressed heartfelt sympathy for Alec's parents and siblings.

Craig Stedman spelled out Bob Beyer's proposal, which he described as a calculated risk. Getting the cooperation of Alec's parents, he suggested, probably tipped the scales in its favor.

The family agreed with him.

39

Tim Kreider came to the police station early on Thursday afternoon. He sat across from Allen Leed at a table in the chief's conference room, flanked on one side by his attorney Robert Beyer and on the other by Corporal Patrick Quigley, yet another in a long line of talented investigators with the state police.

He'd come so the police could interview him about his son Alec's involvement with the Haines killings. He'd come fully aware that this might result in sixteen-year-old Alec's life imprisonment. It was roughly a five-minute drive from Tim's house to the station, through some of the most bucolic countryside in all of Pennsylvania. On that bright and sunny afternoon, however, the drive must have felt like a journey into hell.

Allen Leed shook hands with Tim, who was boyishly handsome and casually dressed in a short-sleeved blue shirt.

Leed took no pleasure in the occasion. He was relieved, of course, that the case was finally solved, but he'd have preferred if the killer were some anonymous drifter. That it was a local kid with deep roots in the community only compounded the tragedy. It meant that the wounds would take that much longer to heal.

He thought back to the episode of a week and a half earlier, when he was called from home to help deal with Alec's threatened suicide. He'd thought at the time that the kid was distressed because of his best friend's grisly murder. He'd tried consoling him, tried helping him through the night. He'd had no idea that it was Alec himself who'd actually committed the murder.

The interview lasted almost an hour. Tim sat with his hands clasped on the table, shoulders slightly hunched, lacing and unlacing his fingers. He'd massage the back of his neck occasionally, or cough into a bunched fist. He seemed emotionally exhausted.

Leed handled the bulk of the questioning. He was smooth and solicitous throughout, trying his best to make a terrible situation at least somewhat less so. He'd give Tim a nod of encouragement at particularly stressful moments, or reach over and touch his arm in a gesture of support.

They discussed Alec's family situation—the divorce, the joint custody, and so forth—and also his stellar performance at school. They talked about his friendship with Kevin and the good times the two boys had had hanging out at each other's houses.

Leed asked about Alec's emotional makeup. Had he experienced any significant problems in recent years?

Tim said that problems had indeed surfaced several years before, in the wake of his and Angela's separation. Alec reacted badly to the separation, he said, so much so that they were forced to take him to a psychologist for anger management counseling. He'd seen the psychologist intermittently since then, Tim said, including once or twice over the past year.

Leed asked if Alec had seemed noticeably upset or disturbed in the days or weeks immediately preceding the triple homicide.

Not noticeably so, Tim said, though Alec had confided in him during this time period about dark and frightening thoughts that he claimed to be having. He hadn't gone into specifics about these thoughts but definitely seemed troubled by them. Tim and Angela had planned on setting up another appointment for Alec with the psychologist.

They discussed Alec's demeanor in the aftermath of the killings, which Tim said was rather what one might expect of a kid whose best friend had just been murdered, and then his threatened suicide and involuntary commitment to Philhaven.

Tim said that the folks at Philhaven had wanted to set up extensive outpatient therapy for Alec prior to releasing him. Before this could be arranged, however, Alec confessed to the Haines killings at the family therapy session on June 12th.

At Leed's skillful prompting, Tim spelled out everything that Alec had said about his involvement in the killings, from the dark clothing and black leather gloves that he'd put on beforehand to his hurried exit afterward through the kitchen door of the Haines home.

Leed asked if Alec had given a motive. Why had he wanted to murder his best friend?

"I got the opinion and the impression," Tim answered, "that it was because Kevin had been annoying him a lot lately."

"Did Alec say that Kevin had been annoying him?" Leed asked.

"He made a reference to that but he didn't give a specific reason," Tim said. "Quite frankly, from the way he talked it isn't any one specific thing."

Leed asked if Alec had attended the memorial service for Kevin and his parents. Tim said that he had indeed done so but that he was upset about it afterward.

"And why was that?" Leed asked.

"He was upset that there were people there that really, apparently, hadn't been nice to Kevin," Tim said. "But they were there grieving."

"That bothered him?" Leed asked.

"Yeah," Tim said. "He's always thought that integrity and honesty are really important, and that really upset him."

Leed asked about the murder weapon. Had Alec given any indication where it might be right now?

Alec had expressed concern during one of their more

recent conversations that the authorities might find the weapon, Tim said. Which suggested that it was still around somewhere, quite possibly at his or Angela's house.

Leed returned to Alec's confession, asking Tim if he'd believed that his son was telling the truth about having committed the murders.

"Unfortunately I did," Tim said. "I didn't want to believe it."

And then he elaborated.

"I hate to admit it, but I've known for years that he's been struggling with anger issues," he said. "That's why I've tried to get him to a therapist. He gets real upset and agitated and sometimes I could calm him down, talk to him and bring him down off of it if I was there. It was hard to do and took a lot of energy, but a lot of the times I could get him to calm down and the anger and stuff would go away, but I have to admit there were times when I knew the rage was in him. There were times after [the killings] that it entered my mind that he had something to do with it. I mean, you don't want to ever think or believe that, but every once in a while you think, you know, could he have had something to do with it."

Finally Leed asked if Alec had communicated any remorse or misgiving about having committed the murders.

"He said it doesn't seem real to him lots of times when he thinks about it," Tim answered. "The other day he said, 'I can't believe I actually did this.' He knows he did it but he actually said, 'Mom, Dad, I can't believe I actually did this.'"

Later that same afternoon, an hour or so after the interview, Tim called the station reporting that he'd found the knife that Alec had used in the murders. John Wettlaufer and Robert Beyer went directly to his house, where they met up with Sergeant Doug Burig and Trooper Mark Magyar of the state police.

The knife was lying on the kitchen counter, next to a black leather sheath. The four-inch blade was made of stainless steel, the black onyx handle plated with chrome. The tip of the blade was broken off and missing.

Tim brought the investigators upstairs to Alec's room and showed them the bookshelf where he'd found the knife. The shelf was cluttered with toys, notebooks, and other childhood paraphernalia.

The investigators asked Tim about the shoes that Alec had worn during the commission of the crime. Might they be somewhere in the house? Tim said that he was quite sure that Alec had them with him at Philhaven.

Sergeant Burig contacted Craig Stedman, who promised to have a warrant for the search and seizure of the shoes ready within a couple of hours. Burig then instructed one of his own men, Trooper Brendan McAnally, to go to Philhaven and make sure that all of Alec's footwear was properly secured.

Trooper McAnally got there at nine in the evening and spoke with the facility's evening manager, and then also with its CEO and chief legal counsel. He told each of them the same thing: He was there to make sure that all shoes belonging to Alec Kreider were properly secured until the warrant authorizing their seizure was issued. Only after this was done would he consent to leaving the premises.

A psychiatric assistant went into Alec's room in the second floor adolescent unit and had him remove the shoes he was wearing. The assistant then took these and another pair of shoes that were in the room and placed them in a secured closet.

McAnally told the evening manager that he wanted to check personally to verify that all of the shoes had indeed been collected. The manager arranged for him to do so, and shortly afterward Trooper Mark Magyar arrived with the search warrant.

McAnally served the warrant and took possession of the shoes: a pair of black Hush Puppies and a pair of black Reebok sneakers.

The Hush Puppies were the shoes that Alec had worn while committing the triple homicide, and that he was still wearing a month later at Philhaven.

There were traces of blood on the soles.

40

Angela Kreider sat down with her attorney Robert Beyer in the chief's conference room at nine-forty in the morning on Friday, June 15th. Brent Shultz and Corporal Patrick Quigley sat facing them from across the table.

Allen Leed wasn't there, mainly because Beyer had complained that he'd been overly aggressive in his questioning of Tim Kreider the previous day. Best to sit this one out, Leed thought, in the interests of having things run as smoothly as possible.

Angela was an attractive, earnest woman just then approaching middle age. Her blonde hair was tied back, and she wore a white blouse with a black shawl draped over her shoulders. She made good eye contact with the investigators throughout and answered their questions in a rich and precise voice. She'd occasionally break into nervous laughter, which only thinly veiled the anguish that she must have been experiencing. At particularly difficult intervals—while discussing what she described as Alec's inner turmoil, for example—she'd convulse in sobs and daub her eyes with a Kleenex. But then she'd quickly regain her composure and carry on much as before. It was a brave and impressive performance.

The interview covered much the same ground as Tim's the day before, with Corporal Quigley handling most of the questioning in Leed's absence. When Quigley pressed her for specific details about Alec's confession at Philhaven, Angela seemed in a state of shocked denial, not yet quite capable of admitting that her very own son was a cold-blooded killer.

"Did Alec specifically say that it was he who committed the murders?" Quigley asked.

"Well, I mean, yeah, it was him but it wasn't," she said. "I mean, he even sat there and said he looks back on it. And hopefully I'm not taking this out of context, but what I got from this was that it was him, I mean, obviously, but it wasn't him."

"Okay," Quigley said.

"It was almost like there was this—I really hesitate using the words 'split personality'—but it was almost like there was this other being or thought pattern or something inside of him that just wasn't him. That's how I took it, now, I mean, that's my opinion. So I can't, you know, I can't . . ."

"Okay."

"That's not anything that's been clinically said," Angela went on. "That's just my opinion of how I took that comment that evening."

She was no less at a loss when Quigley asked why Alec might have wanted to kill his best friend. Had he given any sort of a reason?

"Um, I don't think, I think in the way of really explaining why, I don't believe so, other than that he's been, like, feeling annoyance, um, and I'm not even sure if I can convey what it is I'm trying to say. I mean, from everything I've learned in the past couple of days, he doesn't think, you know, he doesn't think like you and I. It's distorted. So what may sound kind of odd to us is something he took very seriously."

"Sure," Quigley said.

"I don't know, I mean, I don't think there was anything that was really said that you would like say, 'Oh, well, that was the reason why.' At least there wasn't anything I got from that evening that I could honestly say, 'Oh, this is what he was thinking, this is how he was feeling.' There wasn't anything I took from that, um, that I could answer your question of why."

Quigley next asked if Alec had mentioned anything at Philhaven about his state of mind while committing the murders.

"I can remember him mentioning a couple of things," Angela said. "These are the couple of things that at least stuck with me, okay, that stayed with me. While he was [at the Haines home] he just felt this detachment. I guess rage is the best way of putting it. I do believe I remember him saying, yeah, that he felt very detached and he felt this rage that was, you know, beyond any type of control, um, and that once he got back home he was literally ill. It was like, it was like once that whatever inner bad feeling went away, the good conscious part of him came back and he felt remorse. He felt ill to his stomach and he just felt horrible."

Quigley asked her about Alec's friendship with Kevin and Warren Tobin ("They're the Three Musketeers," Angela said) and also about his favorite pastimes. She said that he enjoyed playing video games, surfing the Internet, and practicing kung fu, and that he'd recently become fascinated with samurai swords. She also said that he was on the rifle team at school and "had a love for firearms." She described him as a straight-A student and "a perfectionist," the kind of kid who'd dedicate himself wholeheartedly to anything with which he became involved.

"That's actually a very admirable trait," Quigley said.

"It is," Angela said. "I mean, he is a fine young man."

"He is a fine young man," Quigley said. "Okay."

Quigley asked her toward the end of the interview if there was anything else that she wanted to tell them.

"All I can honestly tell you," she said, "is that the young man who sat there [at Philhaven] on Tuesday and recounted this to me is not the young man I know. And like I said, I am not a doctor, I am not trying to make a clinical diagnosis but, honestly, it is almost like it is two separate persons to me. Just from what I've experienced these past couple of weeks, it is almost like we are seeing dual personalities. At one moment he'll be talking about something, it will be something very lighthearted and warm, and then he'll . . . It's like there's this change or something and then he'll go on to a completely different topic and then it'll be more detached and maybe even kind of cold."

"Okay," Quigley said.

"And then the look he has, he'll change again."

"Okay."

"And he's back to the point. I don't know."

"Okay."

"That's why I keep saying, I mean, he's such a good boy, and it's not just because he's my son, but I find it so hard to believe that the boy I know is capable of any of this. I honestly can't believe that."

Brent Shultz was quick to follow up on this, asking Angela if the "dual personalities" that she'd hinted at was a relatively recent development.

"Well, actually," Angela said, "I've only actually experienced this in the last couple of weeks . . . Really this is all new to me."

"Okay," Shultz said. "But prior to a couple of weeks ago?"

"I would say he was himself," Angela said. "I mean, from what I've learned he was fighting so hard to keep it all together, but perhaps I don't even know how to put it into words. I'm so sorry. I'm not thinking clearly."

"That's all right," Shultz said.

"It was like he was fighting so hard to struggle within himself," Angela said. "You know, be what he knows is correct or I guess what he gets from society. He even said he was good at hiding everything."

Several hours after the interview was completed, Detectives John Wettlaufer and Brian Freysz, along with a forensics team from the state police, went to Angela's house and served her with a search warrant. They then turned the house upside down, searching for anything whatsoever of possible relevance to the case.

They searched the laundry room and the bathrooms for

incriminating fibers. They searched the closets for the clothing that Alec had worn the night of the killings. They searched electronic and paper files alike for telltale documentary evidence.

Their efforts were richly rewarded.

They found a dark blue coat in Alec's closet, which tested positive for blood upon being sprayed with Luminol. They found a long-sleeved blue T-shirt, a black hooded sweatshirt, and a black sock, all of which similarly tested positive. They found the black leather gloves that Tim had mentioned during his interview with Allen Leed, and some bloodstained carpet fibers on the second-floor landing of the stairway.

They also found an untitled, handwritten poem in one of Alec's dresser drawers. It was a carefully crafted piece, with a bleakly prophetic message. "The man sat in loneliness, waiting," it began. He waits and waits, the man does, longing for the end of history and the Final Judgment. But then, at the poem's conclusion, the truth finally dawns on him. The end time is already arrived, and Final Judgment resides not with God but rather with he himself and other men like him.

The poem was signed *Alec Kreider* in the upper right-hand corner of the page, and dated simply May 5th. Was it written then exactly one week prior to the killings? Was it meant as a manifesto of sorts, a nihilistic call to action? Was Alec claiming for himself the prerogative of final judgment, including the judgment of life or death?

The investigators also found, in the same dresser drawer as the poem, a handwritten note on a loose sheet of paper.

Alexander was born
May 12th at 3:30
2007

This was perhaps the most chilling discovery of all. Alec must have written it shortly after returning home from his killing spree. Was he thrilled with what he'd just done? Exhilarated beyond his wildest imagining? Had the taste of blood made him feel fully alive for the first time ever? In referring to himself as *Alexander* rather than *Alec*, was he declaring himself a new person?

Had he finally discovered his true purpose? His destiny?

41

The investigators had amassed enough physical evidence to convict Alec three times over. They had the murder weapon and the gloves. They had the bloodstained clothing. They had the incriminating fibers from the carpeted stairway in his mother's house.

By this time they'd also matched the tread on his shoes with the bloody shoeprint impressions from the crime scene. And they'd found traces of blood on the baseball cap that he'd worn during the attacks and then lost afterward in the ravine behind the Haines home.

They had all of this, and they also had the statements that Allen Leed and Corporal Quigley had taken from his parents.

What they didn't yet have was a motive. Who really was Alec Kreider and why had he committed such an unspeakable crime? Perhaps his closest classmates in the tenth grade could shed some light on the matter.

They started with Carol Clark, interviewing her at the police station on Friday afternoon, June 15th.

Carol said that she'd gotten to know Alec during the past school year, mainly by virtue of working on a class project with him in October. Her earliest impressions were hardly favorable.

"I thought he was very rude at first," she said. "He did his entire portion of the project all in one night, so I thought he was a procrastinator. He was very sure of himself, confident and blunt, saying whatever was on his mind. He'd attack people verbally but in a funny way. You could never take him seriously because of the way he'd say things, but if you merely read what he was saying you'd take it as really offensive."

As time went on, however, she grew to appreciate Alec.

"I took his rude and blunt comments as sarcasm," she said, "and I found him absolutely hilarious. He'd talk about how much he hated the world, and joke that certain people were so stupid that he wouldn't mind shooting or stabbing or boiling them to death. He'd sometimes even joke about killing some of his classmates. Nobody thought he was serious. We'd say, 'No, Alec, you don't mean that,' and he'd just smile. We thought maybe he enjoyed saying outrageous things just to provoke a reaction."

Carol wasn't alone in finding Alec strangely endearing. For some students, apparently, his contrariness was a welcome relief from the compulsory conformity of high school.

"He became more popular as the year went along," she said. "People liked him because he was different and had a quick but dry sense of humor. He'd butt into conversations during lunchtime in the cafeteria, usually with some hilarious insult. He was always willing to get into debates. The rest of us thought that war was bad, for example, but Alec thought it was great. He said he loved war. He said the world would never have peace since people are programmed to fight. Someone is always above another person, and to be better than that person, you need to be good at war."

If war was his favorite topic of lunchtime debate, religion apparently ranked a close second.

"He loved talking about religion," Carol said, "but he didn't hold to any one religion in particular. He said that he studied the different religions of the earth and picked out the parts of each one that he believed in. Then he assembled all of these into his own religion. He never went out and preached this religion to anyone. It was just something he believed in. But he did once say that the world would end in 2012, and that he'd discovered this through studying the Bible."

There was no denying, moreover, that he was an immensely talented student.

"One of the smartest kids in the tenth grade," Carol said. "Biology was easy for him and mathematically he was brilliant. He rarely had to study but occasionally would cram for an exam. He'd never brag about being smart but knew that he was, and he looked down on people for not being in more advanced classes. He was also really competitive, always wanting to come out on top. I remember him complaining about one of his teachers, saying she was dumb for giving him a B on an assignment."

Though they never hung out together after school hours, he'd occasionally talk with Carol about his home life without going into much detail.

"I know that he was upset about his parents getting divorced and his father planning to remarry," she said. "He'd complain that he was from a broken home. And he thought his little brother was a brat and his big sister was lazy. I also know that he loved studying war and shooting guns and playing paintball and practicing kung fu. I don't remember him talking much about anything else."

What about after the triple homicide? Did Carol observe any significant changes in Alec's demeanor?

"On the Monday right afterward," Carol said, "he was just staring off into space at first. Then another boy came into class and said that he'd just spoken to the police and thought that Alec might be next on their list. This seemed to make him upset. About a week later, after the memorial service, he called me and said, 'This situation makes you think about the kind of person you are.' And my friend Nancy Schmidt told me that he called her, too, saying he didn't think he was a good person and we wouldn't think so either if we really knew him, and someday he'd let us in on all of his secrets.

"We were really concerned, since we knew that he and Kevin were such good friends. But before long he was right back to being the old Alec. One time at lunch, though, a couple of weeks after the killings, he called this girl we knew over to our table and told her she was a bitch and a whore and made fun of a past relationship she'd had. The comments seemed totally unprovoked but everybody took it as a joke and was just laughing. But then somebody told him that he'd been really hard on this girl, which seemed to get to him. He agreed and said that he'd have to find a way to make it up to her. This was surprising because I'd never seen him show any regret for anything or be in the least apologetic. But on the whole the killings really didn't seem to change him that much."

If anything, Alec seemed to blossom socially in the aftermath of the triple homicide.

"Toward the end of the school year, he started to become really popular," Carol said. "Everybody wanted to talk with him, maybe because he was so funny and they wanted to hear what he had to say. He even started to initiate conversations, which he'd never really done before. He was definitely getting a lot of attention."

Indeed he was, and not least of all from Carol and a couple of her friends.

"We started what we called the Happy Club," Carol said. "Nancy came up with the idea for it, mainly because Alec was so pessimistic, talking about how much he hated the world or how he might just as well go home and shoot himself if he didn't study for some test. The goal of the club was to make Alec happy. So whenever he'd say something negative, we'd go, 'You can't be sad, Alec,' or we'd tell him to stop being such a sourpuss. Another girl eventually joined and so, including Alec, it was basically four of us in the club."

The investigators next spoke with Nancy Schmidt, who likewise said that she and Alec became friends during the past school year. They took two classes together, she said, and would routinely eat lunch with the same group of students in the cafeteria.

She described him as smart and opinionated, with an

acerbic sense of humor. He was also intensely private, she said, preferring to maintain a strategic distance from those around him. Becoming his friend, she said, took considerable work.

"He's not an open person," she said, "and so it's really hard getting to know him. He comes across as bitter and harsh, the kind of person who's just never happy. I'd kid around with him about this, telling him he needed to be happier. Eventually I made up the Happy Club in order to cheer him up."

She said that Kevin's murder actually brought Alec and her closer together. He tried consoling her in the days afterward, though he'd known Kevin much better than she herself had. She'd thought at the time that he was coping with the murder remarkably well.

She'd never hung out with Alec after school, she said, and knew next to nothing about his home life. He'd once mentioned to her that he'd seen a psychologist from time to time but hadn't volunteered any details beyond this.

She said that she had last seen Alec just before final examinations. They'd wished one another luck on the exams and talked about their respective plans for the summer.

Both of these girls, Carol and Nancy, were horrified to learn the truth about Alec Kreider. Here was a boy whom they'd gone out of their way to befriend, a boy with whom they'd attended classes and regularly eaten lunch in the cafeteria. If he'd killed Kevin for no apparent reason, might he not just as readily have killed them, too?

Caroline was no less horrified. She sat down with Allen Leed late on Friday afternoon, June 15th, and talked about the cute boy with the sarcastic sense of humor whom she'd gotten to know at the mall over the past several months.

They had met quite by accident one evening in March, she said. The food court was busy and so she and her friend, Amanda, had shared a table with Alec. They struck up a nice conversation and arranged to meet again the following week, and this soon developed into something of a routine.

Caroline said that she found Alec really quite interesting for a tenth-grader. He enjoyed talking about politics and religion, which was alien territory for most of the boys she'd met since moving to the Lancaster area several months previously. He also seemed honest and unpretentious, and he was sometimes hilariously funny. She looked forward to their get-togethers but never saw him as anything more than a friend, and she was quite certain that he saw her the same way.

Toward the end of May, however, all of this somehow changed.

"Suddenly he started to text me constantly," she said. "He seemed really clingy, needy, which wasn't the impression I'd had of him. I found the whole thing confusing. Then he started in with the phone calls."

She discussed these increasingly frantic calls, the last of which culminated in the police intervention to thwart his threatened suicide.

Apart from the suicide episode, Leed asked, was there anything about the calls that stuck out in her mind?

"A couple of things," Caroline said. "During the last call, he mentioned a girl named Monica. I remember him saying he hated her for being so happy. He called her a bitch and a whore and said he'd come close to killing her and her family. It sounded like he was really serious about it. Then, a few minutes later, he told me that he's a very good liar and has lied all of his life. This struck me as odd because Alec comes across as very blunt, very direct and upfront. So I wasn't sure what to believe. Was he telling the truth about wanting to commit suicide, or wanting to kill Monica? Or was he lying to me?"

And now that she knew the truth about Alec?

"Now I don't think he's stable," she said. "And I'm afraid of him."

42

At five o'clock in the afternoon on Friday, June 15th, Trooper Brendan McAnally went to Tim Kreider's house for the purpose of seizing the family computer. Once this was accomplished, he received a call from Sergeant Doug Burig, who told him to change out of his suit and tie into something more casual and report to the Manheim Township PD for another assignment.

McAnally went home and put on khakis and a polo shirt and then drove over to the station. Sergeant Burig told him that they planned on arresting Alec Kreider for the triple homicide the next morning. In the meantime, however, the folks at Philhaven were concerned not only for Alec's safety but also for everyone else's at the facility. There was no telling how he might respond upon learning that his parents had bitten the bullet and cooperated with law enforcement.

McAnally's assignment, then, was to undertake surveillance of Alec while posing as a counselor, never once letting the kid out of his sight. Sergeant Burig said that he'd have somebody relieve him at midnight or thereabouts.

Philhaven's evening manager was waiting for him when McAnally arrived at six o'clock. The two men knew one another from the previous evening, when McAnally had come to retrieve Alec's shoes.

The manager explained that Alec had been designated a

high-risk patient, which meant that two counselors were assigned within arm's reach of him at all times. The idea was that McAnally would pose as one of these counselors.

The manager escorted McAnally up a flight of stairs to the second floor. They went through a secured door and along a brightly lit hallway, which brought them into the facility's secured Adolescent Unit.

Alec was sitting at a table in the unit's common room, with two counselors sitting alongside him. He was engrossed in a Sudoku puzzle book.

McAnally recognized him right away. This was the same kid whom he and Corporal John Duby had noticed behaving so awkwardly after the memorial service several weeks before.

The manager took McAnally into a small conference room and introduced him to a counselor named Jim. Then Jim and McAnally relieved the two counselors who'd been sitting at the table with Alec.

Jim told Alec that McAnally was a counselor from another wing of the facility. Alec merely shrugged and continued working on his puzzle. His manner was cool and calm, almost complacent.

Alec was expecting his parents for dinner. They'd told him that they'd bring Chinese take-out. He didn't yet know that they'd gone to the police and that the wheels had been set in motion for his arrest.

Tim and Angela arrived with the take-out at six-thirty. The manager placed them and Alec in the so-called fishbowl, which was a windowed room where they could talk in private and yet still be observed.

The three of them sat down at a table and began eating. Tim looked through the window at one point and saw McAnally sitting in the common room. He recognized him from earlier that evening, when the state trooper had come to his house to seize the family computer.

It was then that he and Angela broke the news to Alec, telling him that they'd spoken with the police about his having confessed to killing Tom, Lisa, and Kevin. They told him that he was likely to be arrested for the killings early the next day.

From his vantage point in the common room, McAnally could tell that it was an intensely emotional moment. Tim and Angela wept and took turns hugging Alec, who seemed actually less distraught than his parents were.

The visit lasted a full three hours, with Tim and Angela finally leaving at nine-thirty. Jim then told Alec that it was time for him to get ready for bed.

Alec went into his room and changed into sweats and a T-shirt and brushed his teeth. Jim told him that he couldn't spend the night in that particular room, however. Rather he'd have to sleep elsewhere.

Jim then led Alec into a windowless alcove toward the front of the secured unit. The walls were padded and the alcove was completely unfurnished except for a mattress and a blanket.

Alec seemed unhappy with this arrangement. He said that he'd much prefer sleeping in his regular room, where there was a window that looked out onto a stand of trees. He said that he wanted to kneel down by the window and pray.

He finally relented and stretched out on the mattress. He tossed and turned for a while and then fell asleep at about ten o'clock.

Jim and McAnally pulled up a couple of easy chairs and sat at the edge of the alcove, listening to the sound of his snoring.

Corporal Leo Hegarty of the state police relieved McAnally at eleven-thirty. McAnally briefed him on the events of the evening and then went off to give John Duby a call.

"You remember that kid we saw after the memorial service?" he said. "The kid who was interacting awkwardly with the rest of the high school kids, like he was a fifth wheel or something?"

"Sure," Duby said. "I remember him."

"Well, that's him," McAnally said. "That's Alec Kreider."

"Amazing," Duby said. "And to think we had him in our sights all this time."

A bit later that same evening, Sergeant Doug Burig contacted Corporal John Comerford, who was working undercover at the time on a drug detail. Sergeant Burig advised Comerford to go home and grab a couple hours of sleep, since he wanted him to take over for Corporal Hegarty at Philhaven at three o'clock in the morning.

Comerford lived in Manheim Township, not far from the Lancaster city border. While turning onto his street just before midnight, he couldn't help but notice that everybody's porch lights and ground floor lights were turned on. The entire street was lit up like a runway. It had been this way ever since the triple homicide. He wondered if things would ever return to normal.

He slept for two hours and then drove over to Philhaven, wearing his trademark jeans, T-shirt, and baseball cap. He met with the facility's night manager, who escorted him upstairs and into the secured Adolescent Unit.

Alec was sound asleep on the mattress, with Hegarty and Jim keeping watch over him from their easy chairs.

Hegarty said that there wasn't much to report. Alec had been sleeping for several hours now, without showing the least sign of stirring.

Comerford sat down and for the next four and a half hours did little more than keep watch over Alec. There was no reading material, radio, or television, nothing whatsoever to distract him from the job at hand. He'd slip off to the nurse's station now and then so that he could call the command post with an update, or make occasional small talk with Jim, but mostly it was a matter of sitting and watching. The time passed slowly and uneventfully.

At seven in the morning, another staff counselor, a guy in his mid-forties, showed up to relieve Jim. The new guy apparently didn't realize who Alec was, or that Comerford was an investigator from the state police on an undercover surveillance detail. Shortly after arriving, he leaned over and whispered: "This kid must've done something really bad. I've never heard of a two-on-one."

Comerford nodded noncommittally. Sergeant Burig had advised him at the outset to maintain a low profile. The fewer people who knew his true identity, the better.

Alec awoke at roughly seven-thirty. Pasty-faced and still groggy from sleep, he got up from his mattress and stretched. He carried his blanket over to the edge of the alcove and said hello to Comerford and the staff counselor. Then he sat down on the floor so that he was facing them in their easy chairs.

He sat there for almost an hour, with his arms wrapped around his knees and the blanket bunched up on the floor beside him. Occasionally he'd stretch backwards for a bit or lounge over on his side.

Two staff guys came into the unit with Alec's breakfast: cereal with a cup of juice and a banana. They chatted with him while he ate, asking how he was feeling and whether he'd gotten enough sleep.

Comerford thought that these guys had an easy rapport with Alec. He seemed pleased to see them and was responsive to their good-natured queries.

"I slept pretty well, thanks," he said. "And all things considered, I'm actually feeling okay."

They took him to the bathroom after he'd finished eating breakfast, and then he got dressed for the day, putting on blue jeans and a black T-shirt.

A staff psychologist came into the unit at eight-twenty. She asked Alec if he'd spoken with his parents.

"Mom and dad came in yesterday," he said. "They're really stressed, and I feel bad about it because I know I'm responsible."

"How are you feeling right now?" the psychologist asked.

"Better than last night, I think," he said.

"That's good," she said.

"Anyway," he said. "In a few hours I won't have any control any more."

She told him that he might not have objective control

over a situation, but that he'd always have control over how he responded to it.

Alec said that he concurred with this assessment.

After the psychologist left, he once again sat on the floor of the alcove where he'd spent the night. He hugged his knees, lowered his eyes, and appeared to lose himself in thought.

As the morning wore on, the atmosphere in the unit grew considerably more relaxed. Staff members pulled up chairs and talked about politics, television, and the early summer weather. Alec was mostly quiet at first but eventually entered the conversational mix, offering his own views on these and other topics.

Comerford found him sharp and lucid. He was impressed that a mere kid, especially one facing imminent arrest for a terrible crime, could handle himself so well in social interaction with adults.

Alec would sometimes take the conversational lead, addressing comments to individual staff members. He'd sometimes address comments to Comerford.

Comerford recognized the importance of exercising caution here. He was legally prohibited from saying anything that might be construed as some form of interrogation. His solution was simply to echo or second whatever Alec happened to be saying.

At one point, for example, Alec said that he vastly preferred one particular television news channel to its competitors.

"I agree," Comerford said.

At another he said that he'd much sooner watch educational programming than sitcoms or reality shows.

"Me, too," Comerford said.

Alec ate lunch at twelve noon, and afterward it was much the same as before. He chatted with just about everybody in the unit, sounding perfectly calm, betraying not the least hint of anxiety. Several times he retreated into the sleeping alcove and stretched out on the mattress for a short nap.

Comerford continued to keep close tabs on him, though occasionally he'd slip off to the nurse's station for a quick phone call to the command post. He couldn't help but notice whenever he did so that a couple of the women who worked in the station had true-crime Web sites up on their computers.

Alec's attorney Jack Kenneff arrived at Philhaven at three twenty-five in the afternoon. He took Alec into a room down the hallway past the nurse's station, where they conferred privately for an hour or so. When they came back out, Kenneff gave Alec an encouraging pat on the shoulder.

"Remember now, Alec," he said. "Don't talk to anybody."

Just then Brent Shultz appeared at the other end of the hallway, along with Trooper Mark Magyar of the Pennsylvania State Police. Shultz had a copy of the arrest warrant with him, which Magisterial District Judge David P. Miller had issued less than an hour earlier. The warrant was for three counts of criminal homicide and one count of burglary.

Comerford had known that Shultz and Magyar were on their way with the warrant. Now that he saw them, he went over and stood beside Alec.

"Alec," he said. "This is Detective Shultz of the Manheim Township Police Department. There's something that he needs to tell you."

Shultz walked up and looked Alec directly in the eye.

"Alec," he said. "You're under arrest for homicide."

Comerford took Alec by the elbow and maneuvered him around so that his back was to Shultz. Alec then extended his arms backward voluntarily, and the detective handcuffed him.

Shultz also applied leg shackles, and then he read Alec his Miranda rights. At Kenneff's prompting, Alec invoked his right to remain silent and to consult with an attorney.

Shultz gave Kenneff a copy of the arrest warrant, along with copies of the criminal complaint and the Affidavit of Probable Cause. Kenneff in turn gave Shultz a sealed envelope containing Alec's medical records from Philhaven, which he asked the detective to hand over to the relevant prison authorities.

Shultz and Trooper Magyar escorted Alec outside and

across the driveway to where their car was parked. Alec squinted in the bright sunshine but otherwise seemed unfazed. He carried himself straight and tall, with his lips parted in a slight sneer. He had a look of arrogance about him.

Magyar sat in back with Alec while Shultz drove. Comerford and Jack Kenneff followed in separate vehicles. The trip to the courthouse in Lancaster for the arraignment took twenty minutes, and Alec was deathly quiet throughout. He was apparently in no mood for the sort of banter that he'd exchanged with Officer Steve Newman while being transported to the hospital a couple of weeks earlier.

Judge Miller arraigned Alec at five-thirty in the afternoon, and afterward Shultz and Magyar took him to the Manheim Township police station for criminal processing. Once at the station, Shultz offered to get Alec something to eat from the McDonald's across the road. Alec said that he didn't like McDonald's, and so Shultz suggested a sandwich from a nearby Subway shop instead. Tim and Angela were also at the station by this point, and Angela told Shultz that Alec much preferred Quiznos to Subway.

Shultz ordered a sandwich from Quiznos, which Alec ate after the fingerprinting and so forth was completed. Then the detective stood guard outside the open door to the processing room while Alec talked with his mom and dad.

Shultz gave them about twenty minutes together. They spoke in hushed tones, occasionally breaking into nervous laughter. Tim and Angela tried their best to put on a brave front. They speculated about the sort of books that Alec might find in prison and also the view that he'd have from his cell window. They promised that they'd visit him at every opportunity.

Alec chatted amiably throughout this brief interlude, even making several attempts at humor. For the moment at least, he seemed resigned to his fate.

Shultz and Trooper Magyar transported him to Lancaster County Prison at six-forty in the evening. They stood by while the intake officer conducted the standard interview for newly arriving prisoners.

The officer asked Alec about his psychiatric history and mental health. Alec said that he was treated for depression several years previously and that he'd recently threatened to commit suicide. He added that he was no longer suicidal.

The officer asked if he was a threat to staff and other inmates.

"No," Alec said.

The officer asked if he was likely to get into any fights.

"I don't know," Alec said.

The officer asked if he'd ever been a victim of violence.

"No," Alec said.

The officer asked if he had a personal history of violence.

"No," Alec said.

Shultz turned over the sealed envelope containing Alec's medical records. Then he and Magyar watched as the intake officer led Alec into the bowels of the prison, perhaps never again to see the light of day.

43

Chief Neil Harkins announced the news of Alec's arrest at a press conference later that same evening. The chief praised the efforts of his own detectives in solving the case, and also those of the Pennsylvania State Police, the DA's office, and the FBI. The investigation into the triple homicide, he said, was a collaborative effort in the fullest sense.

For the local community, the news was hardly an unmixed blessing. People were relieved, of course, that the killer was finally caught and safely behind bars. But they were appalled that he was a mere teenager and, worse still, one of their very own, a straight-A student who was born and raised in Manheim Township. How could such monstrousness have arisen in their midst?

The school district issued a statement almost immediately following the chief's press conference. "[We] are shocked and saddened by the charges released [today] by the Manheim Township Police Department," it read. "Because this is an ongoing legal matter we will not comment on the charges or the student. All questions should be forwarded to the district attorney's office. This is a difficult time for our district. Please, continue to support one another and keep our community in your thoughts and prayers."

The investigators weren't yet ready to call it a day. Despite all that they'd learned about him over the past few days, Alec remained very much a mystery to them. They'd already interviewed his parents and several of his closest friends in hopes of getting a clearer picture. Next in line for interviewing were his teachers at Manheim Township High School.

The teachers were in a state of shock. They'd all held Alec in high regard and several of them had been genuinely fond of him. They'd also been doing some serious soul-searching. Should they have realized that Alec was deeply disturbed? Was there some telltale sign that they'd failed to notice? Might they themselves have done something to avert the tragedy?

One of the teachers, who'd served as Alec's sophomore class advisor, told the investigators that she'd thought of little else since hearing of the arrest. She said that Alec was clearly one of her brighter students, if not the easiest to get to know. He'd participated well in class, she said, but had nevertheless struck her as rather a loner. He'd seemed socially aloof, comporting himself with a certain air of superiority. But there was nothing to suggest—throughout most of the school year, at least—that he might be harboring some sort of serious problem.

Toward the end of the year, however, there were a couple of incidents that caused her to think that something might be amiss. The first of these occurred shortly after the triple homicide, when Alec got up from his desk one day and abruptly left the classroom without permission. This was the same day that somebody scrawled some nasty graffiti in a school bathroom, accusing a minority student in the tenth grade of committing the murders. She'd wondered at the time if Alec might have had something to do with this. Now, with the benefit of hindsight, she rather suspected that he had.

The second incident occurred in the context of the memorial service for Tom, Lisa, and Kevin. She sat at the back of the church during the service, she said, several rows behind Alec, who was already there when she arrived. The following Monday she made a special point of approaching Alec at school and thanking him for attending.

"I wasn't there," he replied, and then turned on his heels and stalked off.

Alec's physical education teacher said that he was "completely shocked" upon hearing of the arrest. He described Alec as "a clean-cut, good-looking teenager" who steered clear of the usual high school cliques and got along well with just about everybody. He was also "a great kid to have in class," the teacher said, the kind of kid who'd always apply himself fully to the particular challenge at hand.

The teacher said that he was accustomed to dealing with emotionally troubled teenagers. Neither before nor after the killings, however, had he seen anything suggestive of trouble with Alec. Quite the contrary, he said, everything had seemed perfectly fine.

Alec's first-period English teacher seemed equally impressed, describing Alec as sweet, mature, and thoughtful. He could always be counted on to behave "like a gentleman," she said, which was why she'd felt confident putting him in a group otherwise made up entirely of girls for a class project.

He seemed popular with his classmates, the teacher went on, though he had a reputation for being something of a cynic and would frown and shake his head disapprovingly whenever another student said something with which he disagreed. He was also refreshingly honest, she said, never making a lame excuse on those rare occasions when he'd come to class without having finished his homework.

The teacher said that Alec's poetry, which she described as "borderline religious," was one of the things about him that most stood out to her. "He doesn't mind sharing his deep thoughts about the Creator in his verse," she said.

The German teacher said that he'd gotten to know Alec quite well over the past couple of years, not only in his capacity as a teacher but also as head coach of the rifle team. He described him as "a great kid" who'd ask pointed questions in class and "was pretty cool under the pressure of tests." He said that he'd never seen the slightest indication of emotional imbalance in Alec nor had he witnessed anything approaching aggressive or hostile behavior.

He then qualified this somewhat, saying that he did in fact once talk with the guidance counselor about Alec. His concern at the time, he said, was that Alec was rather too much in love with himself, or narcissistic. That he didn't enjoy working with other students on projects, believing that he could do a much better job on his own. The funny thing about this, the teacher said, was that Alec was probably right. The kid was so smart and such a perfectionist that relatively few students were capable of keeping up with him.

The teacher said that he was stunned upon hearing news of the arrest, especially since Alec had seemed terribly upset by Kevin's death. He'd sat next to him at the memorial service, he recalled, and Alec had gotten really quite perturbed, claiming that many of the kids in attendance hadn't cared the least about Kevin when he was alive.

Most of Alec's other teachers added little of consequence. They all claimed to have had a favorable impression of him. They all said that nothing about his behavior or attitude had struck them as unusual. One of them even characterized him as "a run-of-the-mill kid." The very last teacher with whom the investigators spoke, however, proved enormously thoughtful and perceptive.

This particular teacher had taught both Alec and Kevin trigonometry during the most recent semester. He said that Alec could almost have been mistaken for a foreign exchange student, since he seemed not to fit in well with anyone and very rarely spoke. He'd work with Kevin and other advanced sophomores on group projects but otherwise kept entirely to himself.

"He was extremely polite, obedient, and attentive, with limited classroom participation because of shyness and fear of standing out or making himself look smarter than the rest," the teacher said. "He came to school just to come to school. He was so obedient that I could tell him to do anything and he would. He was there to learn."

The investigators asked him if he'd noticed any change in Alec immediately following the triple homicide.

"The killings took place on a Saturday, and by the time

the grief counselor met with my trigonometry students on the Monday, many of them had already been counseled," he said. "While the counselor talked, there were several students who were very upset and crying. Alec seemed mostly the same before and after the incident. He may have cried a little but he was not sobbing, nor was he nonreactive."

They asked him if he thought that Alec were truly capable of committing the triple homicide.

"Yes," he said. "If you watched him, he was always looking off in the distance as though focused on something else, and if you talked to him that focus was broken. It seemed as if he was focused on some outer force, psychologically focused on something else. I wonder about the psychiatric make-up of Alec. I'm concerned about that. Like he could have an alter ego capable of extreme violence. I never saw violence with him, and if I did I would have reported it. I described him before as like a foreign exchange student because of this, and I would encourage you to discover precisely how he spends his spare time."

The investigators pressed him on this point. Might Alec's supposedly distracted behavior have been nothing more than daydreaming?

"No, it's definitely more than that," he said. "It would be interesting to find out what he reads in the privacy of his home, to find out what makes him tick."

They asked him about psychological counseling. Was he aware of Alec having received any during his time at high school?

"Nothing that I know about," the teacher said. "If Alec were participating in SAP [Student Assistance Program] or IEP [Individual Educational Program], myself and his other teachers would've been notified. But if a student is seeing a counselor on his own, we're not privy to that information."

The investigators next visited Alec's various places of summer employment, starting with the McDonald's on the Lititz Pike. The manager told them that Alec had seemed a perfectly capable kid, though he'd worked only a couple of shifts at the restaurant. Just prior to his scheduled third shift, his mother had phoned saying that he'd encountered an unexpected medical problem and would be laid up for a few weeks.

The previous summer he'd worked at an upscale carwash on the Manheim Pike, mostly cleaning windows and vacuuming interiors on the entry-level line. He'd gotten the job through his older sister, who'd been on staff there part-time for a couple of years. He'd specified on his job application that he wanted to work about twenty hours a week and hoped to earn in the neighborhood of seven dollars per hour.

The manager of the carwash told the investigators that he'd found Alec somewhat aloof, though he had no complaints whatsoever about his job performance. He'd show up for work on time, always in proper uniform, and do exactly what was expected of him. The manager said that he wouldn't have minded keeping him on once the new school year started but that Alec's parents wanted him to focus on his studies. He added that he was flabbergasted upon hearing of Alec's involvement with the Haines killings.

One thing seemed certain: However coddled he may have been in some respects, Alec could hardly be accused of idling away his summers. He was especially busy during the summer immediately preceding high school, when he had delivered the daily newspaper and worked part-time for a janitorial company, as well as part-time in the box office at Clipper Magazine Stadium, which was home to the Lancaster Barnstormers baseball club. His supervisors for these various jobs didn't have anything new or startling to tell the investigators. Alec was a quiet kid, they said, who simply showed up and went about his business.

On Tuesday, June 19th, John Wettlaufer and Trooper Mark Magyar visited the Lancaster County Prison with a search warrant in hand. Accompanying them was Detective Scott Eelman of the East Lampeter Police Department, who'd helped out with the investigation at several of its critical early stages. The purpose of the visit was fairly straightforward. The investigators wanted to take photographs and body measurements of Alec. They also wanted to obtain samples of his hair and blood for comparison against trace evidence found at the crime scene.

A correctional officer escorted the investigators to a health room that was located in the basement of the prison. Alec was brought into the same room several minutes later, dressed in a black-and-white striped jumpsuit.

The investigators had him sit on an examination table while they explained what the search warrant entailed. They then had him stand so that they could weigh him and measure his height.

He weighed in at 138 pounds.

He stood five feet and eleven inches tall.

Detective Eelman photographed him from various angles. Alec complained that he was feeling ill. His face was ashen and his eyes began to roll.

"Everything looks black and purple," he said.

The detectives helped him back to the examination table, where he stretched out on his side. They let him rest for a few minutes and then told him that they still needed to obtain blood and hair samples.

Detective Eelman drew four tubes of blood from Alec's right arm. He then extracted hairs from three separate locations on his head and placed them in a paper bindle.

A correctional officer helped Alec to his feet and escorted him back to his cell. His face was still deathly pale. He walked gingerly, with his back hunched over. Just three days in prison, and the old swagger was gone.

Completely gone.

44

Alec's arrest was big news, not least of all on the Internet. True-crime Web sites were rife with speculation. Why had Alec done it? Why had this sixteen-year-old academic prodigy murdered his best friend and his best friend's parents?

Several theories quickly rose to the forefront. One was that Alec was motivated by academic jealousy, that he was fiercely competitive over grades and couldn't bear the thought of finishing second behind his more talented friend. So he slipped over to the house on Peach Lane determined to kill Kevin and anyone else who happened to be standing in his way.

Another theory was that the killings were born out of some sort of neo-Nazi madness, that Alec's intense fascination with Germany and German culture somehow metamorphosed into a lust for violence.

Still another theory, and by far the most popular, was that the killings were motivated by a complex psychosexual dynamic. This theory claimed that Alec and Kevin had been gay lovers, or at the very least had sexually experimented together, and that Alec desperately wanted this kept secret, whereas Kevin was planning on telling his parents. So Alec killed him and for good measure also killed his parents.

Before long this last theory took on a life of its own. People discussed it and dissected it as if it were established fact. Alec must have had some reason, after all, for wanting to kill Kevin and his parents. Surely he hadn't killed them simply for the sake of killing them. Sexually motivated murder at least made a certain kind of sense. The idea of murder without any motive at all seemed impossible to accept.

The theory gained such widespread currency, in fact, that the investigators felt compelled to look into it. Once again they turned first of all to friends and classmates of Alec and Kevin, some of whom they'd already interviewed.

Almost all of the kids with whom they spoke in this latest round of interviewing had heard the theory about the two boys being gay lovers. None of them placed much stock in it, and most thought it outright preposterous.

Prior to Alec's arrest, they said, no one at school had so much as suggested such a thing. Only afterward did the talk of homosexuality begin, probably because people—students and otherwise—were desperate for some sort of answer and this particular theory seemed preferable to none at all. The truth, they said, was that there'd been absolutely no indication that Alec and Kevin were sexually involved. If there'd been even a hint of such, they said, everyone in the tenth grade would surely have known about it.

Several of the girls, furthermore, said that they'd be shocked if Alec were gay, claiming that he positively oozed heterosexuality. And one of the boys claimed that Kevin was "far too conservative to be gay."

Though it was a month and a half now since the triple homicide, most of these kids were still obviously shaken by Kevin's death. They talked fondly about him with the investigators, this sweet, shy, and unpretentious boy who'd just been starting to come into his own. They talked about his passion for scouting and the Quiz Bowl, and the dedication with which he'd pursued his studies. They talked about the simple things that seemed to have given him pleasure, such as hanging out with the usual crowd at lunchtime or watching *Gilmore Girls* on television.

One of the girls said that she was in English class with Kevin during the past semester. As part of the final examination, she said, the teacher had assigned a short essay, telling the students that they could write on anything of significance to them. Insofar as she knew, the girl said, every single one of the twenty-five students in the class wrote about Kevin and his death.

They were also shaken by the news of Alec's arrest. Here was a kid with whom they'd attended classes every school day and perhaps even shared a table at lunch. Here was a kid whom some of them had considered a friend.

One girl said that she had seen him on the school bus on the Monday afternoon immediately following the triple homicide. The school had sent home a letter with students that afternoon, informing parents about the grief counseling that was being made available during and after class hours. Alec was reading the letter when she boarded the bus, the girl said. He seemed so distressed by it that she went over and tried to console him. She asked him to smile but he said that he couldn't, claiming that the situation was too awful.

Another girl said that she often ate lunch with Alec, during which times the triple homicide mostly went unmentioned. One day, however, a boy from history class came over to their table with a news article on the killings, which he then started reading aloud. Once the boy reached the point where the article described the actual stabbings, Alec got up and left the cafeteria. He later told several of his friends that he'd found the article terribly upsetting.

Several students said that Alec seemed to have a negative view of the United States, which he'd frequently characterize as being "totally messed up." They also said that they'd found him a tough kid to read. He'd flare up in apparent anger at the slightest provocation but then break out laughing. They could never tell for certain whether the anger was genuine or merely a show.

A girl who'd sometimes hang out with Alec's crowd at lunchtime said that she'd found him something of an intellectual bully. He'd engage in heated debates over war, politics, and religion but couldn't stand anyone disagreeing with him. He'd raise his voice and pound his fists on the table to get his points across, and once he'd threatened to punch another student in the face. She said that Kevin was just about the only kid who'd dare to stand up to him.

A boy who'd taken both biology and history with him during the past semester said that Alec was popular with his classmates.

"Everybody liked him because they thought he was funny," the kid said. "And he *was* funny, in a dark sort of way. He was dark funny. You could never really tell whether he was joking or serious."

The same boy said that Alec had seemed "sad and depressed" following the killings, and that he'd seen him crying in the hallway between classes on the Monday immediately afterward. He said that he was initially surprised by the arrest, thinking that Alec couldn't possibly have done such a thing. Upon further reflection, however, it seemed to make a certain sense to him.

"He was pretty arrogant," the boy said. "Maybe he thought he was smart enough to get away with doing it."

A girl who'd taken biology with him said that she'd always found Alec rather "mysterious" and more than a little unnerving.

"He was quiet in class and I always got the impression that he was hiding a lot," she said. "And he'd get a certain creepy look on his face whenever anybody said something he disagreed with. He was just this creepy, quiet guy who sat in the corner of the room."

She said that Alec's behavior immediately after the killings had struck her as strange, though at the time she'd simply attributed it to eccentricity on his part.

"On the Monday, a lot of students in class were crying, asking who could do something like this," she said. "All the while Alec sat in the room with a smirk on his face. He seemed relaxed, smug, almost as if he was satisfied with himself. It didn't ring an alarm bell with me though. I thought, that's just Alec. That's just the way he is."

She said that she'd heard the rumors of a sexual

relationship between Alec and Kevin, which struck her as frankly ridiculous.

"I really didn't know Kevin," she said, "but I'd be shocked if Alec was gay. He had this whole tough-guy persona that he was trying to project."

Yet another biology classmate described Alec as "quietly arrogant," the kind of kid who assumed his intellectual superiority without feeling the need to prove it. He added that he'd always found Alec an intimidating presence in the classroom.

"Alec would get visibly annoyed if someone asked a stupid question," he said. "And he definitely didn't appreciate anybody disrupting his concentration. It was like he wanted a bubble around him during class."

He said that he was floored upon hearing of Alec's arrest, and so, too, was just about everybody else whom he knew at school.

"None of us believed that he could've killed Kevin," he recalled. "We kept saying, 'There's no way he did it. These guys were best friends.'"

A girl who'd taken several classes with Alec said that she'd mostly liked him and also appreciated his sarcastic wit. She said that he was essentially "a shy and private person but actually very nice and funny once you got to know him." There'd been one incident, however, that had given her cause for concern.

"We'd talk on the phone occasionally," she said, "and this one time he called and said he didn't know much about me. So I told him he could ask twenty questions, which I'd try answering as honestly as I could. But then he got really perverted, asking what color my panties were and if I was wearing a bra. I got angry and told him that he'd offended me. I told him that I thought he was sick. Then I hung up."

She said that she eventually forgave him, deciding to dismiss the incident as an isolated indiscretion. Nevertheless, she said, their relationship was never quite the same. Try as she might, she found that she no longer trusted him as she once had.

The investigators realized that these impressions of Alec were highly selective and no doubt colored by the news of his arrest. Insofar as they could tell, however, the students were trying as best they could to be fair. Several of them even went out of their way to put in a good word on Alec's behalf.

A boy who'd first met him in the sixth grade, for example, said that he'd always thought well of Alec.

"Alec was different, definitely a little strange, but in a good way," he said. "He was a good guy and very intelligent."

He said that he was surprised upon hearing of Alec's arrest and wondered if perhaps it was some sort of mistake.

"I thought maybe the police got the wrong guy," he said. "I didn't think it was Alec's personality make-up to snap and do something like this. Sometimes at school he'd talk about wanting to kill somebody who said something he disagreed with, but I never really took that seriously. I thought it was just a figure of speech. I don't recall ever seeing Alec really get angry."

For sixth grade English, he said, every student was required to write an original poem. Once all the poems were turned in, the teacher made a special point of reading Alec's aloud in class. She also made copies of it for everyone, saying its literary quality was something that they should all try to emulate.

The boy said that he'd kept his copy of Alec's poem and had recently reread it. He thought that the investigators might be interested in taking a look.

Handwritten in Alec's upright script, it began as follows:

> *Blackness is the shadows in all the dark corners.*
> *Black is all the blackened streets in the world.*

It carried on in similar fashion for half a dozen stanzas, with the bleakness of the imagery deepening by the line. Alec wrote the poem when he was just eleven years old.

45

They'd spoken with Alec's friends and classmates. They'd spoken with the people who'd employed him over the past several summers. Now the investigators also spoke with his neighbors.

Bernie and Brian Freysz handled this assignment, interviewing people who lived in the general vicinity of both Angela's house and Tim's. Most of these people had little to offer in the way of illumination. They'd seen Alec around but didn't know much about him. Nor did they know much about his parents or siblings.

One woman said that she'd heard rumors that Alec had been negatively affected by his parents' separation. She'd also heard that he'd experienced anger management problems in the past. She said that she'd sometimes seen him walking home from the school bus stop with his head bent and a forlorn expression on his face.

Several people said that Angela and Tim had struck them as responsible and affectionate parents. Angela would walk Alec and his younger brother to the bus stop in the morning. Tim would play basketball with the boys in his driveway and take them on daylong outings. Both parents would routinely attend functions at the local school.

A neighborhood kid said that he knew Alec only by reputation. He'd heard that he was super smart and enjoyed playing video games. He'd heard that Alec was rather a loner and that he typically rode the school bus with his nose buried in a book.

A couple of state police investigators also spoke with Alec's older sister, tracking her down at the restaurant where she worked.

She said that Alec was subject to angry outbursts. He'd sometimes yell and scream over seemingly minor things, such as people disagreeing with him or chewing their food too loudly. He'd received counseling for this, she said, and his behavior seemed actually to have improved of late. He seemed to be doing a better job of controlling his emotions.

She said that she wasn't precisely certain why he'd threatened suicide several weeks previously, though she'd heard him complain more than once that he was tired of trying "to live up to everyone's expectations."

The interview was cut short at this point because the restaurant had suddenly gotten busy and Alec's sister had to return to work. Nevertheless, Alec seemed as much an enigma to her as he did to almost everyone else.

Later that same day, Allen Leed spoke with the friend of Angela's who'd lent Alec the gun with which he'd threatened to kill himself.

The guy said that he'd dated Angela casually over the past year or so and in the process had gotten to know Alec. He realized that Alec was interested in pistol shooting and so he'd lent him a nine millimeter Beretta. He'd done so, the guy said, under the condition that Alec would only handle the gun under proper supervision. He'd had no idea that the kid was emotionally unstable.

The investigators had spoken with dozens of people by this point and yet Alec remained a puzzle. They still didn't know why he'd committed the murders. For all of their efforts, they still didn't have anything approaching a motive.

But then a couple of interesting things happened. While going through a duffel bag that contained Alec's personal belongings from Philhaven, Angela came across a black-and-white composition notebook. She thought that it might be important and so she dropped it off at her attorney Robert Beyer's office. Beyer contacted Alec's attorney Jack Kenneff about it, and Kenneff in turn contacted Philhaven.

The folks at Philhaven told Kenneff that patients were encouraged to record their thoughts and feelings in a journal or diary. This was precisely what the notebook was, they said. It was the diary that Alec had kept during his stay at the facility.

Kenneff got back to Robert Beyer with this information. He said that he realized that Beyer was probably obligated to deliver the diary to the District Attorney's office, though he wasn't certain if its actual contents were subject to confidentiality protections and privileges as set forth by law. He requested that Beyer place it in a sealed envelope and advise the DA's office that the envelope shouldn't be opened until the matter of confidentiality was resolved.

Beyer sealed the diary in an envelope, which he then turned over to Detective Michael Landis in the DA's office. Detective Landis passed it along to Brent Shultz, who immediately contacted Beyer for clarification.

Beyer told Shultz that the envelope contained the diary that Alec had kept at Philhaven, and which Angela had just recently discovered. He said that he'd arrange for Angela to drop by the Manheim Township PD so that she could clarify the matter even further.

Angela met with Shultz at the station about an hour later. She said that she'd found the diary quite by accident in a duffel bag that was stuffed with Alec's clothing. She said that she hadn't tampered with it in any way prior to turning it over to her attorney.

"Can you describe the writings in the diary to me?" Shultz asked.

"All I know was that it was a composition notebook," Angela said. "I didn't open it or read it because I respect my child's privacy."

After Angela had left, Shultz and Corporal John Comerford contacted Philhaven's chief legal counsel. They asked him if journals or diaries kept by patients at the facility were considered medically privileged information.

The legal counsel advised them that personal writings of this sort weren't considered medical records, and hence weren't subject to the usual privacy protections afforded by law.

Tim Kreider contacted Brent Shultz at the police station about a week later. He told him that he'd found another journal or diary of Alec's, which was right then sitting on his kitchen counter.

Shultz went over to Tim's house, armed with a search warrant. Tim told the detective that Alec had called from prison two days earlier informing him about this second diary. Alec had said that he'd been keeping it prior to his being admitted to Philhaven. He'd also said that he'd torn out most of the pages and burned them because he didn't want anyone "thinking badly" of him.

Tim said that he wished that Alec hadn't done this. The missing pages, he said, might have helped with his defense.

He then gave the detective a black spiral-bound notebook, which mostly contained aphorisms written by Alec under the title of "My Wisdom."

Shultz searched the house, looking for anything else that Alec might have written. In the end he seized close to fifty items. The majority of these were book reports and other school assignments. One of the last items that he found, however, was a hardback notebook with pictures of frogs on the cover, jammed into a corner of the bookshelf in Alec's bedroom. One glance inside and Shultz knew that this was likely something of more than just trivial importance.

It was yet another journal or diary, with dated entries written in Alec's punctilious hand. The kid hadn't been in the least shy, apparently, about recording his personal thoughts.

Craig Stedman, in the meantime, was busy preparing a search warrant for the seizure of Alec's school records, including any files that Alec may have saved on the high school's computer servers.

Stedman wanted as much information about Alec as he could possibly get. School records, electronic files, journal or diary items: All of this material was potentially of major significance for the case. For one thing, it might help shed light on Alec's motive for committing the triple homicide. And for another, it might help clarify his state of mind in the crucial days immediately preceding and following the crime.

It was no secret that Jack Kenneff was planning a psychiatric defense for Alec. Toward this end, he'd already arranged to have Alec examined by various mental health professionals. In order to obtain a conviction for murder, then, Stedman would have to prove that Alec wasn't legally insane at the time of the crime. He'd have to prove that his mental status was such that he could be held culpable for what he'd done.

Perhaps the surest indicator of Alec's mental status was buried somewhere in these records and documents. Stedman could hardly wait to get his hands on them.

46

Lancaster County Prison is a sight to behold. It was originally built in 1852 in the style of a medieval castle, and its soaring towers, stone walls, and arched gateway are still fully intact. It's one of those rare prisons whose appearance seems contrived to inspire reverence no less than fear.

It's also an impressively run facility, thanks in large measure to the efforts of Vincent Guarini, who's served as warden for the past twenty-seven years. A big man in his early sixties, with a humanistic bent and wry sense of humor, Warden Guarini has always been attentive to the special circumstances of individual inmates. The effective operation of a prison, in his view, calls for a certain creative flexibility.

This was especially so where Alec Kreider was concerned. There was first of all the matter of Alec's tender age. The vast majority of inmates in the nearly thousand-bed facility were eighteen years of age and older, and a good many of these were career criminals. There was also the matter of his tenuous psychological condition. Here was a kid, after all, who'd only very recently threatened suicide and undergone commitment to a mental heath facility. And then, finally, there was the matter of his sheer notoriety. Very rarely in its history had the prison housed someone whose case had garnered such widespread media attention.

Warden Guarini realized that he had to make special provisions for Alec, and he wasted no time in doing so. He assigned him to a camera-observation cell in the medical health unit that was brightly lit night and day. He insisted that he be cuffed and shackled whenever leaving his cell, even if it were only to take a shower or to use the telephone. During every moment of his stay, in other words, Alec was to be kept under exceedingly tight wraps.

Guarini also made special arrangements insofar as visitation was concerned. Only his immediate family members were permitted to see Alec, and at specially appointed times rather than during regular visiting hours.

Because Alec was a juvenile, finally, Guarini was required by law to afford him every opportunity to continue his formal education. This meant working out a suitable curriculum in conjunction with school authorities and then setting him up with a professional tutor.

The medical health unit consisted of two tiers of single-man cells facing onto a common area. In the common area there were several picnic-style tables, a television, and six wall-mounted telephones. The staircases and railings were painted lime green and fluorescent lights hung from the ceiling.

Alec's cell was located on the lower tier of the unit, an eight-by-ten-foot cubicle with two barred windows. The cinder block walls were painted pale green. A cot was attached to one wall and along the opposite wall there was a stainless steel sink and toilet and also a combination desk and storage unit. The door to the cell had a slot through which meals and the like were delivered.

A rather dramatic incident occurred during Alec's first week in the unit, when another prisoner who was under psychiatric watch rushed out of his cell and flung himself over the railing of the second tier or mezzanine. The guy injured himself in the process, and it might very well have been worse had he landed headfirst on the hard floor below. Word got back to the warden that Alec had taken due note of the incident and suggested to a fellow prisoner that he was tempted to try much the same thing. That he might climb the stairs to the second tier at the earliest opportunity and hurl himself over the top. The warden wasn't certain if this was a real threat or not but he couldn't afford to take any chances. He ordered his staff to exercise that much more vigilance where Alec was concerned.

Far from attempting a stunt of this sort, however, Alec was actually quite well behaved. So much so, in fact, that Ed Sutton, a correctional officer assigned to the medical health unit, eventually came to regard him as something of a model inmate.

"He was cooperative and never disrespectful," Sutton would recall later. "Alec caused us no problems."

Alec's days soon fell into a predictable routine. He'd eat breakfast in his cell at six-thirty and then go back to sleep for a couple of hours. At nine o'clock or thereabouts, he'd settle in at his desk and work on school assignments. He'd generally skip lunch and instead spend an hour or so doing a kung fu workout, which mostly consisted of kicking at the wall in his cell.

Inmates were permitted to leave their cells and hang out in the common area for exactly one hour each day. Alec would usually take this so-called block-out time in the early afternoon, and he'd always do so alone. Because he was a juvenile, he wasn't allowed out of his cell with other prisoners. He'd spend the hour talking with his parents on the telephone and perhaps watching some television. Every other day he'd also take a shower.

After the hour of block-out, he'd go back to work on school assignments until dinner, which was served in his cell at five-thirty. Once a week, on Tuesdays, he'd have commissary food for dinner. He vastly preferred this to standard prison fare, and every Sunday evening he'd fill out his commissary menu in eager anticipation of his order being delivered two days hence.

Radios and televisions weren't permitted in individual cells, and so Alec would spend most evenings reading. He was especially interested in books and articles dealing with various aspects of psychiatry and the law. His parents would bring him any reading material that he requested, but only after first getting it cleared with the warden.

Most inmates in the unit were asleep by twelve-thirty in the morning. As often as not, however, Alec tossed and turned for a while before dropping off. The light burned constantly in his so-called suicide cell, which made sleeping a difficult proposition.

Outside of visits from immediate family members, his contact with the outside world was highly restricted. His attorney, Jack Kenneff, would come by occasionally and so, too, would the mental health experts whom Kenneff had enlisted to examine him in preparation for the trial.

He received very little mail, and none at all from his closest circle of friends at high school. In early July, however, he did get a letter from a girl with whom he'd taken several classes over the past couple of years. Though she'd never hung out with him, this particular girl had always liked Alec. She'd found him funny and sweet, and she couldn't quite believe that he'd actually done what he'd been charged with doing. She'd intended her letter as a gesture of support.

Alec wrote back right away, thanking her for the letter and offering a curious account of his troubles.

"I can tell you that I'm not a killer," he wrote. "But I have been struggling with some very strong demons that made me think and do bad things."

His precise meaning is unclear here. Is he speaking metaphorically, or does he actually believe that he's suffering from some sort of demonic affliction? Is this the rationalization that he's settled on?

He picked up on the same theme later in the letter, writing of his struggles with mysterious inner forces, and then closed on a poignant note.

"I will probably never see you again unless you send me pictures," he wrote. "However, you will, no doubt, see me again in the papers and in the news."

On Thursday, July 26th, police constables Randall Kreiser

and Robert O'Brien transported Alec to Magisterial District Judge David P. Miller's office at the county courthouse. The previous week, Jack Kenneff had decided to waive Alec's preliminary hearing. Now the judge wanted to see Alec just to make sure that he was on board with the decision.

Though it was only a five-minute drive from the prison to Judge Miller's office, the two constables took the trouble to make small talk with Alec along the way. They asked him if he was comfortable enough in his handcuffs and security vest, and Alec said that he was. They asked him what he thought of prison food, and Alec said that he didn't much care for it. They suggested that he let his lawyer handle any questions from the media, and Alec said that he was more than happy doing so.

Alec even initiated a bit of conversation himself, asking the constables if this was an unusual assignment for them. He then laughed when one of them jokingly chided the other for saying that it was "just another day at the office."

The meeting with Judge Miller went smoothly. The judge asked Alec some questions concerning the waiver of his preliminary hearing, none of which he had any difficulty answering. Then Kreiser and O'Brien returned him to prison. The entire trip took just thirty minutes. It would be Alec's only respite from confinement for a good long time.

Alec had limited contact with the other inmates in his housing unit, mostly because he took his block-outs alone. There was one inmate, however, with whom he eventually became friendly. This was George Jonas, a slender, heavily tattooed white guy in his mid-forties, who was serving time on a burglary rap.

Jonas was a charming guy, with a gift of gab not uncommon among experienced cons. His cell was on the top tier of the unit, almost directly above Alec's. Two or three times a week during his block-out time, Alec would walk up the stairs to talk with him. The guy in the cell next to Jonas's, Donald Sharp, would usually listen in on the conversations.

Ed Sutton, the correctional officer assigned to the unit most weekdays, would warn Alec against consorting with fellow inmates. He'd tell him that he was best off keeping to himself.

"Remember, Alec," Ed would say. "You have no friends in here. So watch yourself and what you talk about. It'll only jam you up down the road."

Alec would have been well served heeding Ed Sutton's advice.

On Friday, August 10th, he stopped by Jonas's cell on his way back from having a shower. During his time in prison thus far he hadn't breathed a word about the triple homicide, not to Jonas or anyone else. When Jonas asked him about it now, however, he suddenly lost his inhibitions. Perhaps he was trying to impress the veteran con, or simply felt a need to unburden himself. Whatever the reason, he talked and talked and talked.

After he'd finished talking and returned to his own cell, Jonas wrote detailed notes on the conversation. And later the same day he drafted a letter to the district attorney's office. The letter, which was handwritten in black ink, came across Craig Stedman's desk on Tuesday, August 14th. "To whom it may concern," it began,

> *My name is George Jonas and I'm on MHV status in Lancaster County Prison.*
>
> *I don't know if the information I have would be of any use but the last day or so Alec Kreider has been coming and talking to me about his case with the murders of the Haines family. He has told me about motives, the way he feels about it, why he turned himself in, and so on. The guy in the next cell heard these comments, too, but doesn't want to get involved. The cameras record everything here in prison. So if you don't believe me, look at the camera tape between 1:00 PM and 2:00 PM (8/10/07) on my cell in the upper tier and you'll see him sitting there talking to me and laughing as he tells me his story. Please let's not*

make a big spectacle of this and I will help you as much as I can.

Thank you for your time,
George Jonas

P.S. Please let's keep this down. I have a family on the outside that I'm trying to get back to.

Craig Stedman passed the letter along to Allen Leed, who went directly to Lancaster County Prison and met with Jonas in a private room.

Jonas told Leed that he'd chatted with Alec a number of times previously in the housing unit but never at such length as on August 10th. He said that Alec sat down outside his cell and talked in considerable detail about the murders. He also said that Alec seemed quite pleased with himself, speaking in a gloating tone and smiling throughout.

Consulting the notes that he'd sketched out immediately afterward, Jonas then summarized the conversation, or at least his version thereof.

He said that he asked Alec if he felt any remorse for having committed the triple homicide.

Alec said no; none whatsoever.

Then why in the world, Jonas asked, had he confessed to his parents and thereby risked going to jail?

Alec said that the answer to this was really quite simple. It had reached the point where he just wanted to tell somebody. He wanted to brag about it.

Jonas asked him if he was on drugs at the time of the killings, or in any other way artificially intoxicated.

Alec said that he never used drugs. He was perfectly himself when he went into the Haines home to commit the murders.

And why had he done it? Jonas asked. Was there some particular reason why he'd wanted to kill the Haineses?

Alec said that sometimes the best motive was precisely no motive at all. In any event, he added, everyone would learn about his motive soon enough.

And what about Kevin? Jonas asked. Was it true that the two of them were best friends?

Indeed, it was, Alec said. Which made killing him all the more interesting. The entire experience, in fact, was interesting.

Was Kevin scared? Jonas asked.

Yes, he was, Alec said, chuckling. Very scared.

The guy in the adjoining cell, Donald Sharp, had been listening in throughout all of this. Now he chimed in also, asking Alec if he had a thing for Kevin's older sister.

He knew that she was home, Alec said, but she slipped out of the house before he had an opportunity to get to her. After all, he added, there were four of them and he was operating alone.

What would he have done if he'd caught her? Jonas asked. Would he have raped her before killing her?

Sure, Alec said, breaking into a big grin. There was a good chance that he would have raped her first.

What if he hadn't confessed and subsequently been sent to prison? Jonas asked. Would he have killed again?

Yes, Alec said. He likely would have killed again.

Did he think that he might have gotten around at some point to killing his own family members? Jonas asked.

Alec said that he'd once tried killing his younger brother.

What about his dad? Jonas asked. What was his response upon hearing Alec's confession?

Mainly denial, Alec said. He didn't want to admit that his own kid was so horribly fucked up.

Jonas asked Alec if he realized that he was facing three life sentences for the killings.

Yes, Alec said. Which was why he desperately needed an insanity plea. Otherwise he was totally fucked.

Jonas mentioned that a story featuring Alec had appeared in *People* magazine. Was he aware of this?

Really? Alec gushed, quite obviously thrilled with the news. He'd had no idea that he'd made *People*.

Alec went on to say that he'd enjoyed some of the local media coverage of the killings. He'd especially enjoyed watching a news item on television about the FBI visiting the crime scene. It felt good, he said, knowing that he'd outsmarted the top law enforcement agency in the land.

He then said that he really shouldn't say anything more about the case and went back downstairs to his own cell.

Jonas turned over his notes to Leed and signed a statement attesting that everything he'd told the detective was factual.

Leed asked him why he'd decided to come forward with this information. Was he looking for some sort of special consideration from the District Attorney's office?

Not at all, Jonas said. He wasn't interested in cutting any deals. He'd come forward simply because he'd found Alec's attitude deeply disturbing.

Several weeks later, lest there still be any doubt as to Alec's guilt, a DNA report came back from the state police's crime laboratory in Harrisburg. The lab had found traces of Kevin's DNA on Alec's left shoe, the brim of his baseball cap, and both thumbs of his driving gloves.

The lab had also found traces of Tom's DNA on the knife that the police had retrieved from Alec's dad's house.

Alec scarcely missed a beat with his studies while in Lancaster County Prison. This was due in large measure to the efforts of Ruth Goetz, a remarkable woman in her midfifties who served as Juvenile Education Director at the facility. Goetz went about her work with a pilgrim's zeal, treating every single one of the young offenders under her charge as a special project worthy of her full attention.

"I'm dealing with remnants of the thrown-away person," she said recently, reflecting on her job. "Young people who are incarcerated can be so dispirited that it's sometimes hard for them to think of cultivating their minds. So you have to be flexible, always open to new ways of teaching. A few years ago the warden supported me in bringing art and painting into the prison, which we've found can be immensely healing. One way or another, though, it's always a challenge."

She certainly had her hands full with Alec, whose program of studies for the year included chemistry, calculus, trigonometry, German, world history, the Holocaust, and English literature. Ruth was responsible for tutoring him in all of these subjects, which meant working overtime simply bringing herself up to speed.

There was a classroom in the educational department of the prison where she'd generally meet with students. Since Alec wasn't permitted to leave the medical health unit, however, she'd twice weekly take the trouble of walking down to meet him on his turf.

At eight-thirty on Monday morning she'd go down with an armful of books and papers. Correctional officers would lead Alec out of his cell and into an area just beyond the security gate to the unit. Ruth and Alec would pull up a couple of chairs, and go over the previous week's assignments and also discuss those for the current week. Then at two-thirty on Friday afternoon she'd go down again and pick up his week's homework.

Ruth tried everything within her power to get through to Alec. On the whole, however, she found him maddeningly unresponsive.

"He was a tough nut to crack," she now recalls. "He was brilliant, right on target with his course material, but something wasn't quite right with him. He had a dull affect, a dopey look. I could tell that he wasn't there with me as a human being. Plus he was always questioning my motives. Was I out to help him, or out to get him? Usually, though, he wasn't much interested in talking. He revealed more about himself through the written word. He wrote very well, and he was receptive to literature. He just wasn't receptive to other people on a basic human level."

Still Ruth never stopped trying. She brought in readings that went beyond the regular school curriculum. She introduced him to *Beowulf*, Dante's *Inferno*, and other great works of literature. She even tried arranging tutoring sessions for him with an amateur philosopher.

The philosopher was a young, talented guy who'd done volunteer tutoring at several other prisons in the state. He contacted Ruth wanting to know if she had any students who might be interested in studying with him. Ruth immediately thought of Alec, and after first getting clearance from the warden, she went down to his housing unit to broach the idea.

"There's this brilliant young philosopher who wants to work with you," she said. "He's happy coming to your cell to talk, if you're interested."

Alec looked at her with a perfectly blank expression.

"No," he said.

And then again, more emphatically.

"No."

Ruth had no idea why he was so opposed to the idea. Despite her best efforts, she simply couldn't make much sense of him.

Neither, for that matter, could Warden Guarini. During Alec's time in Lancaster County Prison, the warden kept careful watch on him. He was interested in finding out who this young triple murderer really was.

"He was here awaiting trial for a full year," Warden Guarini said recently, "and we monitored him very closely. His caseworker saw him regularly, and so, too, did our staff psychiatrist. I met his parents when they came to visit, and I was impressed with them. They seemed totally devoted to Alec, especially the father. They stood by him the entire time. But whom exactly were they standing by? Who was Alec Kreider? We could never quite put our finger on it. We couldn't figure out who he was. Everything was internalized with him. He was a complete enigma, perhaps even to himself."

In other respects, however, the warden had relatively few complaints with Alec.

"He posed no behavioral problems whatsoever during his time here," he said. "He was compliant, respectful. He did what he was told to do. There was only one issue that came up, which I think was dealt with in a reasonable manner. Because we put him in a camera-observed cell where the lights are always on, he never saw darkness during his first couple of months. This made sleeping difficult, and so he asked if we'd mind dimming the lights at nighttime. We arranged to do this, and it was the only concession that he really ever asked of us."

Alec's telephone conversations were recorded, which is standard practice in prisons across the country. He'd call either his mother or his father almost every day, and his tone while speaking with them was often petulant and whiny. He'd blame them for his current plight, or his attorney or the hypocrisy of the broader society. He seemed to regard himself as the victim.

He also seemed not to appreciate just how serious his plight truly was. He'd talk over the phone about his prospects of gaining admission to a first-rate college. He'd talk about needing to keep up with his advanced courses while in prison, and perhaps also learn another foreign language besides German.

He seemed convinced that he'd be found insane and, at the very worst, serve three to six years in prison as a juvenile. Then he'd walk out and pick up where he'd left off. Who could tell? Perhaps even the Ivy League was still a possibility.

His current situation, in other words, was merely an unfortunate detour, a temporary setback. Soon enough he'd be back on the road to success.

The house of cards collapsed one winter evening, however, when Alec's attorney Jack Kenneff visited him in prison. The mental health experts whom Kenneff had enlisted to examine Alec had submitted their reports. They'd found no evidence of serious mental illness, nothing to suggest that he didn't know precisely what he was doing when he stole into the Haines home and committed mayhem.

Alec phoned his mom after Kenneff had left. He was distraught, sobbing. There'd be no insanity plea. There'd be no Ivy League.

47

Jack Kenneff fell seriously ill during the winter of 2008 and died in early March. A smart and capable lawyer from the Public Defender's Office, David Blanck, succeeded him as Alec's attorney.

Not long afterward there was a remarkable development in the case, when Alec decided to plead guilty to murdering Tom, Lisa, and Kevin. This meant waiving his right to a criminal trial. It also meant a guaranteed sentence of three life terms in prison. The only question remaining was whether the terms would be served concurrently or consecutively.

Alec wouldn't have made this decision alone, of course. He'd have made it in concert with his attorney and also his parents. But he certainly would have had the final say. His attorney David Blanck would have insisted as much.

But why should the defense take so fateful a step? Why settle on a course whereby a mere teenager was practically guaranteed the better part of a lifetime behind bars?

One might reasonably surmise that several factors figured into the decision. The first of these was the sheer strength of the prosecution's case. Craig Stedman had the damning confession that Alec had made to his parents at Philhaven. He had the murder weapon, the incriminating shoes, and a wealth of DNA evidence. The only thing he didn't yet have was a motive. Had the case gone to trial, Stedman was practically assured first-degree murder convictions, especially now that some sort of psychiatric defense seemed no longer feasible.

There was also the human factor. A trial would have been brutally hard on Alec's family, especially a trial whose conclusion seemed foregone anyway. The evidence emerging from it on a daily basis would only have served to highlight the monstrousness of Alec's crime. His parents quite possibly appealed to him to spare them such a spectacle. They'd suffered enough agony as it was.

And then, finally, there was a strategic consideration. Since Alec's prospects at trial would have been grim at best, why not simply plead guilty and go directly to a sentencing hearing? If Alec were able to muster a show of remorse at the hearing, the court might be more favorably disposed to imposing a sentence of three life terms to be served concurrently rather than consecutively. This still would entail his spending decades in prison but at least he'd stand a chance of someday being released. All things considered, it was probably the best outcome that he could reasonably hope for.

Alec would have had to sign off on this, of course, which must have been enormously difficult to do. Imagine a kid of his age and ambition agreeing to an arrangement whereby he wouldn't see the light of day, if at all, until he was in his sixties. Several people who know him have suggested that he did so in order to spare his parents any further pain. They suggest that this shows a side of Alec—selfless, courageous—that runs counter to the terrible crime that he committed. It's an interesting thought.

In order to ensure that Alec fully appreciated the consequences of pleading guilty, David Blanck visited him in prison on June 12th, 2008, with a prominent local psychiatrist in tow. Blanck explained to Alec, as he had several times already, that a guilty plea meant a veritable lifetime in prison, with no chance of release for forty or fifty years. Alec said that he understood this but that it made no difference. He was still intent on going ahead with the plea.

The psychiatrist chimed in at this point, asking Alec how he was feeling. Alec said that he was anxious about the upcoming sentencing hearing but that otherwise he felt fine. His appetite was good, he added, and he'd been sleeping twelve hours daily.

The psychiatrist got more specific. He asked Alec if he'd felt depressed or suicidal in recent days. He asked him if he'd experienced any visual or auditory hallucinations. Alec answered no on all counts, once again saying that he'd felt quite fine of late.

The psychiatrist realized that Alec had been taking various medications since his time at Philhaven. He asked him now if they were making him drowsy or perhaps clouding his judgment. Alec insisted that this wasn't so, saying he'd made the decision to plead guilty with a clear mind.

The psychiatrist pressed him still further, asking if he'd been pressured into the decision by anyone. Absolutely not, Alec answered. Pleading guilty was something that he himself wanted to do, quite apart from the wishes of anyone else.

The psychiatrist found Alec sharp and attentive throughout the course of the interview, very much in control of his thought processes, not in the least delusional. Later the same day he drafted a letter to Attorney David Blanck in which he provided his professional assessment.

"It [is] my opinion with a Reasonable Degree of Medical Certainty," he wrote, "that Mr. Kreider is making a knowing, voluntary and intelligent guilty plea. He fully comprehends the consequences of making this plea and denies that he has been coerced or influenced by anyone to do so. He indicated that he is doing this out of his own free choice. He is not evidencing any symptoms of a major psychiatric disorder that would interfere with his ability to make such a decision."

The sentencing hearing took place on the morning of Tuesday, June 17th. The day was hot and sticky, with rain threatening from the north.

It was held in Courtroom 12, on the fourth floor of the

county courthouse in downtown Lancaster. The room was freshly renovated and elegantly appointed. It was also surprisingly small, with space enough for only a handful of spectators in the gallery toward the rear.

Alec Kreider had held an entire community hostage to fear almost exactly one year before. It was somehow appropriate that the proceedings to decide his fate should be conducted in so unassuming a venue. The community was anxious to dispense with him so that it might finally regain a sense of normalcy. Alec deserved no larger, grander stage than this, nor would he probably have wanted one.

Alec sat at the defense table with his attorney David Blanck. His mother and father sat behind him, offering whatever moral support they could. Craig Stedman sat at an adjacent table, though no longer in his previous capacity as an assistant district attorney. He'd been elected DA of Lancaster County in January 2008, succeeding Don Totaro to the job.

Judge David Ashworth presided over the proceedings. He was an impressively articulate man, well known in local legal circles for his sharp mind and meticulous attention to courtroom protocol.

The judge took his seat behind the bench at nine forty-five and advised Craig Stedman that he could now call the case.

"Judge, this is Alec Kreider," Stedman said, gesturing toward the defense table. "Mr. Kreider is represented by Mr. David Blanck. He is here this morning to plead guilty to three counts of murder in the first degree for Tom Haines, Lisa Haines, and Kevin Haines. Each count carries a mandatory sentence of life imprisonment without the possibility of parole."

Stedman paused for effect, giving the gravity of the occasion a chance fully to sink in.

"There has been no agreement reached as to whether the sentences would be consecutive or concurrent," he resumed, once again addressing the judge. "That is going to be a matter for the Court, should you accept this plea."

Judge Ashworth studied Alec carefully, and then gestured for him to stand up. Alec looked pale and stiff in the dark suit he'd worn for the proceedings.

"Good morning, Mr. Kreider," the judge said.

"Good morning," Alec responded.

"It is my understanding that you would like to address the charges that have been brought against you by means of a guilty plea," the judge said. "Is that correct?"

"That is correct," Alec said, with a slight quaver to his voice.

"Now, we're going to engage in a lengthy discussion called a colloquy," the judge said, "and we're going to review an awful lot of information here today. If at any time you do not understand what I'm saying, please stop me, ask me to explain myself, and I'll be happy to do so. Do you understand that?"

"Yes, I do," Alec said.

"Do you understand that you have an absolute right to a jury trial?" the judge asked.

"Yes," Alec said.

"At which time the Commonwealth must prove all of the elements of all of the charges against you beyond a reasonable doubt?"

"Yes."

"Do you understand that you are innocent until proven guilty?"

"Yes."

"But by pleading guilty, you are waiving those rights?"

"Yes."

The judge then spelled out the various kinds and degrees of criminal homicide, from first-degree murder to involuntary manslaughter. He defined the precise elements of each, pausing often to make sure that Alec was following him.

"So by pleading guilty here today to first-degree murder," he finally said, "you are waiving your right to have a jury consider what are called lesser included offenses. Do you understand that?"

"Yes," Alec said.

"Knowing that," the judge said, "do you still wish to proceed with your guilty plea today?"

"Yes."

The judge was being scrupulously thorough here. If the case actually went to trial, nothing other than a first-degree murder conviction seemed remotely possible.

The judge next addressed the issue of Alec's age. He was born on February 4th, 1991, which meant that he was seventeen now and had been sixteen when he committed the triple homicide.

"Do you understand that as a juvenile you would have the right to file a petition to transfer your case to Juvenile Court?" the judge asked. "Do you understand that?"

"Yes," Alec said.

Once again the judge was simply covering all bases. Given the severity of his crime, the chances of Alec's case being transferred to Juvenile Court were exceedingly slim.

"So in theory," the judge went on, "if you filed a petition to transfer to Juvenile Court, this case could possibly be transferred [there], and you would be subject to the jurisdiction of Juvenile Court until age twenty-one. Do you understand that?"

"Yes," Alec said.

"After which the possibility exists that you could be released. Do you understand that?"

"Yes."

"Again, do you understand that you are waiving your right to have that petition filed and that you cannot go back at a later time and seek to have [it] filed? Do you understand that?"

"Yes."

"Knowing all that, do you still wish to proceed with your guilty plea here today?"

"Yes," Alec said.

The judge next wanted assurance that Alec wasn't entering a guilty plea in order to avoid a possible death sentence had the case gone to trial.

"Do you also understand that in this particular case, because these crimes were committed when you were sixteen, there is not a possibility of the death penalty?" he asked.

"Yes," Alec said.

"So if you choose to not plead guilty here today and you choose to go to trial, you would not be subject to the possibility of the death penalty. Do you understand that?"

"Yes."

"In fact, with regard to all of these charges, the maximum penalty that is permitted by law is life in prison without the possibility of parole. Do you understand that?"

"Yes," Alec said.

The judge went on in this vein for some time longer, making sure that Alec fully appreciated his legal rights and options. Then he asked him a series of questions concerning his mental health. Had he ever been treated for mental illness, or spent time as a patient in a mental institution? Had he ever been placed on medication?

Alec said that he'd spent time in Philhaven almost exactly a year before, where he was treated for depression. Since then, he said, he'd been taking three different medications on a daily basis: Prozac, Risperdal, and Cogentin. The first was an anti-depressant, and the second was an anti-psychotic; the purpose of the third was to counter the side effects of the second.

"Are you presently on these medications?" the judge asked.

"Yes," Alec said.

"Do you understand what you're doing here today even though you're taking the medications?"

"Yes."

"Do you feel that the medications in any way limit your ability to discuss things with your attorney or to understand the discussion we're having here today?"

"No," Alec said.

A guilty plea of this sort, whereby a juvenile essentially signed his life away, was highly unusual. The judge wanted to make doubly sure that Alec knew exactly what he was doing.

"Do you understand that the maximum sentence and the sentence that must be imposed by me is life in prison without parole with regard to the charges in this case?" he asked. "Do you understand that?"

"Yes," Alec said.

"The only issue is whether or not the sentences will be served concurrently, at the same time, or consecutively, one after another. Do you understand that?"

"Yes."

"I've already touched on this, but do you understand that you are presumed to be innocent and that you need not plead guilty? That you're not required or forced in any way to plead guilty here today?"

"Yes."

"Do you understand that by pleading guilty you are giving up or waiving your presumption of innocence, which would require the Commonwealth to prove you guilty beyond a reasonable doubt at a trial before a jury or a judge? Do you understand that?"

"Yes."

"Do you understand that you have an absolute right to go to a jury trial and to have the Commonwealth meet its burden of proof beyond a reasonable doubt?"

"Yes."

"And that, in so doing, you would select a jury and you and your attorney would be permitted to ask questions of any prospective jurors?"

"Yes."

"And that the goal of that is to choose a fair and impartial jury to hear the case?"

"Yes," Alec said.

The judge made some additional points concerning jury selection and then studied Alec with a furrowed brow.

"Do you understand that the Commonwealth has the burden of proving your case?" he asked. "That the Commonwealth would be required to convince all twelve jurors in a unanimous decision of your guilt beyond a reasonable doubt?"

"Yes," Alec said.

"So all twelve jurors would have to agree before you could be found guilty? Do you understand that?"

"Yes," he said again.

The judge next made certain that Alec appreciated the finality of pleading guilty. The possibilities for appeal, he emphasized, were extremely limited. He then raised the issue of Alec's legal counsel.

"Obviously you have a right to be represented by counsel," he said, "and you have been represented throughout this case by Mr. Blanck and before him Mr. Kenneff. And Mr. Kenneff tragically passed away during his representation of you in this case. Do you feel that Mr. Blanck, stepping in after Mr. Kenneff's death, has provided you with adequate legal advice and has done what you have wanted him to do in this case?"

"Yes," Alec said.

"Do you have any complaints or concerns about Mr. Blanck's representation of you in this case?"

"No."

"Do you have any complaints or concerns about Mr. Kenneff's representation of you in this case?"

"No," Alec said.

The judge reviewed some additional matters related to Alec's mental health status, and then asked a question directly of his attorney.

"Mr. Blanck," he said, "is there anything in your representation of Mr. Kreider which would suggest that he is not knowingly, voluntarily, and intelligently entering a guilty plea here today?"

"No, not at all, Your Honor," Blanck said.

The judge could hardly have been more thorough. He'd covered every base imaginable and given Alec ample opportunity to rethink his position. Now he gave him still one opportunity more.

"Again, Mr. Kreider," he said, "considering everything that we have talked about so far, is it still your intention to plead guilty here today?"

"Yes," Alec said.

So that was it. There seemed nothing to do but accept the plea and carry on with the rest of the hearing. The judge advised Craig Stedman that he could now present the actual facts of the case.

Stedman stood and faced Alec briefly before addressing the Court. He'd not seen the young murderer prior to today. He'd thought endlessly about him. He'd plotted strategies for convicting him. But this was the first time that he'd actually come into personal contact with him.

Stedman was grateful for the guilty plea but not because of any doubt about the outcome had the case gone to trial. He had a formidable arsenal of evidence at his disposal. He'd have crushed the defense had it gone to trial.

He was grateful because this was probably a less painful process for the Haines family. The excruciatingly detailed presentation of evidence during a trial, drawn out over the course of a week or so, would only have compounded their agony.

Stedman laid out the facts of the case in a clear, calm voice. There was no need here for courtroom histrionics. The facts spoke for themselves. He described how Alec went into the master bedroom of the Haines home and stabbed Tom and Lisa. How he then stole into Kevin's room and stabbed the sleeping teenager repeatedly in the back. How he then slashed and flailed at Kevin in the ensuing struggle, finally finishing him off with a slash to the throat. How he then returned to the master bedroom and finished Lisa off before washing up and leaving the house.

He discussed the criminal investigation and also the evidence that unequivocally linked Alec to the killings, everything from the murder weapon to the bloody shoeprints.

When he'd finished, Judge Ashworth leaned forward and fixed Alec with a level gaze.

"Mr. Kreider," he said. "With regard to your own knowledge, are those facts true and correct?"

"Yes," Alec said.

"Mr. Kreider," the judge then said. "Did you kill Thomas Haines, Lisa Haines, and Kevin Haines?"

"Yes," Alec said.

Alec's attorney David Blanck was next in line to speak. He did so gamely, though it must surely have been a thankless task. There was little he could say at this juncture that would make much difference. His client was already consigned to the trash heap.

"Your Honor," he began. "Certainly we recognize that mandatory sentences are in effect here. Whether we speak for two minutes or two hours, it simply will not change the outcome."

"Justice is to be neutral and detached," he went on. "It's to be reflective and reasoned. It's to be blind. And the reason for that is that whenever a crime of this magnitude is committed, emotions are high at all levels—the family that's left behind, the district attorney representing the Commonwealth, the public, and Alec's family.

"I respect the family's feelings, but in this courtroom I represent the child standing next to me. I've attempted to choose my words carefully so as not to antagonize those who have suffered such a great loss. I'm concerned, however, that a child of this age in a society that says he can't vote, he can't enter a binding contract, he can't even quit school without his parents' permission, a child at this age whom all neuropsychological research would indicate does not have fully developed, mature cognitive abilities, but he's deemed competent to make a decision which will transform his life forever, the life of his family, and also in some way, hopefully, to protect a grieving family from reliving the horror that happened on May the twelfth, 2007."

It was hardly surprising that Blanck should make reference to his client's tender age. Having done so, he was left with just one more card to play, which was to suggest that Alec's decision to plead guilty might in some way reflect positively on him.

"As an attorney, Judge, my role, as you know, is to attempt to limit consequences to my client," he said. "I'm unable to do that in this case. This child has made a decision that very few adults that stand next to me are able to make, which is that he's going to accept the maximum penalty that can possibly be imposed. He's going to spend, not only the rest of his childhood behind bars, he is going to spend the rest of his life behind bars, and he knows that."

"That is Alec's decision," he continued. "It's a knowing decision. It's a decision that has been reviewed and discussed with him, with his family. It's a decision that he is making to accept responsibility. It's a decision that I respect. It's a decision that his family respects in that he is accepting full responsibility knowing the consequences.

"And I would ask that and suggest that the impact of that decision should not be lost on the Court. This child knows functionally that he will spend the rest of his life in prison without parole. We are asking—I am asking—the consideration of the Court that the sentences be concurrent because, again, as I've indicated, with these mandatory sentences, functionally, it is equivalent."

"It is the hope," he concluded, "that in some way this decision will allow people to move on, to allow the grieving process to continue to completion. Thank you."

Judge Ashworth nodded in acknowledgment and then once again leaned forward and looked directly at Alec.

"Mr. Kreider," he said. "You have the right to make a statement. Is there anything you would like to say?"

Alec let the question linger in the air for the briefest of seconds before answering.

"I have nothing to say," he said.

It was a remarkable moment. Here was Alec's opportunity to express remorse. Here was his opportunity to offer some sort of explanation for what he'd done. Yet he professed to have nothing whatsoever to say.

If Judge Ashworth was surprised, he certainly betrayed no indication of such. He merely nodded and moved on to the next order of business, which involved the matter of a pre-sentence investigation report. Alec had previously indicated that he was content waiving his right to the preparation of such a report. The judge now asked David Blanck if this were really so.

"Absolutely, Your Honor," Blanck said, sounding at this point rather like a man who was late for a train. "There's really no additional information that would warrant the Court's hesitation or consideration. We are asking to waive the presentence [report] and stand for sentencing immediately."

Before formal sentencing was imposed, however, the Court needed to hear from some more people, including several members of the Haines family.

Tom's sister-in-law spoke of the family's irreparable loss. Nothing was the same as before. They were haunted by grief, tormented by the senselessness of Alec's actions. Previously happy events such as birthdays and holidays were now occasions of great sadness. Not a day passed without their missing Tom, Lisa, and Kevin and wondering what possibly could have motivated Alec to kill them.

"When Alec made that choice to murder three innocent people in their sleep on May twelfth, 2007, he left no choices to this Court," she said. "Three separate lives were taken by three deliberate and merciless killings. There must be punishment for each one of the victim's lives that were taken. The only way this is possible is by Alec Kreider being sentenced to three consecutive life terms in prison so that no other family can suffer at his hands."

Another family member, Lisa's brother, spoke of the trust and goodwill that Alec had exploited and then so cruelly betrayed.

"Knowing how protective Lisa was with her children," he said, "she must have approved of Alec Kreider. He was in their home on numerous occasions, and he'd even spend the night with other friends of his and Kevin's. The family trusted Alec to be a good friend of Kevin and encouraged the relationship. What led Alec to commit such a heinous crime is inconceivable to everybody who knew the family. You could scour Lancaster County and not find one person that would make any derogatory comments about their character or lifestyle."

He choked up at this point and struggled to regain his composure.

"Speaking on behalf of the family," he went on, address-ing Judge Ashworth directly, "we would implore you to provide justice for our loss as well as assure that the citizens of Manheim Township and Lancaster County will never have to suffer tragedy of this magnitude again at the hands of Alec Kreider. The premeditated murder of Tom, Lisa, and Kevin by someone this family trusted must be answered by the harshest penalty the state of Pennsylvania can apply. It is our desire to have Alec Kreider spend the rest of his life in prison serving three consecutive life terms without the possibility of parole."

Maggie had decided against attending the sentencing hearing. She couldn't stomach the prospect of being in the physical presence of the teenager who'd slaughtered her fam-ily. She did, however, submit a videotaped statement, which was now shown on the courtroom monitor.

Her appearance on the monitor was the highlight of the hearing thus far. She was the lone survivor of Alec's attack, the daughter of two of his victims and older sister of the third.

"When my parents and brother were brutally murdered by Alec Kreider on May twelfth, 2007, my world was shat-tered," she began. "For twenty years my parents had always been there for me, no matter what. I could not and still cannot comprehend the world without them. I miss them every mo-ment of every day. Some days I don't know how I even man-age to function without them, and it's really hard to wake up each morning knowing that I'm the only one left in my im-mediate family."

"Since the incident," she went on, "I have developed post-traumatic stress disorder and often have trouble sleeping at night. I'm also currently seeing a therapist to help me cope with this tragedy. I often feel very alone because no one knows my parents and brother like I do."

She spoke at some length about how loving and kind her parents were, and then she spoke about Kevin.

"He was my beloved little brother," she said. "He had such a bright future ahead of him. He excelled in school and had a passion for learning. Also, he was such a caring kid. He would never even hurt a fly. The day before he passed away, we were out buying Mother's Day cards for our mom.

"What hurts me most is that Kevin will never have the opportunity to graduate high school, go to college, get married, start a family. I looked forward to being a part of Kevin's adult life and having him in mine. In murdering him, Alec Kreider not only stole Kevin's future from him, but he stole part of my future from me."

To this point, she'd done a remarkable job of keeping her emotions in check. When reflecting back on Kevin's horrific death, however, her voice cracked and it was all she could manage simply to carry on.

"Even though the police have told me that there's nothing I could have done to prevent his death," she said, "I still feel a sense of guilt that I should have protected him. That is what big sisters do. I would give anything for him to be alive today instead of me. I would have done anything for Kevin."

She next spoke of Alec, and there was no disguising her pain and rage. She knew Alec, as a friend of her brother's and a frequent guest in the family home. How could he have done this? How could anybody have done it?

"Alec Kreider is a despicable individual, and that's saying it lightly," she said, her voice rising in anger. "His actions are inexcusable. There is absolutely no justification for what he's done. He stabbed my family to death. I am not sure that I can ever forgive him for that. He has shown no remorse for his actions."

"Because of him, I have trouble feeling safe," she continued. "Sometimes I wake up in the middle of the night to the strange sound of panic that someone has broken in and will murder me. Even though I know it's probably the wind, this feeling of sheer terror can take hours to go away. That is not how I want to live. If I feel this much anxiety when Alec Kreider is in jail, I cannot imagine how I would function if he was ever released from prison. Even if I had passed away before he was to be released, I would fear for the lives of my future children."

"I need him to be given consecutive life sentences without parole," she concluded. "I never want him to be free from prison. He does not deserve that. Moreover, I don't trust him not to kill again. I have suffered so much because of him that I need to make certain that he does not have a chance to victimize anyone else."

Alec sat in his chair at the defense table with his head hung. Not once did he so much as glance up at the monitor.

Allen Leed spoke next, making certain to keep his comments brief. He talked about the panicked reaction of the local community to the triple homicide. He talked about the class and dignity of the extended Haines family. He said very little about the pivotal role that he himself played in the criminal investigation. Nor did he say much about Alec. Anything that still needed saying on that particular front, Craig Stedman would surely take care of toward the end of the hearing.

And so he did. Just before formal sentencing, Stedman advised Judge Ashworth that he had some final comments on behalf of the Commonwealth of Pennsylvania.

"Mr. Blanck indicated that his client was a child," he began, "but I would ask the Court to be mindful that on May the twelfth of last year he wasn't a child. He was a murderer. He was a murderer dressed in black who sneaked into his friend's house and slaughtered three innocent people. The pain of the knife going across Kevin's throat or into the bodies of Tom and Lisa is no less significant because Alec was sixteen. Their deaths are no less final because he was sixteen."

And why had Alec committed so brutal a crime? Stedman believed that he knew the answer to this, having read the journals that the police had retrieved from Alec's parents. Alec had committed the crime simply because he wanted to kill and saw no reason why he shouldn't.

"Alec Kreider was simply being himself on May the twelfth of last year," Stedman said. "We can look at the deeds but we can also look at his own words from some of the journals that we were able to recover.

"[And] there's not one shred of remorse in [these journals]," he went on, "just as there hasn't been one shred of remorse today."

He then quoted excerpts from the journals, beginning with a passage that Alec wrote in June of 2007, roughly one month after the killings.

"'Ever since I was young,'" Stedman read, "'I was defiant of rules and their consequences, which, of course, laid the foundation for my current anger, depression, and violent nature. These feelings and sufferings have found their greatest amplification in school, where the rules and restrictions are the most numerous and strict. However, I'm not sure that it would be accurate to say that these feelings have been continually escalating. No, it is accurate to say that, but my ability to conceal these thoughts and feelings increased as my want/need to kill people increased.'"

It was a stark passage, which Stedman followed up with an even starker one, taken from a journal that Alec had been keeping prior to the murders.

"'Never once,'" the district attorney read, "'did I believe that killing out of cold blood is wrong.'"

So Alec, in his own words, wanted to kill and needed to kill. And he had no compunction whatsoever about killing in cold blood. This was why Stedman had said that Alec was simply being himself on May 12th, 2007. In killing Kevin, Tom, and Lisa, he was doing what came naturally to him.

Stedman now administered the coup de grâce. He told the Court what Alec's fellow inmate George Jonas had reported to Allen Leed. That Alec had come by his cell one day bragging about the Haines killings. Saying that he'd especially enjoyed killing Kevin since they were best friends. Saying that he might have raped and killed Maggie had she not succeeded in fleeing the house. Saying that given the opportunity he'd probably kill again. Saying that the best motive was sometimes no motive at all.

"What we are in the presence of, Your Honor," Stedman said, "is a merciless murderer who kills to kill.

"[Alec] clearly planned this out," he went on. "He picked

a time when his mother would not be home. He picked a
time when no one would see him in the middle of the night.
He picked a time when the Haineses would be most defense-
less, and he knew that they kept the door unlocked. He wore
dark clothes. He geared his hat up, concealed it, took his
knife, and did what he wanted and needed to do. He is a deviant, cowardly triple murderer."

Stedman spoke some more about Alec's cunning. He
spoke some more about his remorselessness. And then he
spoke about Lisa and how horrifying it must have been for
her during those last few minutes of life, stabbed and bleed-
ing, her husband lying dead beside her, listening to the
sounds of struggle coming from Kevin's bedroom down
the hall.

It was a compelling performance. And when Stedman
was finished, Judge Ashworth once again asked Alec if
there was anything that he'd like to say.

"No," Alec said.

The judge was not easily dissuaded.

"Mr. Kreider," he said after a moment's pause. "In order
to plead guilty, our laws do not require a defendant to explain why. Our laws do not require you to explain why you
chose to kill these people. However, this community and,
more importantly, Maggie Haines and her family deserve
some explanation or insight into what could possibly cause a
person to commit such a heinous and violent crime.

"We have heard comments made from writings in your
own words," he went on. "You can't take back what you've
done, Mr. Kreider, and this Court does not have the ability to
take away the pain. However, I do have the ability to ask you
why one last time. Is there anything else you'd like to say?"

Alec glanced at the judge and then quickly averted his
eyes.

"There is not," he said.

So that was it. Alec refused to divulge a motive. He refused to say anything at all. Whatever reason he might have
had for committing the triple homicide, he seemed intent on
keeping to himself.

Judge Ashworth had given him ample opportunity to speak. He saw little purpose in delaying the proceedings any longer.

"Mr. Kreider," he said. "Your actions in taking the lives of Tom, Lisa, and Kevin Haines were wilful, deliberate, premeditated, and with a specific intent to kill. You have demonstrated that you are an extreme danger to this community by your violent and cowardly actions. Based upon everything that I have reviewed and heard here today, I am compelled to conclude that no amount of rehabilitation or any period of incarceration would mitigate that danger."

The judge then formally imposed three sentences of life imprisonment without the possibility of parole.

"These sentences shall not only be served consecutively," he said, "but the sentencing order is to include a notation from me that, in the event in the future there is a possibility of clemency by some governor or future governor, I strongly object to the granting of any clemency."

"Mr. Kreider," he concluded, "you will spend the rest of your life in prison."

48

Three days after being sentenced, Alec was transferred from Lancaster County Prison to the state correctional institute at Camp Hill. Not long afterward he was moved to Pine Grove, a relatively new maximum-security facility designed primarily for male offenders between the ages of fifteen and twenty.

Barring some startling development, Alec will never again see the light of day. The odds of his sentence being successfully appealed, or of his receiving executive clemency, would seem astronomical. He'll most likely die an old man in prison.

No one other than Alec knows precisely why he donned dark clothing that May morning in 2007 and went to his best friend's house with murder in his heart. He wouldn't tell Judge Ashworth at his sentencing hearing, nor apparently has he told anyone else. Perhaps he intends to take his secret to the grave.

It's not entirely a secret, however. The personal writings that he left behind, especially his journals, afford a fascinating glimpse into the mind of this teenage murderer. Though we might not know precisely why he committed the triple homicide, an examination of his writings gives us a pretty good idea. Alec himself may have taken a vow of silence but his writings speak volumes.

The best place to begin is with the diary that he kept at Philhaven, and that the police retrieved from his mother following his arrest. It's a remarkable document, especially considering the circumstances under which it was written. Alec had just threatened suicide and was presumably suffering significant emotional distress. There is precious little evidence of genuine distress in the diary's pages, however. Rather the overriding tone is one of petulant arrogance. Alec despises everything about Philhaven and regards himself as superior, intellectually and morally, to fellow patients and staff alike.

The first entry is dated June 6th, 2007, which is the same day that he was admitted to the facility.

"It is my assumption that [the staff] will eventually read this," he starts out, "which I believe to be a definitive violation of my mind and the sacred grounds of the soul." He laments his lack of privacy, saying that Philhaven's administrators and doctors are "foolish" and "idiotic" enough to think that he requires constant monitoring. "This, of course," he writes, "violates my longstanding tradition of needing to be alone."

He then writes a rather lengthy passage in which he tries to account for his volatile emotional makeup. This is the same passage that Craig Stedman quoted to such powerful effect in the courtroom. It bears repeating here.

"I shall explain my situation for my own sake," Alec writes. "Ever since I was young I was defiant of rules and their consequences, which, of course, laid the foundation for my current anger, depression, and violent nature. These feelings and sufferings have found their greatest amplification in school, where the rules and restrictions are the most numerous and strict. However, I am not sure that it would be accurate to say that these feelings have been continually escalating. No, it is accurate to say that, but my ability to conceal these thoughts and feelings increased as my want/need to kill people increased."

He goes on to decry "the institutions of suffering and pain" in society, by which he means school and presumably everything else. Having to submit to the restrictions of these institutions, he complains, has caused him untold frustration.

"Now I have become exhausted," he writes, "because people keep trying to make me do things that work against my personal wants, habits, and nature."

So here we have Alec's frank admission that he feels a compulsion to kill, and also his professed hatred for social convention. The ordinary rules and restrictions of social life he finds utterly oppressive. The moral guidelines to which most people conform as a matter of course he regards as a source of personal misery. They violate his natural instincts. They torment his soul. They might very well apply to ordinary mortals, these rules and guidelines. They certainly shouldn't apply to him.

Immediately after this bit of self-examination, his writing takes a decidedly self-pitying turn. If routine social restrictions so affront him, imagine his vexation in the highly regimented environment of a psychiatric facility. He rails against Philhaven and "the insolence and idiocy" of its doctors and support staff. He can scarcely believe his plight, stuck as he is in this "institution of evil" where he can't even go to the bathroom without being watched. He yearns for escape and worries that a prolonged stay might have disastrous consequences for his future health. "The inability of this institution to reform itself around my needs," he writes, "ensures that I will suffer a further and more horrible condition than ever."

His mood lightens noticeably the next day, June 7th. He writes in his diary that he's getting along better with the staff and feeling much more positive than before. He says that he's still very much in love with Caroline and looking forward to seeing her upon his release. He also says that he wouldn't mind trying his hand at gardening.

The day afterward, June 8th, he mostly frets about Caroline. He's sent off letters to her and wonders if she'll respond. He says that he's spent part of the day crying and "slowly beginning to realize that [this] isn't a sign of weakness." He says that he'll quit his job at McDonald's after getting released, which will free up more time for gardening.

"It's raining now," he writes just before bedtime, "and as I've said before, god is in the rain. Now that I've acknowledged his presence, he's going away now."

The diary entry for June 9th is quite expansive. He continues to fret about Caroline, who hasn't yet responded to his letters. He worries that he's in danger of losing not only her but also the privilege of owning firearms. He says that guns count as one of the great loves of his life.

He's hopeful of getting out of Philhaven on Thursday, June 14th, and decides that he'll "throw a cookout" shortly thereafter, with Caroline heading up the guest list. "It will require some work to put together," he writes, "but it will be more than worth it. I hope everyone can come to it on Saturday the 16th."

He's grown more comfortable with the support staff at Philhaven, especially a couple of guys on the day shift whom he describes as "fun, cool, and relaxed." And he finds it amusing that two young female patients have apparently taken a liking to him. "They think I'm hot," he writes, "which is funny because the only girls that I have around that like me are carrazy."

This certainly doesn't mean that he's now entirely at peace with his situation. He still hates the regimentation of Philhaven. He still regards himself as vastly superior to everyone else there. He's unhappy that he'll have to return for outpatient therapy after his release, and unhappier still with the psychiatrists charged with treating him.

"He's a smart man but he betrays my personal interest," he writes of one such psychiatrist. "A smart man, but an effective doctor, no."

He concedes that he has a propensity for rage, and claims to know better than his doctors the various things that incite it. These he lists as "extreme stupidity, extreme disrespect, inept authority, and chewing." Coping with these annoyances, he suggests, will require a monumental effort on his part. He'll have to dig deep and somehow find a way to become more tolerant, more patient, more forgiving.

It would be hard to imagine greater arrogance than this. Here's a kid who's still just sixteen years old, who scarcely a month earlier had brutally murdered three people, and yet he feels aggrieved by the stupidity, disrespectfulness, and incompetence of almost everyone else. Alec's biggest fault, apparently, is that he's not sufficiently tolerant of other people's faults. It's other people who tax his patience, who get under his skin. Other people who send him into a murderous rage. He's actually the victim in all of this, forced to contend with rudeness and obtuseness on every front. And yet, magnanimous soul that he is, he thinks that he might try being a little more forgiving of those who are so clearly his inferior. It's Alec's highly peculiar version of noblesse oblige.

He carries on with his self-examination, such as it is. He complains about various other matters that cause him stress, such as the responsibilities of school and family. He complains about not having enough money to buy all of the things that he wants. He complains about having to work part-time. He complains about feeling envious of other people's good fortune. He complains about the build-up of pressure from these accumulated stresses, which sometimes results in an explosion of rage.

And then the next day, June 10th, he finds something else to complain about. He's just had his first session of group therapy, which struck him as a complete waste of time. "It was quite stupid," he writes, "and I'm quite sure that it didn't help me." Still, he resolves to participate more fully in subsequent group sessions so as not to jeopardize his projected June 14th discharge date.

He's still lovelorn, and more concerned than ever about his standing with Caroline. "I still haven't received anything from her," he writes. "So now I'm in great fear of what my future will be like."

The diary entries for the next two days, June 11th and 12th, are mostly unremarkable. He grouses some more about his doctors and, of course, stews over Caroline. He worries that forces beyond his control are pushing them apart.

He's also upset because his discharge date has been pushed back to June 17th. He's not certain if this is because of his indifferent performance in group therapy or rather something else. He sees it as a terrible injustice but decides that his most prudent course for the moment is "accepting it with grace."

On the positive side, however, he believes that he's made additional progress in coping with the sound of other people chewing. "I managed to make it through two messy eaters," he writes. "The foods that they challenged me with were pretzels, corn, and slurping grape juice."

On Tuesday evening, June 12th, Alec's parents come to Philhaven for their fateful session of family therapy. They tell him that Caroline's aunt won't permit her to have a relationship with him, thereby confirming his worst fears. It's as if his world has ended, and in a fit of teenage pique he confesses to the Haines killings.

For his diary entry the next day, June 13th, this is how Alec begins: "Now I have a problem because the cat's out of the bag. I failed to undergo the proper cautions and regulations to make everything go correctly."

Now I have a problem because the cat's out of the bag. So cold, so utterly heartless: He's just confessed to murdering three people, and this is his prevailing sentiment? *The cat's out of the bag.* Tom, Lisa, and Kevin? They scarcely figure in his thinking. He's concerned with them only to the extent that their deaths suddenly pose a problem for him. He let his guard slip and so now he's at risk, as he also writes, of not making it through "this incident." The insouciance on display here—the sheer matter-of-factness—is staggering.

He goes on to grouse yet again about his doctors, and also to bemoan his lack of physical exercise of late. He even throws in a bit of film criticism. "Right now I'm watching this stupid movie called *Ernest Goes to Africa*," he writes. "[It's] the dumbest thing I've seen in a long time."

He then turns reflective, saying he tried praying the previous evening but doubts that God was listening.

He says that he feels entirely at a loss and fears that he's now "condemned to loneliness and agony."

The entry for the next day starts off more optimistically. He says that he plans on pledging his allegiance to God, which is the only path to true deliverance. He says that it was God who placed him in his current situation, perhaps as a sort of spiritual test. "God has tested me many times in my life," he writes, "and after each test have I risen again to fight the next and so my greatest hope is that God shall allow me to rise again, above the sins I myself have committed." He says that God will surely forgive him if he does the right thing, though he's not yet sure what this is.

It's always risky judging the authenticity of somebody else's spirituality. In Alec's case, however, this surge of piety seems transparently self-serving. Where was his concern for forgiveness prior to his telling his parents about the triple homicide? Where was it when he was still exercising all of the necessary precautions? Where was his spiritual yearning when he was still confident of getting away with the killings? And the idea that God somehow brought all of this to pass as a way of testing Alec? As if the lives of his three victims counted for nothing more than this? Could anything be more grotesque? There isn't a shred of genuine remorse here, a morsel of concern for the Haines family. The verdict seems clear. This is a sham spirituality, born of desperation and extreme narcissism.

Amazingly, moreover, he still seems to think that he can simply go home and carry on with his life. He writes that he's hopeful of leaving Philhaven on Sunday, June 17th, and throwing his cookout later the same day.

Alec would not record another entry in this particular diary, nor would he ever get around to throwing his cookout.

He was arrested on Saturday, June 16th.

There are two other diaries that cast light into the mind of this young murderer. The first of these he kept in the black spiral-bound notebook that was retrieved from his father's house. Unfortunately, most of the pages from this notebook are missing. Alec apparently tore them out at some point, not wanting to take the chance of somebody reading them and thereby thinking ill of him.

Most of the surviving pages contain aphorisms written by Alec under the title of "My Wisdom." They're hardly earthshaking, these philosophical nuggets, though they do attest to his intellectual precocity. An illustrative sampling should suffice.

"A good man does not live by good rules, but rather lives by good intention and with a good heart."

"The most nagging and irritating thing in the world is another man's ignorance."

Tucked away in the back of the spiral-bound notebook is a single entry from February 2007, when Alec was fifteen years old. Here he talks about his disenchantment with school and his nagging suspicion that he might actually be insane. "Other than this," he writes, "my pains come from my lust for girls/women and violence." He goes on to discuss his belief that wisdom is something that's lived rather than learned, and then he closes the entry on a chilling note: "My misery will not end until my existence with other people ends."

On the face of it, a passage of this sort might be interpreted as simply an outpouring of teenage angst. Given Alec's personal history, however, it takes on incendiary significance.

Even more illuminating is the diary that he kept in the hardback notebook whose cover was decorated with pictures of frogs. This, too, was found at his father's house, stuffed into the corner of a shelf. It consists of several undated entries that were almost certainly written sometime prior to the Haines killings.

He starts off by writing in poignant detail about the breakup of his parents' marriage, saying he knew that henceforth he'd never be happy. He mentions the anger that he feels toward the world and contemplates his chances of ever knowing true love. "Love's counterpart is hate," he writes, "which I have plenty of." And several lines later: "I hate most of all happy people. They just try to get those who hate to not hate."

Shortly afterward he veers off on a tangent.

"I hate so many people because they do not live up to my expectations," he writes. "Also because I must live here instead of Germany. Whether I can become chancellor or not, I will make Germany the most powerful country in the world."

He makes several additional claims of this sort in the diary, which would seem to reflect not only his obsession with Germany but also his grandiosity of mind.

Time and again, however, he returns to the theme of hatred, which is often yoked to that of violence. "I don't know if God wanted me to hate so much," he writes at one point, "but things have been very hateful lately." And at yet another: "I dislike many white people. I wish I could kill them because I know I could."

And then there's the line that Craig Stedman quoted at the sentencing hearing: "Never once did I believe that killing out of cold blood is wrong."

The most disturbing passage concerns a local girl whom Alec claims to despise for being so consistently upbeat.

"[She] drives me insane because of her happiness," he writes, "but soon she'll fall into my world and she'll wish she never knew me."

Was Alec plotting the murder of this girl? Did she occupy a place on his list of prospective victims? This would indeed seem to be the case.

Also worthy of consideration, finally, are separate letters that Alec sent Caroline and her aunt from Lancaster County Prison, fully a month after his arrest.

The letter to Caroline has a tone of desperation about it. He'd written her from Philhaven without receiving a response and now he's taking one last shot. He opens on a preachy note, saying that he's placed his trust in God and entreating her to do likewise. He credits her with talking him out of committing suicide, saying that she thereby spared him a fate far worse than death. "[God] sent you to me," he writes, "and you have saved me from eternal damnation."

He discusses his feelings for her and says he wishes that things had gone differently between the two of them. Then he pleads with her not to judge him too harshly. "I ask that you not hate me for the evil that lives in my mind," he writes. "I believe you will forgive me for the genuine goodness of my heart and soul."

A bit later he makes an implicit reference to the Haines killings, admitting his culpability but then retracting it in the next breath. "I know what I did was horribly wrong," he writes, "and I hope you realize that the good Alec, the Alec you know, would never have done it."

Elsewhere in the letter he mostly comes across as manipulative and self-pitying. He pleads with her to write and to send pictures of herself, saying that he needs her now more than ever. He says that there's a good chance that he'll never see her again. "But I suspected that this would happen," he writes. "God takes all things that I love from me."

The letter to Caroline's aunt is a transparent effort at ingratiation. He thinks that getting on her good side might help him gain easier access to Caroline. Here, too, he opens on a preachy note, extolling God's infinite power and wisdom. He thanks the aunt for intervening on his behalf during the threatened suicide episode, and claims that both she and her niece are his guardian angels.

He strives for a tone of humility but his arrogance shines through at every turn. At one point, for example, he discusses how much it would mean to him to hear back from her. "I beg of you," he writes, "(and if [Caroline] has told you anything about me, you may know that I don't beg for anything) please write back." At another point, he says that though Caroline once promised to stand by him through thick and thin, he's prepared to let her off the hook should she now want nothing further to do with him.

Toward the end of the letter, he goes into full preaching mode, as if he were a sage instructing some naïve disciple.

"Words of wisdom, I have acquired some in my time," he

writes. He then goes on to denounce video games, telling Caroline's aunt that she should dissuade any young men she knows from wasting time on them. And for sheer chutzpah, consider the following passage:

"Pray to God when things are tough," Alec writes. "If you live by his command he will answer you. But don't forget that we must not neglect the Lord when times are good, then crawl back to him in times of bad."

Keep in mind that this is a mere teenager addressing a responsible adult. A mere teenager, moreover, who just several months previously brutally murdered three people. In Alec's world, however, the murders don't seem to count for much. It's all about him, the philosopher-king, the man of high moral principle, the man who would save Germany if only given the chance.

He closes the letter by entreating the aunt not to believe any negative things that might be reported about him in the news media.

"I truly am a good person at heart," he writes.

49

So why did he do it? Why did Alec Kreider kill Tom and Lisa and Kevin? Why did this sixteen-year-old academic prodigy commit cold-blooded murder?

One possibility we can dismiss right away. He certainly didn't do it on the spur of the moment, driven by a burst of blind rage. He went over to the Haines home fully intent on killing Kevin and then for good measure he also killed Tom and Lisa. At every point he knew exactly what he was doing. He even had the presence of mind to wash up before making his escape through the kitchen door.

This was no psychotic episode. Alec comported himself as coolly as if he were a trained assassin.

Then afterward it was business as usual. He went to school the following Monday without arousing an inkling of suspicion. He sailed through the rest of the semester without missing a class or skimping on an assignment. He attended a memorial service for Kevin and his parents, where he pulled off a convincing impersonation of a grieving friend.

He kept up the charade for weeks on end, with such aplomb that even seasoned criminal investigators were taken in by it. Imagine a mere teenager being roused from sleep on a Sunday morning for an interview with the police concerning a triple homicide for which he himself was responsible. Imagine this same teenager somehow getting through the interview without betraying so much as a twinge of guilt or anxiety. But this is precisely what Alec did, demonstrating preternatural composure under circumstances that would have induced panic in just about anybody else. The kid had ice water running through his veins.

Which isn't to say, of course, that he was a paragon of psychological health. We know that he had problems. We know that he was prone to depression and anger. That he was deeply narcissistic and quite possibly suicidal. But all of this is rather beside the point. The question is whether these problems were the decisive factor, the driving force, behind the triple homicide.

It's quite certain that they weren't. Otherwise his attorneys wouldn't have given up so easily on the possibility of a psychiatric defense. Nor would Alec's family have agreed to forego a trial and proceed directly to a sentencing hearing, which essentially sealed his doom.

If not insanity, then what else might have driven Alec to such savagery? We know that drugs weren't involved. We know that money wasn't a factor. And we can rule out sex as a motive, despite speculation on the Internet and elsewhere that Alec and Kevin were having a secret gay relationship. There's simply no reliable evidence that this indeed were so.

So what was it then? It had to be something. No one wants to believe that a sixteen-year-old kills simply for the sake of killing. The very thought is anathema to us. We yearn for an explanation that fits our conventional categories. We want to believe that the killing is linked to lust or greed or some other deadly vice. We want to believe that it's the consequence of social or psychological pathology.

In some cases, however, the conventional categories aren't quite up to the job. This is one of those cases.

Alec went to the Haines home that spring night for one simple reason. He wanted to kill Kevin. His only motive was killing. He wanted the experience of killing in cold blood. He wanted to see if he'd enjoy it as much as he expected that he would.

And why did he target Kevin?

Here again the answer is disarmingly simple. He knew that Kevin was home and almost certainly asleep. He knew that the Hainses always kept their doors unlocked. He knew the precise layout of the house.

The Haines house, moreover, was only a short distance by foot from his mother's house, which was where he was staying that week. Since he didn't yet have his driver's licence, this posed an obvious tactical advantage. Still another advantage was his familiarity with the neighborhood, which meant that he had an escape route mapped out in advance.

His reasons for targeting Kevin, in other words, were entirely tactical. Alec might very well have harbored petty grievances against Kevin but he certainly didn't hate him. He probably cared very little about him one way or another. Targeting his so-called best friend was simply a matter of convenience. Under different circumstances, it could just as well have been somebody else.

He ended up killing not just Kevin but Tom and Lisa also. And afterward he showed not the slightest trace of guilt or remorse. The lives of his victims meant nothing to him. His only concern was getting caught. Imagine the inconvenience that this might cause him. It might slow his academic progress. It might hurt his chances of gaining admission to a top-flight university. It might—heaven forbid—even dampen his prospects on the high school dating scene.

Eventually he was caught, of course, after suffering a lapse of discipline and confessing to his parents. Not that this really mattered. It was only a matter of time before he was caught anyway. Allen Leed and company wouldn't have retreated an inch until the case was solved. They were utterly relentless.

Imagine, however, a different scenario. Imagine if Alec had somehow gotten lucky and slipped through the net. What then? From the evidence of his personal writings, it seems likely that he would've struck again. And kept on striking until his luck ran out.

Alec enjoyed murdering the Haineses. He found the

experience exhilarating, intoxicating. It had the power of revelation for him. Almost immediately upon returning home he wrote the chilling note implying that the true Alec had now finally emerged.

Alexander was born
May 12th at 3:30
2007

The true Alec was someone who derived immense pleasure from killing in cold blood and who hadn't the least qualm about doing so. The true Alec was a fledgling serial killer. In murdering the Haineses, he'd found his life calling, his raison d'être. At the time of his arrest, he was probably already plotting his next victim. It may have been the girl whom he claimed in his diaries to despise for being so happy. It may have been one of his teachers from school. It may even have been a member of his own family.

Alec displays most of the characteristics of the classic sociopath. He's incapable of genuine empathy and utterly devoid of shame or remorse. He's prone to pathological lying and subject to delusions of grandeur. He's contemptuous of anyone attempting to understand him. In the lexicon of contemporary psychology, he's almost certainly suffering from antisocial personality disorder.

But a diagnosis of this sort only takes us so far. It doesn't really get to the core of Alec, to the inner workings of his soul. It doesn't tell us why he committed cold-blooded murder and quite likely would have done so again. For this we need to turn to philosophy and theology. We need to look for parallels in literature, to characters such as the treacherous Raskolnikov of Dostoevsky's *Crime and Punishment*. Because with Alec we're brought up against a mystery for which neither psychology nor sociology has a satisfactory answer. It's the mystery of evil. At his core there seems something intrinsically evil about Alec.

Authors generally don't want to demonize the people they're writing about. They want rather to find a spark of decency beneath the surface. They want to find evidence of a beating human heart.

This particular author tried meeting personally with Alec in the hope of finding a spark of human decency. Alec ultimately rejected the idea, though at one point he did take the trouble of sending a letter. He apologized for not writing sooner, and then raised a series of questions, mainly having to do with the author's point of view and primary sources. "It would be appreciated if you would respond with the answers to my questions," he wrote.

Perhaps Alec will be willing to talk at some point in the future. Perhaps he'll even express remorse. For the moment, however, we're stuck with the ghastly images of his brutality. We're stuck with the chilling testimony of his diaries.

We're stuck with a portrait of evil.

Alec killed because he wanted the experience of killing. He saw nothing wrong with doing so. On the contrary, he thought that he was entitled to kill. That he was an exalted being for whom ordinary rules of morality simply didn't apply. He confessed to his parents not out of guilt but rather adolescent frustration over the state of his love life. And afterward he remained monumentally indifferent to the suffering that he'd caused. "Now I have a problem," he wrote in his diary, "because the cat's out of the bag."

At the sentencing hearing, District Attorney Craig Stedman characterized Alec as "a deviant, cowardly triple murderer."

The district attorney was being kind.

AFTERWORD

Alec Kreider has recently moved to Coal Township, a medium-security prison located near the town of Shamokin in east-central Pennsylvania. He's also found an advocate of sorts. The advocate is a professional educator from Pennsylvania, a guy who sees Alec as victim rather than predator. Never mind the confession and the guilty plea. Never mind the thoroughgoing criminal investigation. The advocate isn't buying. Alec is innocent, he believes—railroaded by the police and the DA, persecuted by the media, betrayed by the system.

He claims, the advocate does, that he's undertaken intensive research on the case. He says that Alec's straight-edged knife couldn't possibly have been responsible for the jagged wounds that were found on the bodies of the victims. He says that Maggie's account of the fatal night is riddled with inconsistency. He says that Alec's confessions might be interpreted as simply the confused outpouring of a troubled and tormented teenager.

The advocate is tilting at windmills. The knife in question was perfectly capable of inflicting the lethal wounds. Maggie's account is truthful and consistent. Alec's confession is supported by a mountain of forensic evidence. Still the advocate carries on. He seems obsessed with Alec, totally dedicated to his cause. He visits him twice a month and speaks with him several times weekly by phone. He pores over autopsy reports and police files, trying to find the elusive detail that might prove the difference. Alec apparently strings him along, not denying that he committed the murders but not admitting it either. Perhaps he simply appreciates the support and attention—any port in a storm, after all—or perhaps he, too, has come to perceive himself as a victim.

Alec wrote to the author again recently. His letter suggested that he might finally be open to talking frankly about his crime. He asked if the author valued accuracy and suggested that he'd be happy reviewing a written list of questions pertaining to his case. "Until I hear back from you, take care and may the Lord be with you!" he concluded.

The author responded with questions covering a variety of themes. Why had Alec agreed to enter a guilty plea? Had anyone placed undue pressure on him to do so? Was there any truth to persistent rumors that the murders had been fueled by sexual intrigue? Had Alec experienced a religious awakening of sorts while in prison? Did he harbor hopes of someday winning his freedom?

Afterward there was dead silence from Alec's end. He neither answered the questions nor explained why he'd decided not to. Perhaps they failed to reflect the kind of accuracy that he was looking for.

It's possible, of course, that Alec has nothing further to say about the murders. That he's already banished the topic to some distant, unreachable province of his mind. Even so, fascination with his case will persist, with new information likely emerging in dribs and drabs. The resourceful proprietor of the *CrimeSlam* Web site, for example, has recently claimed that Alec enjoyed playing online combat games and that he may also have posted online reviews of pellet guns.

The situation remains bleak for Alec. His appeals have thus far come to naught, which is hardly surprising. It's hard imagining a court—*any* court—reviewing the facts of the case and finding grounds for reducing the sentence. It's also hard imagining Alec finding even a semblance of peace without first coming to terms with the horror that he inflicted not only upon a family but also an entire community.

In the meantime, life goes on in Lancaster County. Tourists still come to soak up the pastoral pleasures of the Amish countryside. Locals still tend their gardens and spend quiet evenings at home. The cruelties of recent years have taken a toll but the community remains a place of civility and charm.

Life goes on for Alec's parents, too, both of whom have displayed a special brand of courage in staying put rather than moving elsewhere. They remain loyal to Alec, and also protective of him. As a way perhaps of making partial amends to the community, Tim Kreider has created a Web site dedicated to helping troubled teenagers. "[Alec] became lost in front of my face, in front of my eyes, and I couldn't do anything about it," he confides on the site, sitting before a video camera. "[He] was a straight-A student who had every privilege, every opportunity available to him in this world."

For Maggie Haines, of course, things will never be the same. No one goes through so terrible an ordeal without suffering lasting damage. But she's smart and resilient, and having graduated college now, she seems poised to strike out on a fresh path.

DA Craig Stedman remains as busy as ever. He's had to contend with several other killings in the very recent past, all of which he's handled with his customary aplomb. If ever somebody were ideally suited for a job, it's Stedman for this one.

And what about Allen Leed, Bob Beck, and the other detectives in the squad room? They're cops, which means they can't afford to dwell much upon the past. It's the cases they're currently working on—the crises of the moment—that demand their attention. Whenever they do happen to cast a backward glance at the Alec Kreider case, however, they can't help but feel a certain chill.

ACKNOWLEDGMENTS

I'm grateful to everyone who spoke with me during the research for this book, some of whom requested anonymity. Special thanks to Lancaster County DA Craig Stedman, Corporal John Duby of the Pennsylvania State Police, FBI Special Agent J. J. Klaver, and Warden Vincent Guarini. Special thanks also to Chief Neil Harkins, Lieutenant Doug Sing, Sergeant Keith Kreider, Lieutenant Wayne Wagner, Sergeant William Sindorf, Officer Daniel Jerchau, and Sergeant Bob Baldwin of the Manheim Township Police Department.

I owe a large debt of gratitude to Detective Allen Leed and, indeed, all of the detectives with the Manheim Township PD: Bob Beck, Rich McCracken, Brent Shultz, Cleon Berntheizel, Brian Freysz, and John Wettlaufer. It's hard imagining a better group anywhere in the world of law enforcement.

Thanks as always to Margaret Cuneo, Rebecca Cuneo Keenan, Brenda Cuneo, and Ryan Cuneo. And also to Shane Cuneo, without whom the book quite simply couldn't have been written.

I'm indebted also to the Lancaster *Intelligencer Journal* and WGAL (NBC) for their predictably excellent reporting on the case.

Thanks, finally, to Charles E. Spicer, Jr., and Allison Strobel of St. Martin's Paperbacks, and also to Claudia Cross.